Faith in Flux

CONTEMPORARY ETHNOGRAPHY

Kirin Narayan and Alma Gottlieb, Series Editors

A complete list of books in the series
is available from the publisher.

FAITH IN FLUX

Pentecostalism and Mobility in Rural Mozambique

Devaka Premawardhana

PENN

UNIVERSITY OF PENNSYLVANIA PRESS

PHILADELPHIA

Published by
University of Pennsylvania Press
Philadelphia, Pennsylvania 19104-4112
www.upenn.edu/pennpress

Printed in the United States of America
on acid-free paper

1 3 5 7 9 10 8 6 4 2

Library of Congress Cataloging-in-Publication Data

Names: Premawardhana, Devaka, author.
Title: Faith in flux : Pentecostalism and mobility in rural Mozambique / Devaka Premawardhana.
Other titles: Contemporary ethnography.
Description: 1st edition. | Philadelphia : University of Pennsylvania Press, [2018] | Series: Contemporary ethnography | Includes bibliographical references and index.
Identifiers: LCCN 2017047730 | ISBN 978-0-8122-4998-9 (hardcover : alk. paper)
Subjects: LCSH: Pentecostalism—Mozambique. | Social mobility—Mozambique. | Residential mobility—Mozambique. | Makhuwa (African people)— Mozambique. | Mozambique—Religious life and customs. | Conversion. | Pentecostal churches—Mozambique.
Classification: LCC BR1644.5.M85 P74 2018 | DDC 276.79/083—dc23
LC record available at https://lccn.loc.gov/2017047730

For Kalinka

The sedentary life is the very sin against the Holy Spirit.

—Friedrich Nietzsche, *Twilight of the Idols*

CONTENTS

Introduction 1

PART I. *OTHAMA*—TO MOVE

Chapter 1. A Fugitive People 29

Chapter 2. Between the River and the Road 51

PART II. *OHIYA NI OVOLOWA*—TO LEAVE AND TO ENTER

Chapter 3. Border Crossings 73

Chapter 4. Two Feet In, Two Feet Out 93

PART III. *OKHALANO*—TO BE WITH

Chapter 5. A Religion of Her Own? 117

Chapter 6. Moved by the Spirit 138

Conclusion 159

Notes 173
Works Cited 193
Index 213
Acknowledgments 219

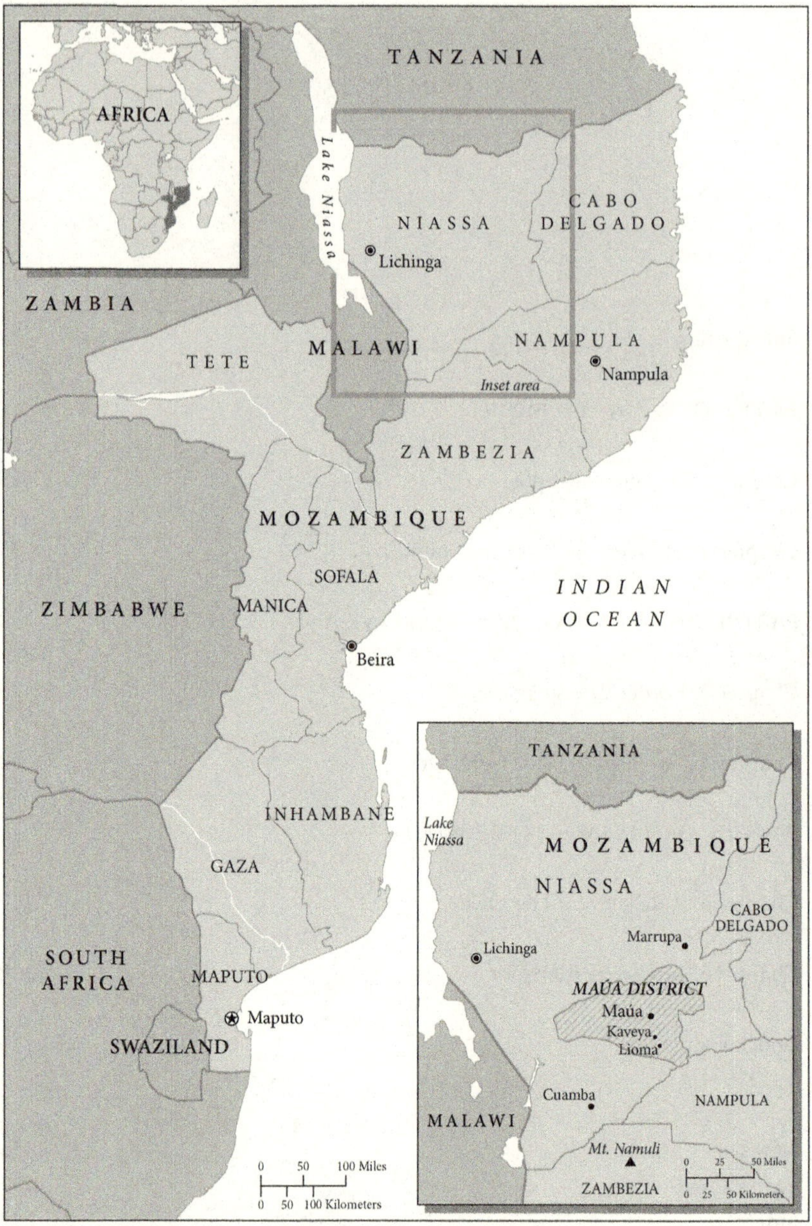

Figure 1. Map of Mozambican field site.

Introduction

I clapped twice to announce my presence, then ducked into the mud-plaster longhouse that Mutúali built soon after the rains had ceased. It was dark inside, except for the day's last sunrays passing through the rear. It was empty except for Mutúali and Leonardo standing toward the front. On a bamboo platform before them sat what was, as late as 2012, only the second television set to appear in Kaveya village. An empty box to the side revealed it to be a fourteen-inch Sharp Multisystem. To repay the loan needed for its purchase, Mutúali would be operating his longhouse essentially as a village cinema, charging visitors an entrance fee of three *meticais* (at the time, around five U.S. cents) per night. Of course, not always would he be able to show videos and take in revenue. "Depends on the gasoline," he said. The fee would also go toward this: the cost of diesel for his electric generator, and the labor of biking, jerry cans in tow, to the service station forty kilometers away.

For this inaugural occasion Mutúali invited his fellow worshippers at Kaveya's Pentecostal church to join him early. I arrived with Jemusse, a church member with whose family my wife and I were living that year. We greeted Mutúali and Leonardo, then sat down in the front row—a broad log on the dirt floor. Silently and admiringly we watched our friends maneuver through a tangle of wires and devices.

Other church members trickled in. After Deacon Nório arrived, technical preparations ceased. Or, rather, they took a new form: we got to our feet and prayed. Jemusse started by recalling Mutúali's previous failed projects—a dilapidated sewing machine, a malfunctioning motorbike—yet affirming that God was behind those opportunities just as God is now behind this one. "Bless us, Lord, so that all the machines work well," he said. We each then took to shouting our own prayers. Our eyes were shut and our voices loud. A few arms were raised, others punched the air. After some minutes, Deacon Nório raised his voice above the rest: "We thank you, God, for the miracles you are doing in this home. Here on earth no one can do these miracles. Thank you, Lord! But whoever wants to spoil this place, stay away. Evil spirits, you cannot come near! Let Jesus Christ reign. I hand over all to you, my God." We all yelled in unison, "Amen!"

I reclaimed my seat, and Mutúali and Leonardo resumed their setup. Out of some foam casing they removed a DVD player. They connected it to an extension cord that snaked out the side entrance. There the generator sat, whirring hesitantly, then more persistently. It was soon emitting the pungent odor of burning fuel.

Meanwhile the rows behind me were filling silently, everyone seemingly awed by the novelty before them. One man finally broke the silence with a joke, telling us to look and see the television already on. He was referring to what the screen reflected beyond the rear passageway: the open sky and a mango tree, under which children could be seen playing.

Those children rushed in when, finally, a test bulb flickered overhead. The screen lit up and the word SHARP appeared as if to signal the substitution under way: bold blue pixels displacing the faint blue reflection of the evening sky. Afro-pop beats soon resounded from the speakers. Everyone cheered and fixed their eyes on Mr. Ong'eng'o, the Kenyan megastar on screen. Though the Gusii words he sang were meaningless to us, the images and sounds were electric.

The bass lines thumped so intensely they would nearly drown out the beats that sounded a short time later from elsewhere in Kaveya. Summoning villagers to an all-night *mirusi* ceremony, these rhythms were amplified not by sleek new speakers but by the goat hide of hand drums, their source of power not diesel but deities. These deities were the ancestral spirits integral to all healing ceremonies, the same spirits Deacon Nório had just called evil and banished from Kaveya's new longhouse cinema.

The distant throb of drums presented me with a dilemma. I was tempted to go; it was one of my first opportunities to witness a traditional healing ceremony. But I worried about how I could be present for both it and this signal event in the life of my friends. I hung around a bit longer, then rose to leave, apologizing for having to break away. No one saw the need for apologies; everyone respected my desire to go. Leonardo, tireless in his offers of research assistance, even promised to join me later, once his services at the cinema were no longer needed.

I thanked him and began the ten-minute walk down the laterite road. In the darkness I made out the profiles of children and teenagers sharing the path with me. We exchanged greetings as we crossed: *Munetta phama?* (Are you walking well?)

I knew I had arrived when five or six fire pits came into view, all at a single compound where usually just one burns through the night. Around each fire sat clusters of people on the ground or on stumps, their hands alternately extending toward the flame and tearing balls of porridge paste from a common tin plate. I was invited to sit and share in the meal.

After eating, a number of young people got up and left. They headed in the direction from which I had come, and I realized that those whose paths I earlier crossed were not just heading to Mutúali's cinema. They were leaving the *mirusi* grounds to do so. It was tempting to see this as a harbinger of things to come. Were we at a tipping point where people increasingly opt for transnational pop over ancestral ceremonies? The short journey from the ritual grounds to the cinema seemed suddenly a passage of great import. The only one swimming upstream was the anthropologist.

The *mirusi* ceremony eventually got under way. All the women—and only the women—made their way into the healing hut. But they scarcely remained there. At various points through the night, they exited in single file, shaking gourd rattles and chanting rhythmically: "Let's go to the mountain and seek out wood for the pot." "Let's seek the *naruru*, the medicine from the bush." "I'm returning from where I came, to take the *nihiro* bath." Each verse named an element of ritual significance. Firewood was used to heat the medicine consumed by the afflicted. The *naruru* (water strider) was brought into contact with the patient, then released to return her vertigo to the bush. The *nihiro* was a river bath, taken just before sunrise, wherein, I was told, "the sick person moves from the old environment to a new life." Transformation, in all these cases, presupposed motion: from inside to outside, from land to river, from village to bush. Yet there was always, also, a return.

In so many ways the *mirusi* ceremony differed from what was simultaneously occurring just up the road. One event was retrospective, done because "this is how our ancestors did it"; the other was prospective, evoking electronic futures from which ancestral spirits were explicitly expelled.

There were also, though, similarities. As central as motion was to the healing ceremony, the same could be said of the motion pictures, mostly of dancers, broadcast at the cinema; and both events summoned forces from other worlds—whether ancestral spirits or the Holy Spirit, whether bush animals or pop stars. Two seemingly disparate events were connected by movement. The past and the future conjoined in a mobile present.

That mobility manifested most clearly in the youths whose paths I had crossed earlier that night. It turned out I would see them again, when they returned to rejoin their mothers. Back on the healing grounds, they tended their own fire pits, varyingly following the ritual and entertaining themselves with riddles. It struck me as I observed their seamless inhabitation of parallel worlds that although radical changes were afoot, such changes were not one-way. There was, it seemed, a return route on the path to modernity.

I saw it not just in the ease of young people's movements but in the fact that many women at the *mirusi* ceremony had been, and would perhaps again be, involved with the village Pentecostal church. I saw it in the good cheer with which my friends wished me off to what, for them, is a forbidden ceremony. I saw it in the enthusiasm with which Leonardo, though Pentecostal, arrived around midnight to aid my introduction to it.

All this made me rethink what had so troubled me earlier that day: "How would I be able to attend both the cinema's inauguration and the healing ceremony? How terrible that both had to fall on the same night!" I now wondered whether the sense of this as a dilemma was uniquely mine.

Continuities of Change

This is a book about change, about how it is conceived and experienced, received and initiated. Dominant discourses, following Michel Foucault's (1972) view of history as a series of epistemic ruptures, have come to present historical change in terms of discontinuous epochs. Attending this is usually a strong sense of the exceptional nature of the present, its radical alterity from the period just past. Hence, the present world, the one we are *all* said to inhabit, is that of the "post": postmodern, postcolonial, postsecular. Germane to this book's opening narrative is the "postelectronic world" now upon us, one in which media technologies connect even remote corners to far-off places (Appadurai 1996: 5).

Of course, there are exceptions. As late as the year of my fieldwork (2011–12) no cell phone signals reached Kaveya or other rural parts of northern Mozambique; electricity was confined to the core of the district capital. Yet plans for constructing cell phone towers were in the works. And, as seen at the longhouse cinema, living off the grid could not keep resourceful villagers from accessing hitherto unknown styles and stylings. Mr. Ong'eng'o was just a hint of things to come. On future visits I saw villagers enjoying videos from as far away as Nigeria and Hollywood.

Especially popular among the latter was the film *Undisputed II: Last Man Standing*, promoted on the DVD cover as "Intensive! Explosive! Mind Blowing!" Major changes under way, indeed.

There is indisputable value in seeing often-overlooked locales as developing in these ways. Worried by globalization trends, anthropologists once made it their mission to document and thereby salvage "tribal" folkways before modernity could render them extinct (Gruber 1970). Well-intentioned though they were, the anxieties driving these efforts also betrayed a measure of ignorance about how cultures have always been dynamic, adopting and adapting to foreign and unfamiliar forces. An anthropological alternative to the caricature of vulnerable natives powerless before homogenizing pressures arose in the late twentieth century along with similar developments in postcolonial theory (Bhabha 1994). The argument here was that however universalizing its rhetoric and however expansive its ambitions, no cultural, religious, or political formation succeeds in taking similar form in dissimilar settings. People do not passively accept the new. They hybridize and syncretize it, they localize and indigenize it, all in accord with underlying, context-specific logics.

With his 1996 book *Modernity at Large*, anthropologist Arjun Appadurai marked yet another shift, not by denying processes of hybridization but by intensifying possibilities of change. Due not only to electronic media but also to greater means of long-distance travel, a far wider set of possible lives has become imaginable, if not achievable, for more people than ever before. It is not just that people appropriate the new in terms of the old. Today most have it in their power to transcend their places of origin. Consequently, "the world in which we now live . . . involve[s] a general break with all sorts of pasts" (Appadurai 1996: 3).

Nothing better illustrates this turn from hybridity to rupture than the oeuvre of anthropologist Charles Piot. In *Remotely Global*, Piot (1999) argues compellingly against the tendency to see remote African villages, such as those in Togo where he worked, as untouched by global processes of interaction and exchange. One decade later, in *Nostalgia for the Future*, Piot (2010) claims to stand by those earlier insights, but with the premise that something has changed, something epoch defining in fact: the end of the Cold War. Dictators and chiefs lost power and prestige as global superpowers ceased propping them up. The resulting, radically new sovereignties have generated radically new temporalities and subjectivities, in Togo and elsewhere.

Piot acknowledges the arguments against seeing history in terms of momentous breaks.[1] Yet "despite the continued presence of . . . hybridities—of the cultural mixing that is emblematic of the postcolonial moment and celebrated by postcolonial theory—this is nevertheless a world that has turned a new page" (2010: 14). Quotidian concerns have been reoriented from untoward pasts to indeterminate futures. Figuring most prominently in this is the extraordinary spread of Pentecostalism. This is the branch of Christianity—distinct from Orthodox, Catholic, and Protestant branches—that traces its institutional origins to the early twentieth century and manifests in such visceral displays as speaking in tongues and miracle healings. It is also the Christian tradition most belligerent toward non-Christian (sometimes simply non-Pentecostal) ways of being.[2]

Precisely through its disparaging and demonizing of "tradition," Pentecostalism exemplifies just how new is the page that has been turned (Piot 2010: 53–76). From elsewhere in West Africa, political scientist Ruth Marshall frames her own work on Pentecostal renewal movements against what she calls anthropology's "domestication of modernity" paradigm. This approach "depends on tracing, not the ruptures that 'conversion to modernity' brings about, but rather the lines of cultural and historical continuity" (2009: 6). Yet Marshall's critique of anthropology may be overdrawn, since, as seen, more than a few anthropologists have come to emphasize rupture over hybridity.

Indeed, it is within—though also against—the anthropological discipline that the anthropology of Christianity has arisen; and it is within this subfield that the trope of rupture most thrives. Most of its studies of conversion reference Birgit Meyer's (1998) essay, "'Make a Complete Break with the Past': Memory and Post-Colonial Modernity in Ghanaian Pentecostalist Discourse."[3] In the case Meyer describes, to break with one's past means to sever ties with kin and to desist from ancestral rituals. The global reach of this injunction has helped generate much interest in and theorizing of contemporary Pentecostalism.[4]

Leading anthropologist of Christianity Joel Robbins not only documents evidence of Pentecostal discontinuity; he makes of it a critique of his discipline. Anthropology is biased toward continuity, he argues, wedded to a view that "culture comes from yesterday, is reproduced today, and shapes tomorrow" (2007: 10). Robbins contends that Pentecostalism's discourse of disjuncture and ritualization of rupture compel a retheorizing of how people relate the new to the old. Pentecostalism refuses capture by standard models of hybridization and localization. It does, in fact, demand discontinuity.[5]

There is much to commend in the shift from hybridity to rupture, from continuity to discontinuity. Regarding Pentecostal practitioners, first of all, it takes them at their word. Many Pentecostals do claim to be making a "break with the past." The prayers offered at the cinema's inauguration are a clear example, evidence that Mutúali's entrepreneurial project is inseparable from an ethical project of remaking the self in particular ways. Moreover, it is significant that the cinema appeared in the compound of members of Kaveya's Pentecostal church. In the prayer to banish evil spirits from the space of the cinema, the rupturing dynamics associated with mass media's proliferation converged with the rupturing dynamics associated with Pentecostalism's proliferation. Finally, anthropological models that reduce people to one or another cultural matrix do indeed perpetuate a pernicious notion that certain people, usually labeled "traditional," are prone only to reproducing their past, such that even as they change, they essentially stay the same. As argued in an important review essay on the anthropology of Christianity, scholars who hold such views tread perilously close to "suggest[ing] that people are incapable of ever learning anything new" (Bialecki, Haynes, and Robbins 2008: 1145).

Efforts to avoid such perils must be applauded. It would be the height of ethnocentrism to deny non-Westerners existential possibilities that most Westerners assume for themselves—possibilities of transcending one's formative context, of breaking with the past, of taking on the new. But what is implied by associating these capacities with Pentecostalism and other aspects of modernity now said to be at large? Renewal certainly may be occasioned by them, but does it require them?

In line with existential anthropology's insistence on the irreducibility of the self, this book affirms the recent theorizing of rupture but also seeks to radicalize it. The men and women among whom I lived showed me that experiences of migration, models of change, and rituals of transformation are not mere by-products of contemporary global forces. Rather, these preexist and prefigure engagements with those forces.[6] Change, even rupturing change, is endogenous, intrinsic to "tradition."

Theorists of rupture never explicitly state that some people could never, absent "modern" catalysts, engage discontinuity. Just this, however, is implied by the exceptional status granted to such novelties as long-distance migration and Pentecostal conversion. This book can be read as an attempt to render rupture less exceptional, to see Pentecostal conversion at least potentially—and certainly in what I witnessed—as a mundane extension of an already convertible way of being. Conversion, so understood, is less a matter of continuity *or* change than of the continuity *of* change (Bergson 1998: 23).

Beyond Pentecostal Explosion

Helping underwrite the theoretical turn toward rupture is Pentecostal Christianity's global rise. Few studies of the tradition begin without asserting, or at least assuming, its "explosive" growth.[7] Robert Hefner summarizes the consensus in the opening line of just one recent state-of-the-field overview: "It is by now a commonplace in sociology, anthropology, and comparative religious studies to observe that Pentecostalism is the fastest growing religious movement in the contemporary world" (2013a: 1). Were such a claim not sufficiently superlative, consider the words of two renowned religion scholars—Peter Berger, who has written, "In all likelihood, Pentecostalism is the fastest-growing movement in history" (2012: 46), and Harvey Cox, who has described "the tsunami of Pentecostalism that is sweeping across the non-Western world" (2009: 197).

With little more to go on than accounts such as these, I arrived in Mozambique's northern province of Niassa in 2011. I knew what I would be finding; the only task was to make some original analysis of it.

I did not find it.

Not in Niassa Province anyway. To be sure, charismatic ministries have spread throughout Mozambique, including in the historically less Christian, more Islamic north.[8] Moreover, Niassa's capital city of Lichinga is not without a Pentecostal presence. The most visible and well-known among Lichinga's churches is the Brazil-based Universal Church of the Kingdom of God (Igreja Universal do Reino de Deus, or IURD). Fifteen branches had opened in the ten years prior to my arrival—evidence, indeed, of Pentecostal explosion.

Yet in that same time span, as many as three of those branches had folded, while others had moved into smaller buildings.[9] The most graphic illustration of Pentecostalism's tepid reception was written on the cracked, whitewashed façade of a two-story building near Lichinga's municipal prison. During the time of my fieldwork, the building served as a storage

Figure 2. A church building turned storehouse, Lichinga.

and operations facility for Humana People to People. A banner displaying this NGO's Portuguese acronym occupied the top right corner of the exterior wall. However, in faded yellow letters that the banner only partially concealed appeared the faintly legible words *Jesus Cristo é o Senhor* (Jesus Christ is the Lord), the slogan affixed to IURD buildings throughout the world. The narrative of Pentecostalism's dramatic rise is commonly expressed in terms of former cinemas, factories, and storehouses turned into churches. Here I encountered the reverse.

It is not that IURD churches in Lichinga were uniformly empty. Many services were reasonably well attended. However, I soon learned, the attendees were primarily *vientes* (newcomers). This Portuguese term refers not to Yao-, Makhuwa-, and Nyanja-speaking peasants arriving in the city from Niassa's countryside. Rather, *vientes* are formally educated business and government elites who relocate from the more prosperous cities of Mozambique's southern and coastal regions, usually with employment contracts in hand. One worship service I attended in Lichinga included a praise song recited in Changana, an indigenous language of Maputo Province, located nowhere near Niassa. The pastor, himself a *viente*, preached against the demonic influence of "traditional healers, false prophets, and *mazione*." The latter word referred to the prophets of Zion churches that are ubiquitous in southern and central Mozambique but scarce in the north (Seibert 2005: 126). The preacher was clearly contextualizing his demonology—in response, though, not to the reality around his church but to the *vientes* within it.

When I asked one pastor how many of his congregants hailed from Lichinga or elsewhere in Niassa, he estimated around 3 percent. He added that in Lichinga's peripheries, where migrant laborers live, "it's sometimes hard to get fifteen people in the church, even on Sunday." Every time a new congregation opened, he told me, masses of locals would flood in. But within a few months, most would leave. Curiously, many would appear again—too sporadically, though, to be counted among the faithful. I observed such patterns repeatedly during my time in northern Mozambique—of churches arriving, but without always thriving.

Scholars have rarely explored such seeming anomalies, though calls to do so are on the rise.[10] Hefner, while framing his volume on global Pentecostalism in terms of extraordinary expansion, also notes an increase in defections, which "may prove to be an important horizon of research" (2013a: 27).[11] In their edited volume on Pentecostalism, anthropologists Simon Coleman and Rosalind Hackett note that "cases of failure or half-hearted engagement" may disclose new dimensions and fresh insights (2015: 28). Stimulated by such suggestions, I intend with this book to advance what is clearly an emerging research agenda, one that eschews triumphalist accounts by querying rather than assuming the linearity of Pentecostal growth.

My aim, however, is not to replace conventional narratives of Pentecostal explosion with an equally generic account of Pentecostal decline. I have neither the data nor the inclination to make sweeping claims of this sort. A guiding premise of this book—the principle of existential mobility, which I detail later in this Introduction—holds that religious identity is an imperfect indicator of religious activity. I therefore critique the narrative of Pentecostal explosion not because I find the statistics behind them to be wrong, but because there is more to the story than statistics can convey.

One quantitative study, though, deserves special consideration. It not only poses one of the most original, and pointed, challenges to assumptions of a generalized Pentecostal surge. It also happens to be based in Mozambique. Analyzing national census records from the past many decades, Éric Morier-Genoud (2014) concludes that there is no basis for commonplace claims of a massive demographic shift toward Pentecostalism. What *did* change, in 1989, is that Mozambique's erstwhile socialist state adopted policies of economic and cultural liberalization. New religious movements stepped in, suddenly free to project themselves into public space. They constructed large buildings, dominated mass media, and proselytized in the streets. It is the considerable visibility of these movements, argues Morier-Genoud, that has created the impression of extraordinary Pentecostal growth. It is an impression, however, belied by the data.

Researchers who predefine their studies as being about Pentecostalism are especially susceptible to reading too much into such impressions. That is because framing one's work around any single tradition draws one, understandably enough, to where that tradition is most vibrant—and away from everywhere else. The recent effort of cultural anthropologists to organize a research program under the rubric of the anthropology of Christianity illustrates the bias. This subfield arose in response to anthropology's historical neglect of Christianity as an object of inquiry.[12] Avoidance came increasingly to be seen as untenable given Christianity's—particularly Pentecostal Christianity's—apparent rise in the very locales anthropologists have long gone for fieldwork. But if those outside the anthropology of Christianity have neglected the religion, while anthropologists of Christianity focus on where it most stands out—where "members practice their faith in ways that make their commitments hard to ignore" (Bialecki, Haynes, and Robbins 2008: 1141)—a large middle terrain remains largely unexplored.[13]

This book aims to help fill that gap. It shifts attention from the amply documented places where Pentecostal churches flourish to the relatively unknown places where they fail, from the centers of global Christianity to the fringes. In those places where Pentecostals are present but not prominent—where they are, in fact, easy to ignore—might there still be a story worth telling, a story in part about Pentecostalism itself?

Circular Migrations

What scholars tend to report about Pentecostal conversions—that they are universally on the rise—is just as often assumed about urban migrations (cf. Potts 2012). There is no disputing that most African cities are growing rapidly. So too are rates of transnational migration. In his more recent work on post–Cold War Togo, Piot pairs this "exit strategy" with conversion to Pentecostalism: "If Charismatic Christianity represents one response to the current sovereignty crisis, playing the visa lottery is another" (2010: 77).

But, as with conversion, so too with migration there is no shortage of stories to puncture the prevailing narrative. Consider Gildon, whom I met in Niassa's rural district of Maúa, where I based my fieldwork and also where Gildon had grown up before pursuing advanced studies in Lichinga. He recalled the optimism with which his teachers had filled him: "They said about a person who studies that some will be presidents, some nurses, some teachers, some engineers." Yet upon finishing school, reality set in. Since urban survival required a cash income, Gildon needed a job to survive. But since public examiners demanded bribes, he also needed cash to get a job. Lacking the money and the connections he needed, Gildon's education eventually came to nothing. He took to selling tomatoes at the market, tomatoes that were always too quick to spoil. Unable to make ends meet, he decided finally to return to Maúa. He was devastated, but at least there he would have land off which to live.

In his study of the once vibrant Zambian copperbelt, anthropologist James Ferguson (1999) dismantles what he calls "the myth of permanent urbanization," part and parcel of modernization narratives. These narratives refer to the "progress" and "development" attending labor migrations, relocations to that which Westerners consider the pinnacle of civilization: the polis, where people settle, work, and prosper. Yet the overwhelming evidence from copperbelt towns—of deindustrialization and depopulation—points to quite the opposite. On the basis of that evidence, Ferguson argues against evolutionary models that posit linear movement from one discrete stage to another. Such modernist teleologies have devastating effects well beyond the social scientific disciplines that promote them: "For the workers at the Nkana mine, the breakdown of the myth of modernization was no mere academic development but a world-shattering life experience" (1999: 14). The same could be said of Gildon's sense of failure in the city. He had, after all, been promised that school, the great motor of modernization, opens boundless opportunities.

Not everyone from Maúa district had a chance to advance in their studies, though, and so not everyone imbibed the myth of modernization. Cewalusa, for example, is a middle-aged man who tried his fortune in Cuamba,

Niassa's second-largest city, before returning to the Maúa countryside. In Cuamba, rather than employment he encountered only hunger. Yet, despite my suggestive questions, he said he never associated return with resignation or with a sense of shattered worlds. When an opportunity arose to try his fortune in the city, he went. When it failed to bear fruit, he returned. Regress was as seamless as egress.[14] Cewalusa's perspective is by far the more common in Maúa, where formal educational opportunities and thus modernist thinking are scarce. Yet whether accompanied by despair or dispassion, both Gildon's and Cewalusa's stories put the lie to unidirectional conceptions of urbanization trends.

None of this is to imply that people who return do so permanently. Retreat to the countryside did not preclude forays back to the cities—whether to visit relatives, seek treatment in hospitals, or sell surplus crops. Better than "reverse migration," the notion of "circular migration" (Potts 2010) captures such patterns, marked as they are by both transience and repetition. They entail not so much the permanence of outward movements as the multiplicity of lateral movements.

Modernization narratives, by contrast, presume a trajectory. Teleological assumptions about civilizational progress are explicitly denied by those who have recently theorized rupture (e.g., Appadurai 1996: 9). Nevertheless, the trajectory remains. Pentecostalism, it is argued, differs from hybrid forms of religion (e.g., popular Catholicism and African Initiated Churches) in the same way that urban and transnational migration differs from nomadic forms of habitation. Against such thinking, there may be value in applying the same critique made of "permanent urbanization" to the comparable issue of "permanent Christianization." If migrations are circular, so too may be conversions.[15]

Phenomenology and Critique

How might anthropology better account for such deviations from the standard narrative of unidirectional breaks and irreversible shifts? It turns out that Piot, despite purveying this narrative in his more recent work, provides therein an answer. Extending his thesis that both Pentecostalism and emigration independently bespeak discontinuity, Piot notes that the two reinforce one another: "Not surprisingly, perhaps, prayer is routinely called on to enhance peoples' [*sic*] chances in the [visa] lottery. Entire Lomé congregations have even been known to engage in prayer . . . so that members will get visas." Yet, Piot adds, "the lottery fuels not only church attendance but also visits to spirit shrines. One selectee I know hedged his bets and did both, stepping up church attendance while also *returning* to the village to consult a diviner" (2010: 91; emphasis mine). An important shift has taken place from one passage to the next: from "entire Lomé congregations" to "one selectee," from the general to the particular, from ethnography to ethnographic biography.[16] Although his book centers on wide-scale, post–Cold War aspirations to break with villages and spirit shrines, Piot in this brief but telling anecdote reveals what his theoretical model conceals: the often circular and situational character of both migration and conversion.

Inherent in much academic writing is a tendency to eclipse such variations in lived experience with grand theories and metanarratives. Inherent specifically in much social science is a tendency to reduce human thought and behavior to social structures, cultural meanings, and other antecedent conditions amenable to conceptual grasp. Arguing for the disciplinary integrity of the anthropology of Christianity, Robbins (2007) contrasts this subfield with Jean Comaroff and John Comaroff's (1991, 1997) influential work on Christianity and colonial capitalism. According to Robbins, the Comaroffs fail to do what an anthropology of Christianity must: take up Christian culture "as a system of meanings with a logic of its own" (Robbins 2007: 7). Logocentric concerns with meaning and logic—often centered on what people say, what they claim to believe, and what "language ideology" they ascribe to—have driven much of the anthropology of Christianity.[17] Yet while there is no disputing the need to take informants at their word, there are obvious limits to discourse and representation. As Meyer makes plain in the subtitle of her seminal essay, the Pentecostal claim of rupture—conveyed in the phrase "make a complete break with the past"—is a *discursive* claim. In practice, most notable is "believers' *inability* to make a complete break with what they conceptualize as 'the past'" (1998: 318; emphasis mine).

Phenomenological approaches go further than most in stressing the limits of language. Anthropologists working in this vein attend to the frequent disjuncture between ideology and experience, between worldviews and lifeworlds.[18] A phenomenological perspective on the anthropology of religion would take as its starting point not the reified terms whereby institutional religions are conventionally classified—Buddhism, Islam, Christianity—but the idiosyncrasies and indeterminacies of everyday life

(Schielke and Debevec 2012).[19] Crucial to this book, as a work of specifically *existential*-phenomenological anthropology (Jackson 2005; Jackson and Piette 2015), are its detailed portraits of the individual in situation. It employs storytelling techniques that eschew the consolations of category thinking, privileging instead the messiness of mundane events and interactions.[20] Narrative ethnography has the added virtue of resonating with the pluralistic approach to life that characterizes societies relatively less encumbered by the West's outsized Greek metaphysical inheritance. That Africa, as theorized by Négritude philosophers, offers tools for deconstructing Western rationalism and reductionism perhaps explains why phenomenological approaches have been so generative in Africanist anthropology.[21] Out of their respective fieldwork engagements in West Africa, phenomenological anthropologists Paul Stoller and Michael Jackson have helped pioneer a more humanistic mode of anthropological research and writing.[22] I follow their lead in accentuating the textured, multiplex lives of my interlocutors. Those lives are worthy of attention in their own right, but also as a critique of the disembodied epistemologies that are as alien to African villages as they are paramount to Western academies.

Without discounting the impact of global forces and discursive formations, phenomenological anthropology recognizes that macro-scale phenomena, "explosive" though they may be, never exhaust the intricacies of life as lived. These intricacies often present themselves at such easily overlooked registers as corporeal dispositions, mundane metaphors, and quotidian practices. Robbins's starting point for the anthropology of Christianity is much different—more discursive than experiential, more intellectual than embodied, more structural than existential. Concerned to identify that which uniquely characterizes Pentecostal culture, Robbins ultimately settles on a negative definition—"a culture 'against culture' " (2010: 159–62). He insists nonetheless that it is meaningfully spoken of as a whole. In his rejoinder to Robbins's initial critique, John Comaroff argues that by "treat[ing] the faith primarily as culture," Robbins commits the once common flaw of analyzing cultural or religious traditions separately from their historical and material entailments (Comaroff 2010: 529).[23] I could not agree more with Comaroff on this point, though I do not endorse the Comaroffs' alternative that reifies impersonal powers and processes of another type—for example, neoliberalism, commodification, and modernity.[24]

Against all forms of abstraction, phenomenological anthropology intervenes by reinserting the individual and refusing to infer lived experience from identities and epochs. Comaroff is as dismissive of this approach as he is of the anthropology of Christianity. He faults it for fetishizing the local and failing to deal with theory. Yet a turn to critical situations and lived events need not imply disregard for global dynamics (Abu-Lughod 1993: 8). It is simply a refusal to see what Comaroff calls the "macro-cosmic forces and determinations in the world" (2010: 528) as so forceful or so determinative that they leave people with little to do but acquiesce.

Existential Mobility

Along with identifying and characterizing "Christian culture," a parallel research priority for anthropologists of Christianity has been that of specifying what it means to be a "Christian self." Social theorists have long noted the role of Christianity, particularly Protestantism, in individualizing and interiorizing subjectivity. Among those for whom the self is defined relationally, conversion to Christianity involves conversion not just to a religion but to a modern conception of autonomous personhood.[25]

Yet just as surely as unidirectional models of conversion and migration oversimplify, so too do trajectories of individualization and the typology they assume. Against claims anthropologists once made about the mystical interrelations of "primitive" people, Godfrey Lienhardt highlights the eccentricities, slips of tongue, and clever calculations at the heart of traditional African folktales. Without foreclosing relationality, these reveal an "African concern, also, on occasion, with individuals as individuals" (1985: 143). Conversely, against claims that Christian converts become self-governing free agents, numerous recent studies show that, after conversion, forms of sociality get newly formed while others persist from the past.[26] To honor this variability, Simon Coleman proposes replacing the language of trajectory with that of negotiation, since "the spiritual, moral, and ethical movements involved in such negotiation are not one way and certainly do not seem inevitable" (2011: 244; see also Bialecki and Daswani 2015: 272–73). Rather than reducing subjectivity to one relatively stable modality or another, phenomenological anthropologists similarly call attention to the variety of ways of being—egocentric *and* sociocentric—that remain viable and negotiable whatever the cultural context (Jackson 2012).

Philosophers associated with the existential branch of phenomenology emphasize this irreducibility of the self to any singular essence or identity. Martin Heidegger (1962), for example, describes the existing human as ever entangled, and therefore as ever changing, with the temporal world; Jean-Paul Sartre (1968) defines freedom as the individual's ability to make something of what he or she has been made; and Lewis Gordon (2000) develops his critique of antiblack racism on the grounds that human beings are incomplete possibilities. Presupposed in all these views is the epistemic openness of lived experience, the indeterminacy of individuals in the immediacy of their situations.

Rather than taking Pentecostal religion and indigenous culture as themselves objects of analysis, I follow such insights by privileging critical events: moments of being that are existentially most imperative and analytically least conducive to closure.[27] This book records a series of such events—snakebites and elephant invasions, chronic illnesses and recurring wars, disputes within families and conflicts with the state—each of which stretches individuals in ways not always predictable by or reducible to their ascribed identities. Existential anthropology aims to honor such ambiguities. Against the tendency to pin personhood to one sort or another, it endeavors to disclose life in all its aspects: its contingencies no less than its norms, its shadows no less than its centers.

To reject the myth of the essential self, continuous and constant across space and time, is to recognize that identities are not identical with experience and that the individual is multiple (James 1950: 294). We do not have cultural identities but cultural repertoires. Which aspect of one's repertoire will come to the fore, and which will remain latent, depends on the particular demands and opportunities of the moment. Those I came to know over the course of my fieldwork limited their actions to neither a "Pentecostal" nor a "traditional" frame, neither an urban nor a rural one, neither an individual nor a relational one. Rather, they experimented with and oscillated between the various options available to them. Such options are open to all who inhabit the kinds of complex, pluralistic worlds that have recently led a variety of scholars to question anthropological frameworks focused narrowly on Christianity, Islam, or any other single religion.[28] It is in line with such critiques that I present this book. What follows is less an anthropology of religion than an anthropology of religious eclecticism.[29]

It is, thus, an anthropology of mobility—or, better, of existential mobility. For Ghassan Hage, existential mobility expresses the imperative to feel that one's life has direction, that one is not in any way "stuck." Well-being is contingent on things *going well*, not necessarily on people *going places* (2005: 470–74). Similarly, Jackson describes existential mobility as inclusive of but more fundamental than geographic migration. It is the proclivity for improvisation that manifests in "the minor, fugitive, and often unremarked events that momentarily change a person's experience of being-in-the-world" (2013: 229). What these movements—imagined or physical, local or translocal—point to is a situational, shape-shifting mode of existence, a capacity to navigate different societies, different people, and different moments in the life course. By so emphasizing the plasticity of personality, the notion of existential mobility portrays the human being as several rather than singular, shifting rather than settled. If there is an essence to this kind of selfhood it would be its inbuilt multiplicity, its intrinsic mobility. Existentialists have captured well this paradox, coining such terms as the "journeying self" (Natanson 1970) and the "homo viator" (Marcel 1962).

Those among whom I lived would have their own metaphor to deploy—that of the polygamous man. He must provide for the well-being of each of his wives and all of their children, a less than enviable role in a society so wracked by scarcity. Given matrilocal residence patterns, discharging this responsibility requires that he spend much of his time walking—sometimes all day, usually alone, between the widely dispersed compounds of his wives. Once, while returning to the district capital after a week of work in the villages, I happened to cross paths with an acquaintance, a man I knew to have multiple wives. After exchanging greetings I asked whether he was also heading home. He replied with a hearty laugh. "The polygamous man has no home. He lives on the road!"

Mobility in Context

So, in a sense, does the ethnographer. Although I started off in Lichinga, intending to conduct fieldwork exclusively there, the evidence I encountered of circular migrations moved me to partake in my interlocutors' own movements. I followed them back to their rural homes.

Thus I found myself, by the start of the 2012 dry season, in the savanna woodlands of Maúa district, in the Makhuwa-speaking south of Niassa Province. Half of Maúa's fifty thousand inhabitants lived in the district capital, also called Maúa—or Maúa town, as I will refer to it. Getting there from Lichinga required a half day's drive along mostly unpaved roads. I foresaw numerous benefits to carrying out the remainder of my research in a rural district like Maúa. First, Pentecostal churches are present there. It is an important but overlooked fact that the Pentecostal movement is not limited to the urban centers where most studies of it are set.[30]

A second reason is inherent to long-term, localized fieldwork. Ethnography as a method involves researchers in the practical exigencies of life in a place. It allows one to essay some understanding only after prolonged periods of concentrated immersion. Delimitation is key. As a Makhuwa proverb asserts about another kind of fieldwork, *Wunnuwa ematta kahiyene oruwerya* (To have too big a field is to fail to produce), a recognition of the greater crop yield resulting from a well-defined plot. Living in so nondescript a locale as Maúa may have afforded me little to work with in terms of breadth, but much to work with in terms of depth. It forced me to account for individual lives rather than collective types, to learn an indigenous language rather than rely only on Portuguese, and to consider the history of a specific set of communities rather than collapse it within that of Africa writ large. In so circumscribing my focus, the intent was not to satisfy that romantic yearning, once common among anthropologists, to live in a remote village assumed to be self-contained. Even seemingly isolated settings, as this book shows throughout, are replete with instabilities and encounters (see Tsing 1993; Piot 1999).

Narrowing my field to Maúa also allowed me to study Pentecostalism in terms not solely of transnational flows—a prevailing thrust in the scholarship—but of the *reception* of churches that in every case originate elsewhere. This book focuses on the recipients more than the transmitters of Pentecostalism, on that *from which* more than that *to which* people convert. It attempts to trace the local dynamics that illuminate the counternarrative at the heart of this study.

As already mentioned, phenomenological approaches to anthropology are criticized for attending so much to the fine-grained and experience-near that they lose sight of the big picture. They are regarded as decontextualized—indifferent to social forces and cultural formations. The notion of existential mobility is likely vulnerable to the same critiques. Existentialism, after all, is a philosophy of the individual, while mobility suggests context transcendence, not context dependence. Neither of these commonplace assumptions, however, applies to the ethnographically grounded works of existential mobility that inspire this study.[31] Indeed, as stressed by the anthropologists who first elaborated the term, existential mobility may manifest as resilience and endurance, not only as resistance and escape (Hage 2009; Jackson 2013: 207–8).

More basically, assumptions about the deracinated self miss key features of the existential tradition itself. Existentialism is not so much a philosophy of the individual as it is a philosophy of the individual in relation. The first person to call himself an existential thinker, Søren Kierkegaard, defined the self as "a relation which relates to itself, and in relating to itself relates to something else" ([1849] 1989: 43). As with Kierkegaard's (1985) famous example of the biblical Abraham, who risked making himself monstrous so as to be true to the divine, the self only comes into being through means of an unconditional commitment. Similarly, Heidegger (1962) casts his project as a critique of Cartesian subjectivism and individualism. His notion of being-in-the-world—of subjects and objects as intertwined, of the self as inseparable from surroundings—sought to correct for founding phenomenologists' emphasis on the ahistorical, transcendental ego (Zigon 2009). As with Kierkegaard, so too with Heidegger: commitment and passion, involvement and care, are constitutive of what it means to be human.

Mobility, by definition, also seems antithetical to contextual analysis. Social theorist Charles Taylor considers migration one of two quintessential expressions of what he calls modernity's "great disembedding"—the ability "to imagine the self outside of a particular context" (2004: 55). The other, suitably enough for this study, is conversion. But there is no good reason to counterpose migration and milieu, conversion and context. Mobility always transpires within a field. Moreover, some contexts and some cultures promote mobility from within. A central argument of this book is that the Makhuwa culture, in the paradoxical way I use this term, is one; the Pentecostal culture is another. The more committed to either (in a Kierkegaardian sense) or involved with either (in a Heideggerian sense) that one finds oneself, the more prone one is to making moves: sometimes within it, sometimes beyond it. Hence, the title of this book, *Faith in Flux*, which conveys the idea of an inconstant faith, but also of faith in the virtue of inconstancy, and thus in any tradition that helps foster it.

By exploring existential mobility ethnographically, through fieldwork among a particular people in a particular place, I endeavor to show that contextual and cultural analysis is entirely compatible with the aims and assumptions of existential anthropology.[32] Existential mobility is not only about going beyond what has been prescribed by custom or internalized as habit. It is, at least potentially, about going beyond *because of* what has been prescribed by custom or internalized as habit. Of Virginia Woolf's famous line "I am rooted, but I flow" (1998: 83), one could posit a paraphrase befitting this point: I am rooted, so I flow.

The Peripheries of Pentecostalism

In the rural district of Maúa, no less than in the provincial capital of Lichinga, the few Pentecostal churches present have been tepidly embraced. The first to arrive was the African Assembly of God (Assembléia de Deus Africana, or ADA), which originated in Southern Rhodesia (Zimbabwe) in 1968 but crossed national borders almost immediately.[33] After establishing itself in Mozambique's central provinces, nearest to Zimbabwe, the ADA gradually spread north. In 1992, it arrived in Maúa, brought by a local schoolteacher who discovered it in Cuamba. When I began my fieldwork in 2011, Maúa was home to one central ADA congregation in Maúa town and two congregations in outlying villages. At the central congregation I regularly observed twenty-five to thirty worshippers at Sunday services. Approximately half of these were *vientes*, those residing in Maúa town for employment purposes but who considered home to be elsewhere.

When I first met Pastor Simões, the locally born but externally trained head of the central congregation, he seemed proud to tell me that wherever he ministers he gathers congregants every morning for prayer. His enthusiasm waned, however, when I expressed interest in attending the next day. He may not have wanted me to see what I later learned to be the case—that the only regular attendees (except on Sunday) were Pastor Simões, his wife, and their children. The satellite congregations fared similarly. In Kaveya, the seven-hundred-person village where this book's opening narrative—and most of its ethnographic material—is set, approximately a dozen adults regularly attended the local ADA's Sunday services. (Here there were no weekday gatherings, nor any pretense of them.) The third ADA congregation, in another distant village, counted only four regular attendees who held their weekly meetings in one of their homes.

The other Pentecostal presence in the district was the Evangelical Assembly of God (Evangélica Assembléia de Deus, or EAD). Unlike the ADA, the EAD operated only in Maúa town. When it was brought by itinerant Brazilian missionaries in 2001, a few dozen individuals took part. But those numbers steadily declined. In 2004, the structure of the building disintegrated. It is common enough that mud walls incur damage during the rainy season. What varies is the level of commitment to replastering them. This time, when the church walls collapsed, so did the church. Yet six years later, slightly before I began fieldwork, the national EAD organization sent a young Mozambican pastor named Manuel to revive its Maúa ministry. He succeeded. On Sunday morning visits during my fieldwork year, I could always count on worshipping alongside twenty-five or so others. Yet most, even more so than at the central ADA congregation, were *vientes*.

Altogether, these numbers may seem paltry; relative to the district's total population, they are. Either for simple distance from one or (an argument I elaborate in the Conclusion) for the reputation these churches have developed, most locals never set foot in the ADA or the EAD. At the heart of this study, though, are those who did. Whether identifying as members of a congregation or by chance living close to one, these men and women involved themselves situationally and selectively. While the relationship of *vientes* to the churches may have been more stable (though this is an open question), this book takes as its study population the vast majority of Maúa's inhabitants who, by contrast to *vientes*, are locally born, Makhuwa-speaking, and economically disadvantaged. Insofar as they relate to Pentecostalism, I argue, they do so powerfully, but they do not do so permanently.

Pentecostalism is only the most recent religious body to arrive in Maúa. Already on the scene were Islam and Catholicism. Still today these are the two most prevalent religious traditions, each claiming almost half the district population.[34] Islam came first, spreading from the Swahili coast in the late nineteenth century. This was, and continues to be, an Islam integrated with ancestor-based practices. In 1938, Catholicism arrived via Italian missionaries. Initially, these missionaries proscribed ancestor veneration and denied baptism to healers and diviners. The Church's stance opened radically in the 1960s, such that today Maúa's Catholic leaders go so far as to sponsor annual initiation rites.

The openness of Islam and Catholicism to "tradition" fosters considerable resentment among Pentecostal leaders. It makes Maúa, as they see it, singularly sinful and thus unusually unreceptive to God's truth. As Pastor Manuel once told his congregation (clearly one of *vientes*): "This is a battle we brought from Maputo, from Nampula, from Beira. When we arrive here, sometimes people come with energy, with great energy, but just crossing the border into Maúa, it seems like angels of the devil stop us. Yes, the word of the Lord here is difficult. If not for us, I would say that here there is no Holy Spirit, only evil spirits." So framing his struggle as a cosmic battle serves, in part, to rationalize his failure to attract locals to his church. It also goes far toward assuring him of the valor in waging this struggle where he does—on the uncharted peripheries of Pentecostalism, at the farthest fringes of the faith.

Conversion as a Spatial Practice

Besides pastoral claims of demonic impediments are scholarly explanations for why Pentecostalism does not or would not thrive in a place like Maúa. Conventional assumptions that the tradition grows most rapidly in previously Christianized areas imply that growth would be weak in places where Christianity has not established itself. It may well be that "the more Muslim north" of Mozambique is itself a barrier to Pentecostal growth (van de Kamp 2016: 11n20). However, it should be noted that although the region is indeed heavily Islamic, Catholicism also has long been prevalent.[35] Another demographic sector frequently associated with Pentecostalism is that of the urban and upwardly mobile. An implication could be drawn from this as well, that a rural district of subsistence farmers lacks the socioeconomic conditions for Pentecostalism to flourish. There may be more explanatory value here, although, as already noted, the provincial capital of Lichinga seemed scarcely receptive to Pentecostalism despite being an urban setting. Meanwhile, researchers in other rural parts of Africa have reported significant Pentecostal impact (e.g., Jones 2011).

In attempting to understand the ambivalence displayed toward Pentecostalism, what struck me most was that whenever I asked people why they joined, why they left, or why they circulated in and out, most struggled to articulate an answer. This absence of ideological formulations and reasoned justifications should be taken seriously (Ahmad 2017). It suggests a need to think beyond the explanatory impulse typically guiding outsiders, whether religious leaders or academic scholars. Rather than trying to find ways to reduce complex and contradictory phenomena to some sensible pattern of cause and effect, I was forced by the pragmatism of those I worked with to turn elsewhere: to mundane metaphors and everyday practices. In the Makhuwa case, these were largely metaphors and practices of mobility.

According to one Portuguese-Makhuwa dictionary, *converter* (to convert) translates as *opittukuxa murima*, literally "to change heart" (Filippi and Frizzi 2005: 1034). Yet whenever villagers talked with me about switching religious allegiance, they never used that term. Much more common were routine verbs denoting spatial movement: to move in the sense of migrating (*othama*) or in the sense of leaving one religion and entering another (*ohiya ettini ekina, ovolowa ettini ekina*). In contrast to introspective conceptions of conversion presupposed in Western thought (Swift 2012), conversion among the Makhuwa is embodied and embedded. It is a migratory movement—less spiritual than physical, less a change of heart than a change of place.[36]

While, in local parlance, *othama* and *ohiya ni ovolowa* translate "conversion," neither term is particular to religious change. Both designate all sorts of geographic relocations. In order to understand the nature of conversion, therefore, I had to study the nature of migration. I discovered in short order that movement—going, but just as often coming—is foundational to the Makhuwa sense of self. One may speak of a Makhuwa disposition toward mobility, a kinetic conception of being that finds expression in migration histories, agricultural techniques, and life-cycle rituals. A typical greeting—what I was met with on the path between the cinema and the healing grounds—is not "are you well?" but "are you walking well?" And as seen on the healing grounds themselves, restoration to health entails bodily transformations, bodily transformations premised on bodily transportations.

Plan of the Book

This book thus unfolds as a series of variations on the theme of mobility—religious, regional, and above all existential. Part I (*othama*, to move) and Part II (*ohiya ni ovolowa*, to leave and to enter) are named for the two commonest renderings of "to convert." Chapter 1 and Chapter 2 (in Part I) attend to histories and mythologies of geographic movement, evidence of how wrong it would be to restrict mobility to modernity. To be "rooted" in Makhuwa tradition is paradoxically to be grounded in a transient, seminomadic way of life. Makhuwa historical experience and selfhood manifest an ability to adapt quickly to changing political and environmental circumstances, circumstances that remain unpredictable and precarious up to the present.

Part II begins by shifting attention to the lived body. In Chapter 3, I argue that initiation rituals serve not only to express mobility but also to cultivate dispositions toward it. This chapter also highlights the resonance of discontinuous spheres—between, for example, male and female, young and old, bush and village, night and day—even prior to what I discuss in Chapter 4: the colonial-era fragmenting of social life into discrete domains, and of spiritual life into reified religions. Thus, movement, including interreligious movement, is best seen not as frictionless flux but as the crossing, and recrossing, of borders.

Part III takes its title (*okhalano*, to be with) from another Makhuwa term, not one for "conversion" but one that sheds light on the symbiotic manner by which the Makhuwa carry out their lives. Chapter 5 documents the matricentric character of Makhuwa society, contending that women, especially, maintain Makhuwa pluralistic propensities amid the ever-increasing hegemony of market logics. Chapter 6 takes up what it means "to be with" Pentecostalism. No less than ancestral traditions, Pentecostalism also is marked by mobility. It presents itself, thus, as continuous with Makhuwa ways of being, continuous precisely through its dynamics of change.

All of this points up a profound irony, the nuances of which the Conclusion explicates and the implications of which it explores. That is the irony of radical change as a cross-cultural constant. Convertibility as a mode of being is present as much in Makhuwa traditions as in Pentecostal traditions, and therefore also in people's oscillations between the two.

This insight sheds valuable light on the ambivalence with which the Makhuwa have received Pentecostalism. It also suggests a need for nuance in the largely unchallenged narrative of Pentecostalism's worldwide "explosion." The propensity for novelty and change that contributes to the rise of Pentecostalism can also contribute to its decline. For just as Makhuwa mobility draws people to the churches and finds reinforcement in the churches, it also facilitates exit from the churches. The Makhuwa are predisposed to convert. But having done so once, they feel little need to stop.

PART I

Othama—To Move

CHAPTER 1

A Fugitive People

The opening chapters of this book take *othama* (to move) as their guiding motif. Just one of the local metaphors used for religious conversion, it is a term whose relevance lies in its everydayness. Those among whom I lived, although not precisely nomadic, have a propensity for dealing with problems by leaving them behind. Their predilection for flight suggests that to be grounded in Makhuwa tradition is paradoxically to be mobile. It is this fluid way of being, I argue, that informs the facility with which many of the same people who move across space move across religions. In situating historically the regularity and reversibility of both migrations and conversions, the current chapter also demonstrates that the small set of African villages where I worked bears no resemblance to the static enclosure once considered the ethnographic ideal. Hence, as further introduction to the setting of my research, this chapter attends less to the place than to the people—people who inhabit the land not by rooting themselves to it but by moving themselves through it.

Luisinha

The sun just beginning to fall below the forested horizon, ten-year-old Luisinha was doing what she normally did when not helping her mother pound grain or fetch wood.[1] She was playing with age-mates on the main road connecting Kaveya village to Maúa town. She likely had on the same tattered dress I always saw her wearing and the same sweet smile I relished whenever she wandered near. I would look up from the water I was boiling or the notebook I was filling, nod toward the 50cc Lifo parked close by, and whisper our secret word: *muttuttuttu-ttu-ttu-ttu*. Covering her face and laughing, she would reply with the same—our play on *muttuttuttu*, the Makhuwa word for motorbike.

It was here, in the mud hut compound of Luisinha's parents, that my wife and I lodged during our stays in the Maúa countryside. Jemusse and Fátima belonged to Kaveya village's African Assembly of God (Assembléia de Deus Africana, or ADA) congregation. They were among its most earnest participants. While from them I learned the rudiments of Makhuwa domesticity and Pentecostal piety, I had their children to thank for helping me most with the language. They tired less of speaking with me, perhaps because of our comparable verbal skills, perhaps because they found endlessly amusing all the mistakes I made, and the game of turning each mistake into a new and silly word.

I was away that day—in the district capital, catching up on correspondences and square meals—but it was told to me that shortly before her mother would have called her in for the evening, Luisinha strayed into the low brush along the road's edge. Something sharp pierced her bare left foot, and the swelling came immediately. Vomiting ensued. It was not long before she passed out.

Snakebites were uncommon, but not unknown, in the area. In the recent past, health dispensaries offered the most effective remedy. There had been one nearby, initiated by the Catholic diocese, but Mozambique's health ministry had recently closed it for reasons unknown to villagers. Lacking that option, Jemusse and Fátima consented to the application of traditional medicines by a local healer. Meanwhile, they focused their own efforts on prayer. I had seen my friends pray on many occasions for their three young children, always with unbridled intensity, frequently with weeping and wailing, even in times of health. I can only imagine how agonized their cries to Christ must have been that night, cradling their little girl as she struggled to stay alive.

At various points it was debated whether to transport Luisinha to the district hospital. The elder of Fátima's clan dissented, insisting that hospitals cannot cure this kind of bite. He meant that the snake that bit Luisinha, locally known as the *evili*, was no ordinary snake. He may also have been expressing the common knowledge that even Maúa's foremost medical facility was so under-resourced that the time spent getting there—hours by bicycle over a deeply rutted road—could be put to better use.

Jemusse and Fátima resolved to keep doing the best they could with the little they had, at least until daybreak when a truck would likely pass by and its driver hopefully take pity. Devastated by these details when I first learned them, I could not help but recall Luisinha's "*muttuttuttu-ttu-ttu-ttu*," and wish with all my being that it had been there that night. It was not, and before the sun rose again, Luisinha breathed her last.

The Ends of the Earth

Bereft not only of health facilities but also of paved roads easing access to one, the village of Kaveya could be classed as an "out-of-the-way place" (Tsing 1993). It is located forty kilometers from the district capital, which lies four hundred kilometers from the provincial capital, which, in turn, lies nearly two thousand kilometers from the national capital. Mozambique itself is relatively unknown and unprosperous, even by African standards. A recent report in *National Geographic* describes it as the planet's third poorest nation and calls special attention to the wretched of the rural north: "their ragged clothing, their swollen bellies, their sod houses, their obvious poverty" (Bourne 2014: 71). The article ultimately celebrates signs of development under way. During the past decade, agribusiness multinationals originating in Brazil and China have taken over much of the land, introducing electric power, mechanized equipment, and cash incomes.

They have also transformed much of the landscape, repairing roads first laid by Portuguese concessionary companies and laying many others for the first time. Development workers tout modern infrastructure as the linchpin of progress; roads connect peripheries to centers, people to power. Yet anthropologists have traditionally seen things differently. Roads were reckoned as little more than conduits of contamination. Aiming to investigate unknown people in unreached places, anthropologists took care to accentuate the abysmal quality of the roads leading to their field sites (Dalakoglou 2010: 145).[2]

In the 1980s, anthropologists came to revise radically the bounded and static conception of culture that undergirded this earlier suspicion of roads.[3] No longer a source of anxiety, the trope of mobility came to figure prominently; routes became as interesting as roots (Clifford 1997). The timing of this shift is not incidental. In the late modern world—characterized by decentralized industries, diminished state sovereignty, and advanced transport technologies—migration rates have accelerated at every scale and in every place. Rootedness is now a rarity. Recognition of this has offered not only empirical insights into the present but also a framework for rethinking the past. As Renato Rosaldo argues, "Rapidly increasing global interdependence has made it more and more clear that neither 'we' nor 'they' are as neatly bounded and homogeneous as once seemed to be the case" (1989: 217).

Yet the very dependence of this argument upon the "rapidly increasing" dynamics of globalization leaves open the question of mobility's historicity. Most commonly, mobility appears as a feature not of the human condition but of the *contemporary* human condition (e.g., Urry 2007). It characterizes, exceptionally, the present "age of migration" (Castles and Miller 1998). Indeed, Arjun Appadurai's own conjecture that place-bound natives "have probably never existed" (1988: 39) is belied by the title and thrust of his influential book *Modernity at Large.* Wide-scale population movements, he argues there, are among the "brute facts" that ethnographies pertaining to the present must confront. "The landscapes of group identity—the ethnoscapes—around the world are no longer familiar anthropological objects, insofar as groups are no longer tightly territorialized, spatially bounded, historically unselfconscious, or culturally homogeneous" (1996: 48).

But were they ever? Are "traditional" societies historically dynamic only by virtue of their contact with such "modernizing" forces as colonialism and capitalism, radios and roads? The commonplace conflation of mobility and modernity finds classic expression in G. W. F. Hegel's *Philosophy of History.* After a mere handful of pages disparaging "the Negro" for lacking consciousness of such universal principles as God and Law, Hegel hastens his readers along: "At this point we leave Africa, not to mention it again. For it is no historical part of the World; it has no movement or development to exhibit" ([1837] 1956: 99). The subject chosen for action is revealing: "we" world-historical people (non-Africans, for sure) uniquely possess the agency to leave Africa, and should do so forthwith to avoid becoming mired in its morass.[4]

One suspects such urgency in the speed with which Land Cruisers charge through Maúa's woodland landscapes. For their occupants, point A and point B—rather than the unmarked spaces between—are what matter.[5] Villagers, upon picking up the distant hum of an engine, invariably pause what they are doing and crane their necks to see. When the vehicle emerges from a cloud of dust, someone calls out who among the district's known *akunya* (whites) is passing by. Whether lumber extractors from China, game hunters from South Africa, or state administrators from the capital, the pace of these *akunya* contrasts sharply with that of the subsistence farmers watching from the roadside. These women and men travel by foot, "step by step, like the chameleon" (*vakhani vakhani ntoko namanriya*). The chameleon, honored through this and other proverbs for its deliberate motions as well as for its chromatic mutations, is mostly admired for the lateral positioning of its eyes. This allows it to see peripherally, to take in the margins—something fleeting motorists cannot possibly do. For such passersby, the blur of roadside peasants can only confirm Hegel's view that novelty and vitality come from without, that internal to Africa there is "no movement or development to exhibit."

While such thinking prevails to varying degrees among most of Maúa's *akunya*, it is particularly pronounced among the recently arrived Pentecostal missionaries.[6] Usually from Mozambique's coastal cities and southern provinces, these young men express satisfaction at having arrived at "the ends of the earth" to which Jesus directed his disciples (Acts 1:8, New Revised Standard Version). As Pastor Manuel of the Evangelical Assembly of God (Evangélica Assembléia de Deus) church said with what seemed a mixture of pride and concern: "People back home warned me: Maúa is a place where you arrive alive and leave dead." Yet the very ubiquity of death—Luisinha's was just one of many during my fieldwork year—also goes far toward assuring outsiders of the urgency of their work. Here, at the ends of the earth, live the damnable and destitute—men and women badly in need of being saved, of being changed, of being moved.

Irreversible Breaks

Pastor Simões surprised me by appearing at the door of my residence in Maúa town. As district head of the ADA, he often wore the sleek, ill-fitting maroon suit that, on this occasion, contrasted with the rags of the shorter man beside him. That was Nório, the deacon of the ADA's Kaveya congregation, who had just biked in to summon his pastor back out. Knowing the usually jovial demeanor of both men, I sensed something amiss when my boisterous greeting fell flat. "The girl of Papá Jemusse and Mamã," Pastor Simões muttered in Portuguese before switching to Makhuwa, "*òhokhwa*." I froze with shock. Nório filled in the details. Our heads dropped and we all stood still, a silence only breached when I whispered a curse. We made plans to depart together before daybreak, to be with Jemusse and Fátima just as soon as we could.

We arrived to the sight of dozens holding vigil: members of the Kaveya congregation intermixed with members of my friends' respective clans. The men were gathered together in and around the *muttheko*, the open-air shed used for receiving visitors. The women, seated on reed mats across the compound, were wrapped in *capulanas* (lengths of printed cloth), Fátima bare-breasted as is customary for mourners. I spotted Jemusse off to the side, cradling himself on the dirt ground. Dropping my helmet, I walked over, fell to my knees, and embraced him. He never looked up. "Papá," is all his throat emitted. I held him close. And he cried.

An onlooker with knowledge of Makhuwa cultural codes might have found this unusual. Makhuwa men are not supposed to cry (Macaire 1996: 284). If they do, they do so only on the inside. I often heard the same said of Pentecostals. A charge commonly leveled by villagers against their Pentecostal neighbors is that, when a family member dies, they do not cry (*winla*), a way of saying they callously neglect the proper funerary rites. It is true that pastors, no less than initiation masters, teach stoicism in the face of hardship, even in the face of death. It is possible, then, that in sobbing uninhibitedly for his daughter, Jemusse was violating norms of both the Makhuwa culture and the Pentecostal church to which he belonged. It is possible that I too was violating norms of my community—the social scientific community—failing to keep my research subjects properly at bay.[7] But in the face of death, codes of conduct meant very little. Jemusse's head buried in his knees and my head buried in his shoulder, I held him close. And we cried.

Luisinha's body had already been interred. What remained was the third-day visit in which we would carry to the burial plot a floral arrangement the women had put together and a small wooden cross the men were working on. On the crossbar, Luisinha's name was tenderly inscribed with ink produced from charcoal dust and the sap of a banana flower. During this period, by Makhuwa tradition, immediate family members were also to shave their heads (*okhweliwa*), though this had not been done.

The procession began at daybreak the third day. We walked silently in single file behind Pastor Simões, still in his maroon suit, who carried the cross in one hand and his Bible in the other. Turning off the main road onto a narrow footpath, we followed it deep into the bush until we reached a clearing studded with mounds of dirt. The men snapped off leafy

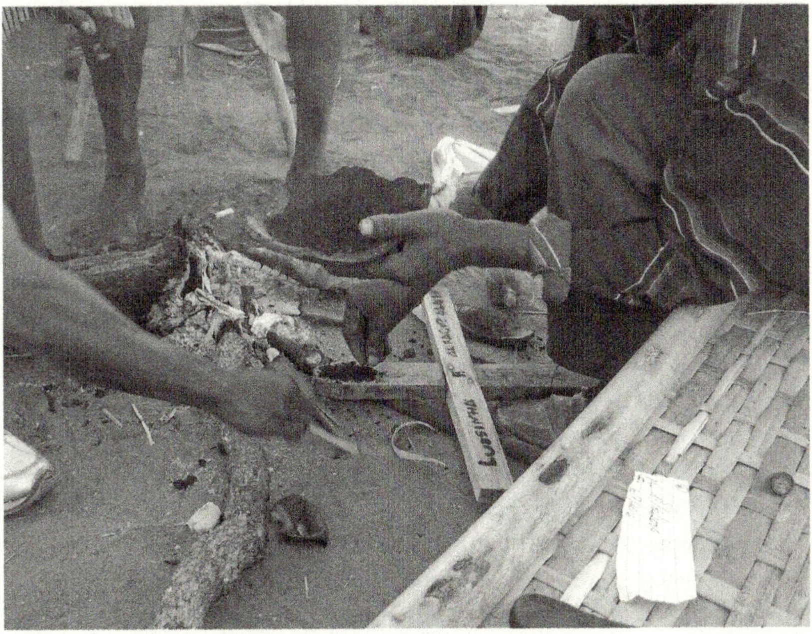

Figure 3. Preparing the cross for Luisinha, Kaveya village.

branches from surrounding trees and used them to sweep around Luisinha's plot. Cross planted and flowers set down, all of us then crouched low and turned to Pastor Simões.

He opened with a short prayer before launching into his homily. Rather than reminisce about the dearly departed, he used his time to excoriate Makhuwa conceptions of the afterlife. Luisinha's *munepa* (spirit; pl. *minepa*) is now in heaven, he instructed, and she will not return. She will remain with God and with Jesus. It is only evil spirits (*minepa sonanara*) who return to the living, demanding food and drink. "But if you do the will of God, you will arrive in heaven and you will return no more." Luisinha had done the will of God. She would not return; she had already forgotten all the troubles of the world, not least her terrible final hours: "Now she hears nothing, sees nothing, thinks nothing, eats nothing. Everything is forgotten. Therefore, we cannot do *esataka*. Many people, when somebody dies, they go and buy rice, buy a goat, to go and do *esataka*. They say it is to help the person who died. Why did they not help the person when he was alive? They say that we do this because our ancestors did it. But to follow the ancestors is a lie! Jesus abolished this." Pastor Simões was painting an opposition to Makhuwa traditional beliefs about death, grounded as they are in the funerary rite known as *esataka*.[8] This ceremony is understood to join the living to the dead in an act of accompaniment, accompaniment on the recently deceased's journey to the ancestral abode. Yet just as there is a passage out, there is also a return. *Minepa* revisit the living, appearing in dreams and requesting to be fed, offering help to some and causing havoc to others.

It is precisely such regressions that Pastor Simões labored to denounce. His message was that Jesus introduced a new conception of death: one without return, a permanent state of rest at God's side. There was thus no need for *esataka*, nor, for similar reasons, for *okhweliwa*: "Even if you shave your head, the child has already gone." Our responsibility is not to the dead but to the living, particularly at this time to the bereaved. There was a good deal of compassion in Pastor Simões's message for my grief-stricken friends, consistent with his willingness to overlook that they permitted the use of traditional remedies on their daughter. He seemed to respect that in such dire straits, they simply could not refuse any of the few measures available to them. But he was going to make sure no more backsliding (*voltando atrás*) occurred. He knew, no doubt, that it is at times of death that the threat of backsliding looms largest.

Mobility Beyond Modernity

The insistence on rupture, on a total break with the past, is not unique to Pentecostal forms of Christianity. Historians trace it to the first-century apostle Paul. In his classic study on conversion, A. D. Nock (1933) describes Paul's as the first Christian conversion insofar as it made the new a substitute for, rather than a supplement to, the old.[9] Conversion as transference between mutually exclusive faiths was the evangelical ideal in colonial-era missions as well, and consequently became part of social scientific discourse (Comaroff and Comaroff 1991: 248–51). That discourse changed significantly beginning in the 1980s, with such terms as bricolage, hybridity, and syncretism soon permeating historical and anthropological studies of cross-cultural encounter (McGuire 2008: 185–213). Only in a more recent recalibration have anthropologists studying Christianity swung the pendulum back to the rituals and rhetoric of rupture, doing so largely in response to their prominence in the Pentecostal ministries flourishing today. These do, in fact, instantiate the Pauline ideal.

The intensification of rupture—historically, through Pentecostalism, and theoretically, through the anthropology of Christianity—coincides with coterminous shifts marked by critical theorists and political economists: from modern to postmodern conditions, from Fordist to post-Fordist economies, and from centralized to neoliberal governance (Piot 2010: 12–13). Underwriting each of these are the "meta-narratives of modernity" that posit the modern as a break from the traditional (Englund and Leach 2000). Assumptions about irreversible time thus govern processes of both conversion and modernization. Anthropologists of Christianity have noted the consonance well: "Insofar as [modernity] implies an irreversible break with the past, after which the world is utterly transformed in mysterious ways, it is itself modeled on the Christian idea of conversion" (Cannell 2006: 39).[10] With respect to Pentecostalism, in particular, while its enchanted supernaturalism gives it something of a nonmodern cast, its emphasis on discontinuity "maps neatly onto modernist ideas about the need for radical change and about transformation as progress" (Robbins 2010: 168). Conversion to various forms of Christianity, but particularly to Pentecostal forms, can thus be readily viewed as "conversion to modernities" (van der Veer 1996), both formations entailing or at least enjoining a break with what comes to be seen as a backward past.

Pentecostal pastors in Maúa district, as elsewhere, see themselves as implementing this progressive agenda through their efforts to "mobilize" what they regard as a stagnant population stuck in its ancestral ways. Yet here a paradox emerges. While the kind of movement characterizing Pentecostal conversion may be a movement of rupture, the end of this movement is repose. It is a conversion to end all conversions, a move to end all moves. Pentecostals are not the only recent purveyors of such thinking in Mozambique. At the height of its program of socialist reform (1975–80), the Mozambican Liberation Front (Frente de Libertação de Moçambique, or Frelimo)—the anticolonial guerilla force turned postindependence ruling party—conceived its work as the "mass mobilization" of the peasantry (see Bowen 2000: 53–57). Yet, simultaneously, it adopted from Karl Marx what Marx adopted from Hegel: the view that the successful revolution is less about movement than about the end of history, that the telos of radical change is perennial stasis. Political and religious reformers operating in postcolonial Mozambique share in common what modernization programs most basically assume: border transgressions permitting no regression, great leaps forward allowing no slides back.

This same theme suffused Pastor Simões's graveside homily. Luisinha's transition from life to death, he taught, is not a passage from one zone to another. Rather, it is a shift from one state to another: from movement to rest, from flux to finality. Thus death, like the ideal conversion, is a rebirth—rebirth conceived as an irreversible break, a point of no return, a deliverance unto rest. Rest and permanence, stability and serenity may be self-evident ideals for self-conscious modernizers; they often are for academics under the sway of Western philosophy's "search for the immutable" (Dewey 1929: 26–48). Yet immutability—and, likewise, immobility—is impractical, if not downright odd, for many Makhuwa. For them, rebirth is entirely compatible with return, rupture with reversal. Of course, no shortage of Makhuwa men and women, Jemusse and Fátima among them, have embraced Pentecostalism. That embrace, however, is less helpfully seen as a marker of their modernity than as the latest (and not necessarily the last) marker of their mobility.

Fight or Flight

Soon after Pastor Simões returned to the district capital, discussions at the compound turned to the tragedy's real cause. The elder was deemed correct. This was not just any snake. The bite of the *evili* is usually not fatal—all the proof needed that this one had been transformed. A sorcerer had sent it, and the identity of that sorcerer—Atata Mukwetxhe, an estranged uncle (*tata*) of Fátima's—was known to all. This same man had caused a similar death only one year earlier. The occupants of that compound responded by abandoning it and reconstructing a new one in a distant corner of Kaveya village.

Jemusse and Fátima were now making similar plans—"to leave Atata Mukwetxhe here alone to do his sorcery," Fátima said. Because the rainy season was fast approaching, and because they wanted to remove their two surviving children from further danger, they planned quickly. After consulting with clan elders, it was decided they would decamp to the district capital. Among Maúa town's twenty-five thousand inhabitants were both biological kin and surrogate kin (members of the ADA's central district congregation). Jemusse and Fátima would be able to lean on them for support. Jemusse also foresaw opportunities to reestablish his carpentry trade; although timber was only available in the forested regions of outlying villages, the clients who bought his doors and window frames all resided in town.

Only two concerns held Jemusse and Fátima back. One was limited means with which to transport their belongings—corn and beans, mortar and pestle, carpentry tools, a bundle of clothes. The other concern was for me. With as much generosity as they had shown in allowing me into their lives, they worried about abandoning the compound I had come to use as my rural base. I begged them not to think at all about the second problem and to let me help with the first. I hired a truck from town that could pick them up and transport them there. It was a small and inadequate reciprocation for their hospitality and companionship. Just before the rains arrived, they returned to the cemetery to tell Luisinha they were leaving, loaded their belongings and children onto the flatbed pickup, and set out for the district capital.

I was happy to see my friends do what they thought was best, as were their family and fellow congregants. Not, however, Pastor Simões. "It's not correct to just get up and leave," he said. "They should have remained there. They should have had the courage to fight." Turning sermonic, though it was just us talking, he invoked Jesus's response to Satan testing him in the desert. Jesus did not flee, but remained firm. He stood up to Satan. "A strong person would stay, use the power of prayer and fasting. Only if the person is weak will he leave the situation, change locations." Besides, merely fleeing the problem does nothing to solve it. "You cannot flee from Satan. If this is sorcery, you cannot flee from sorcery. People here say that the sorcerer travels by night."

Pastor Simões did not deny that the occult forces of the sorcerer were real and responsible. He merely maintained that the Holy Spirit is stronger, that it holds the power to protect those who serve it. If only their faith were firm, Jemusse and Fátima could have stayed, fought, and prevailed. This emphasis on fixity recalled the pastor's graveside message from only a few weeks earlier: his insistence that Luisinha's *munepa* would go to heaven and rest eternally there. Nearly everyone and everything around Jemusse and Fátima, however, told them differently. Not only was Luisinha's *munepa* on the move. So, too, to protect their remaining children, must they be.

Evident in Pastor Simões's critique, besides the value of fixity, is the value of ferocity. One also hears this in his frequent sermons enjoining militaristic vigilance against "traditional" customs and practices. At least two discursive contexts help situate this bellicosity. One is that of spiritual warfare, wherein conflicts of the physical world manifest conflicts that are metaphysical in nature (DeBernardi 1999). This takes a particular form in Pentecostal discourse: of a vigorous struggle between the Holy Spirit and satanic forces. Pentecostalism's aggressive antagonism toward alternative religious options has proven alarming to governing authorities, (non-Pentecostal) religious leaders, and scholars alike (Hackett 2003). Yet shorn, perhaps, of its extreme Manicheanism, the idea of cosmic conflicts redounding to the mundane is not uniquely Pentecostal. In fact, as theologian Ogbu Kalu (2008) argues, one reason for Pentecostalism's takeoff in indigenous African societies is a basic ontological compatibility on this point.

A second context for Pastor Simões's elevation of fight over flight is the political project of nation-state formation. Historians note two complementary factors behind Mozambique's independence in 1975: the wearing down of Portuguese militants by Frelimo guerillas in a war that began in 1964, and the overthrow of the Salazar regime in Portugal's 1974 Carnation Revolution. While these factors are interconnected, the Mozambican nationalist narrative, unsurprisingly, accentuates the former, often to the exclusion of the latter (e.g., do Rosário 2004); independence was hard won on Mozambican soil—the result of fierce, armed struggle against the Portuguese. Nothing promotes or celebrates this narrative better than the Kalashnikov on Mozambique's flag, one of very few national flags to feature a weapon and the only one to feature one so lethal. Significantly, the current flag—which foregrounds a hoe (symbol of agricultural productivity) along with the rifle—was officially adopted in 1983, at the height of the civil war between Frelimo and the Mozambican National Resistance (Resistência Nacional Moçambicana, or Renamo). Through its slogan and rallying cry—*a luta continua* (the struggle continues)—Frelimo presented this civil war as an extension of its war of independence, this one also to eliminate a foreign adversary (Renamo's organizational and operational support came from the white ruling regimes of South Africa and Southern Rhodesia).[11] The weapon on the flag therefore not only honors the valor of Frelimo warriors battling Portuguese imperialists, it expresses the need for continued vigilance against threatening foes.

These two larger contexts—the occult one of spiritual warfare and the nationalist one of physical warfare—are not entirely distinct. This is the argument of anthropologist Harry West (2005) in his exploration of sorcery discourse among the Makonde, an ethnolinguistic group of adjacent Cabo Delgado Province. For the Makonde, sorcery attacks do not go unchallenged. Against sorcery of ruin, sorcery of construction (Makonde: *kupilikula*) is deployed to defend one's self and one's kin. Most insightful about West's ethnography is its argument that, for the Makonde, this dialectic of sorcery and countersorcery has provided an idiom for comprehending and controlling a long history of entanglements with unfamiliar forces. Thus, the projects of Portuguese colonizers and Catholic missionaries, of Frelimo modernizers and neoliberal reformers, have all been subjected to inversion and overturning through Makonde sorcery discourse. Arguably the most pernicious of those forces was that of the Portuguese colonial regime. For their central role in combatting this foe, the Makonde until today hold a privileged place in the narrative of Mozambican nationhood.[12]

If, among the Makonde, the idiom of countersorcery expresses opposition to powerful forces, ought not the same hold for their Makhuwa neighbors, Jemusse and Fátima among them? In fact, in the days following the death of their daughter, some clan members contended that the only way to solve the problem once and for all was to eliminate the cause, to kill the relative who sent the snake. This could be done by enlisting the aid of a *mukhwiri*, an occult specialist with the powers of countersorcery. They decided, instead, to move. When I asked Jemusse why he dismissed the advice of some of his kin, he cited the Pentecostal injunction against sorcery and other ancestral practices. "It's because I handed everything over to God. 'God, you are the one who made everything, heaven and earth, our entire body.' I didn't go to the *mukhwiri*. It's true." Yet as we have seen, even their church's leader encouraged a kind of countersorcery. Spiritual warfare is common to both Pentecostalism and indigenous traditions. What differ are the weapon (prayer or sorcery) and the cosmic collaborators (Holy Spirit or ancestral spirits). Eschewing counterattack of either sort, Jemusse and Fátima opted instead for simple flight, one among other "weapons of the weak" (Scott 1985).

This choice of migration over confrontation is consistent with a relatively nonmilitant approach to adversity that, at least during the colonial period, characterized Makhuwa history. Unlike the Makonde, the Makhuwa never held a prestigious place in Frelimo's narrative of anticolonial resistance and nation-state formation.[13] To the contrary, Frelimo has long treated the Makhuwa with contempt and suspicion for not adequately contributing to the liberation cause (Funada-Classen 2012: 289–91). The possibility of a real divergence in values came across in conversations I had with Makhuwa elders and chiefs. In early visits with them, I would ask who the Makhuwa understand themselves to be. Consistently, their responses made reference to two "pillars": cultivation (*olima*) and procreation (*oyara*).

Noting that the first of those appears on Mozambique's flag through the image of the hoe, I asked one elder what the symbols of a Makhuwa flag would be. He hesitated to answer. Perhaps it never occurred to him that what I insistently called "the Makhuwa" needed a flag.

"For Mozambique, it is the hoe and the Kalashnikov," I said, trying to help. "For the Makhuwa, maybe the hoe and . . . ?"

This time, with no hesitation, "the child."

Migration Histories

If Mozambique's nationalist values of defense and vigilance suggest a hunkering down, a posture of defiance premised on rootedness to a land, the Makhuwa value of *oyara*, by contrast, evokes natality. As defined by Hannah Arendt, this is the capacity of human action to initiate new beginnings, to release the future from bondage to the past (1971: 247). An equally apt metaphor for this regenerative capacity is mobility, particularly existential mobility, which (as discussed in the Introduction) connotes human improvisation, experimentation, and opportunism.

Notwithstanding the impression created by postpartition maps of Africa —of definitive boundaries separating discrete populations—the norm for the continent's inhabitants has long been one of unsettlement and instability, of fluidity and flux.[14] Many historians and linguists hypothesize "Bantu expansion" to explain the coast-to-coast distribution of a single language family. In a mere matter of centuries, beginning in West Africa around 1000 BCE, emergent iron-using agriculturalists speaking a proto-Bantu language pushed east and south, eventually spreading across an entire third of the continent. More recent scholarship has problematized the notion of a singular rapid expansion (e.g., Ehret 2001), but it is beyond dispute that the distant forebears of most African peoples migrated over long distances—

episodic, gradual, and resistant to historical modeling though their migrations likely were.

Makhuwa, one of an estimated six hundred Bantu languages, is currently mother tongue to some four million inhabitants of Mozambique's northernmost provinces, those situated roughly between Lake Niassa (also known as Lake Malawi) and the Indian Ocean. Because European contact with the Makhuwa in the early colonial period was limited to the maritime coast, little has been recorded about the lives of those in the interior. Whether they entered the region from the north or the south is a matter of speculation (Newitt 1995: 63). What archaeologists do know is that the current inhabitants did not originate on the land they now call home.[15] Their present location owes to migration tracks or *miphito*, "collective movements [that] were far from random but . . . were very strategic" (Funada-Classen 2012: 109).

The strategic nature of their movements owes to a series of pressures imposed by external forces. Among the most brutal were slave raiders and slave traders in the eighteenth and nineteenth centuries, a dreadful and devastating period throughout northern Mozambique (Newitt 1995: 247) that fell particularly hard on the Makhuwa (Alpers 1975: 219). The Arab slave trade predated that of Europe, but it was only when French sugar plantations emerged on Indian Ocean islands and when Caribbean and Brazilian interests turned to East Africa that slave trading came to define northern Mozambique's regional economy (Alpers 1997). Lacking the kinds of large political units that lend stability, flight emerged as the surest means of resisting capture. Whole chieftaincies relocated in the early nineteenth century in search of less easily reached, more easily defended homes.

Far more vivid in the memory of the living are the displacements that attended war. The elders I came to know have lived through two: that of the Frelimo liberation movement against Portugal (1964–74) and that of the postindependence Frelimo state against Renamo (1977–92). The first scarcely reached this part of the countryside. Such was far from the case with the second. Harrowing memories haunt much of the adult population, memories of rebel fighters entering villages, plundering grain, raping women, and kidnapping men (see Newitt 1995: 569–74). The most common response to this latest upheaval was, once again, flight. Nationwide, nearly five million people fled their homes during the civil war (Hanlon 1996: 16). The few villagers of Maúa who were willing to open up about that period told of escaping into forests and mountain caves; others found refuge in large cities or across national borders. Of course, exile did not always, or immediately, solve the problem. Food could not be carried, nor clothes, nor the reed mats used as bedding. The priority was carrying the children. Yet in the most treacherous moments, when speed was of the essence, so too was silence; mothers of crying children had to be left behind, retrieved only when safe to do so. The Makhuwa of Maúa district lived this way—"running like chickens" as Fátima recalled it—for much of the 1980s. They moved from one temporary settlement to another. Lack of land to cultivate and the rapid spread of disease in refugee zones motivated regular relocations, which is why when the fighting finally ended, return routes were soon established. Few lost ties with the people and the lands from which they (temporarily) loosed themselves, certainly not to the degree suggested by the image of refugees as "uprooted" victims (Englund 2002). The current inhabitants of Kaveya village returned to the same area along the Nipakwa River they had earlier occupied. Rebel fighters had burned everything to the ground, so they had to reconstruct their homes and renovate their crop fields, but, as many put it to me, they were content simply to breathe (*omumula*) again.[16]

Slavery and warfare infuse the historical consciousness of those among whom I lived.[17] Yet the response has typically been neither to resist identifiable adversaries nor to stay put and acquiesce. More commonly, people have solved their problems by leaving them behind. In stark contrast to the view of traditional societies as static, the Makhuwa have long lived their lives this way—on the move. In this regard, they are not unlike nomadic, pastoralist, and other "traditionally" transient peoples in numerous African societies, peoples for whom immobility, in fact, is the anomaly.[18]

Even in northern Mozambique, it is not only the Makhuwa who have customarily moved in response to ever-changing, ever-precarious circumstances. Flight from slavers is how the Makonde came onto the plateau on which they now live and into the ethnicity by which they now identify. As one of Harry West's informants told him, "We [Makonde] are really Makua. . . . We took refuge here from the slave caravans" (2005: 27).[19] Significant about the Makhuwa, however, is that they not only came into being as a people on the move, they actualize their being by staying on the move. Makhuwa mobility is evident in the response Jemusse and Fátima chose to their predicament. It is equally evident in what could be called the Makhuwa "culture of mobility," a paradoxical phrase that highlights the irreducibility of the Makhuwa to a single "culture." Their characteristic mobility predisposes them to exceed the bounds not only of their geographic "home" but even, as suggested by West's informant, of their ethnic one as well.

A Culture of Mobility

Humanitarian discourse represents refugees in terms of acute suffering and dramatic loss: helpless victims "stripped of the specificity of culture, place, and history" (Malkki 1995: 12). Distinct from labor migrants, refugees of war—and, one might add, of slave raids—are cast as *involuntary* migrants, reflexively moving in pursuit of bare survival. Yet the decision to migrate is rarely forced upon people wholly devoid of agency. As Stephen Lubkemann argues in his study of social life amid Mozambique's civil war, men and women on the move continued to meet the complex demands of everyday existence—cultivating crops, raising children, performing ceremony. Fugitive acts did little to erase their "culturally scripted life projects, most of which . . . had little to do with the macropolitical interests usually taken to define 'the war'" (2008: 14).

Indeed, migration not just preserved but enacted such scripts insofar as movement itself was a "well-established coping mechanism forged through a long history of crisis and political duress" (Lubkemann 2008: 196). For the people of Manica Province with whom Lubkemann worked, evasion emerged as a strategy of resistance to a series of resettlement schemes visited upon peasants by the Mozambican state. A similar history, I show in Chapter 2, has long weighed (and still does) on populations of the north. Yet, for the Makhuwa at least, the roots of mobility lie even deeper than that. As with the Ndembu—a central African people famously studied by anthropologist Victor Turner—so too with the Makhuwa, one may readily identify "traditions of migration" that make certain villages constitutionally centrifugal (Turner 1957: 59). These are villages prone not to stability and continuity but to periodic displays of fissure and motion. Consequently, what Turner calls the "modern changes," such as monetization and immigration, that would seemingly disrupt social continuity and spur spatial mobility in fact "do no more than accentuate tendencies inherent in the indigenous social system" (1957: 51).

Peoples deemed "native" are typically identified with a determinate land to which they are presumed to definitively associate. Cosmogonies are largely responsible for this, referencing as they do a fixed point of origin. For the Makhuwa, that would be Mount Namuli. Situated in the northern part of Zambezia Province, just beyond the borders of Niassa, Mount Namuli is the second tallest landmass of Mozambique and by far the tallest of the region. "She who made others to see the sun"—that is to say, the first human—is said to have originated atop Mount Namuli. Setting off to explore the verdant plains below, she tripped on the perilous slopes and hit the ground hard. Upon regaining consciousness, she opened her eyes to see that blood from her wounds had mixed with water from a stream. As it wound its way down the mountain, the mysterious mixture formed into a solid shape. It was man. From the blood of the first woman came the first man; and from their union came all future generations. These generations followed the pattern of the first: flowing like streams and voyaging long distances, all the while bringing forth new life.[20]

Conflicts developed, as they inevitably do, between the various lineages born of the first woman and first man. Each lineage group then descended the mountain and spread throughout what is today northern Mozambique. Thus, while the myth of Namuli certainly orients the Makhuwa toward a particular mountain, the myth itself evokes the opposite of geographic fixity. Particularly telling is that, unlike other foundation myths (the Abrahamic, for example) in which the place of origin is also one of departure, Mount Namuli is the place of origin, departure, *and* return. Upon death, the *munepa* of a person is restored to its first home: "From Namuli we come, to Namuli we return" (*Nikhumale onamuli, nnahokolela onamuli*). Contained within all references to Namuli is this dialectic of egress and regress, of risking oneself in the world only to later retreat. Being is thus predicated on mobility or, more precisely, circularity.

So too is well-being. The myth of Namuli constitutes what anthropologist Francisco Lerma Martínez calls the backdrop (*pano de fundo*) of Makhuwa healing ceremonies insofar as it expresses the human being *en passage*—from health to illness and back. Lerma Martínez connects this trajectory to the movement all humans make from Namuli to the world and back (1989: 181–82). Virtually every component of the *mirusi* healing ceremony in particular contains an allusion to the myth of Namuli (Frizzi 2008: 1336–1501). This is as true of the songs chanted through the night as it is of the embodied actions of the ceremony's participants. Repeatedly between sunset and sunrise, these participants (almost entirely women) leave the healing hut, walking in single file with slow deliberate steps and the slightest twist of the torso. In this manner they venture into the bush, where the healer (*namuku*) earlier obtained medicinal herbs and roots, and where regenerative energies abound. The last of many such excursions, shortly before the cock's crow, takes participants to the nearest river—the place of encounter with ancestral spirits (*minepa*) approaching from the river's far side. A propitiatory offering there "gives to the spirits the opportunity to come from Namuli and enter the body of the afflicted, thus enabling his or her physical recovery" (Frizzi 2008: 1350; translations mine). It is at the moment of this encounter that the afflicted person's turn toward health occurs. The procession back from the river is vigorous and triumphant. The remaining ceremonial action transpires outdoors, in the light of the dawning day, with frenetic dancing, singing, and running—evidence that the circular journey to the bush and back is ultimately one of return to life itself.

For the Makhuwa, this oscillatory dynamic describes not only the performance of their ceremonies but even their preservation. The communal ceremony known as *makeya* consists of sorghum flour offerings made to *minepa* under the sacred *mutholo* tree. This ancestor shrine is akin to that of the Ndembu, consisting of "quickset muyombo saplings," a prime feature of which is the ease with which they may be abandoned when Ndembu villagers move to a new site, as they often do. The impermanence of shrines for the Ndembu, as for the Makhuwa, speaks to the ancestor cult's association with what Turner calls "the transience of settlement . . . and with the mobile human group itself rather than its specific habitation" (1957: 173). For the Makhuwa, such sites are not only easily abandoned, they are readily renovated. During the civil war, rebels ransacked and razed villages, forcing inhabitants to flee in haste. When safe to do so, two or three clan members would return and remove a single branch from the abandoned *mutholo* tree. Near the new site of refuge, another *mutholo* would be chosen and the lone branch from the old would be laid up against the new. With time, the branch and the trunk would fuse, assuring villagers that to whatever destination they moved, their forebears were there with them. No ancestral practice rivals, in regularity or in importance, the *makeya* offerings at the *mutholo* shrine. It takes place at every life-cycle ritual, before any venture is undertaken, whenever adversity strikes. It must be relevant, therefore, that the word *makeya* derives from *omakeya*, the modal form of the verb *omaka*, meaning "to inhabit"; *omakeya* means, literally, "to be inhabitable" (Frizzi 2008: 1690–91). This suggests that the ceremonial invocation of ancestors arose first and foremost in pursuit of basic habitability—of security, prosperity, and vitality in one's ever new, though never final, home.

Well-being, for the Makhuwa, is tied less to location than to this capacity for relocation, a capacity instilled and distilled over a long series of situations wherein the inability to move easily meant the immediacy of death. Yet, it is worth recalling, even after death *minepa* are understood to migrate back to Namuli—"From Namuli we come, to Namuli we return"—then back again, reappearing in the nightly dreams and daily affairs of the living. Mobility is clearly no mere by-product of our contemporary, globalized age. Egress has always been a part of even this most "traditional" of cultures, egress followed almost always by regress.

Religious Movements

When Jemusse and Fátima moved to the district capital, I lost my base in Kaveya village. I did not care to sleep alone in their now empty compound, in part for fear of the *evili* that could just as easily have bitten me. It was also my final few weeks in Mozambique, and spending the time in town, synthesizing a year's worth of material, seemed fitting for where I was in my work.

So we remained neighbors—not cohabitants of the same compound as in Kaveya, but now coresidents of Maúa town. But the rhythm of life there did not allow for the idle palaver I so enjoyed back in Kaveya, sharing stories and sugarcane under the shade of a mango tree. While working hard to reinitiate his carpentry trade, Jemusse's first priority was securing a means of feeding his family. He and Fátima had managed to transport surplus grain for the impending rains, but they were already behind schedule for the next year's harvest.

Given how much busier Jemusse became, I accepted that in the remaining weeks of my fieldwork I would not be seeing much of him. It therefore gave me great joy when, after an obviously long day in the fields, Jemusse showed up at the compound where I lodged in town. After exchanging greetings, I asked him to wait while I fetch him some water. Before letting me do so, he opened his mouth to speak.

"Papá, there's something I want to tell you."

"Go ahead, Papá," I said sitting down, struck by the change in tone.

"You know, my thought was to attack Atata Mukwetxhe," he said. "I was thinking a lot of things right after my daughter died. I was thinking of doing countersorcery. The family of Mamã was telling us to attack him because there have been five deaths because of him now."

One week after Luisinha's death, he told me, he had traveled to Cuamba. There he consulted with a powerful *mukhwiri* about visiting deadly force upon the man responsible for his family tragedy. Despite the distance, Jemusse made sure to complete the round-trip in one day, so as not to make public the extent to which he nearly engaged the occult forces barred by his Pentecostal faith. He eventually did not go through with it, opting instead to solve his problem by fleeing from it. But that he had come so close was news to me.

I was touched by Jemusse's openness, his revelation of a secret I had not pried into, nor even suspected. It was common knowledge that he and Fátima had permitted a traditional healer to offer aid on that terrible night, also that Fátima shaved her head (*okhweliwa*) when Pastor Simões was no longer around, and that an *esataka* ceremony was eventually conducted by Fátima's clan.[21] Yet this admission of consultation with a *mukhwiri* seemed transgressive in a much deeper way. It probably would have incensed Pastor Simões and provoked the reprimand that the other offenses did not. It certainly shocked me, as I struggled to reconcile my experience of such gentle and generous friends with my new knowledge that they nearly tried killing a man.

I thanked Jemusse for sharing but wondered aloud why he chose to do so just then. His answer had to do with a desire to externalize what he had done. He worried that once word reached Pastor Simões, he would be made to feel guilty. To Jemusse, I served simultaneously as an outsider able to carry off this anticipated feeling, and as an insider unconcerned with making him feel it. "When I inform you," he said, "I don't have to think any more about this because I am speaking what I did, and when I speak it my words have left my body and are now with you."

"I am free now," Jemusse went on, "because I don't have to think any more about what I was thinking. Now I can forget all of this and begin thinking about other things, about my plans. I can begin again."

I was silent, moved by the eloquence and expectancy of what my friend had to say—by his arrival, yet again, at what he saw as a fresh start.

"Besides," he smiled, "it will only go into your little notebook."

I had nothing to write with just then, but Jemusse knew from observing me at the end of each day (studying me not unlike the anthropologist studying him) that most of what I saw and heard eventually made its way into my field journal. I asked if it would be okay to write his story down to include in the book I planned to write. He said it would. In a context where nearly all are illiterate—even Pastor Simões weaving the Bible into his sermons more from memory than from the text in hand—it is the spoken word that carries real power. That is why Jemusse felt an urge to verbalize his sentiments to me.

Jemusse and Fátima ultimately chose geographic relocation as the solution to their dilemma. Yet, crucially, the option of occult warfare that they also entertained involved a similar sort of displacement, a violation of their church's prohibition against sorcery, against *returning* to "tradition." This kind of religious mobility is best seen as a variation on the perennial theme, explored throughout this chapter, of physical mobility in Makhuwa history and culture. The prevalence of dislocation, of routinized rupture, in Makhuwa life suggests the centrality of mobility to any understanding of the Makhuwa in general. Its real relevance, however, owes to the semantic point explored in the Introduction—that in the parlance of villagers, *othama*, "to move," also translates as "to convert." Conversion is not an internal transformation but an embodied one, and the regularity and reversibility of spatial shifts give insight into the regularity and reversibility of religious shifts.

Accompanying no act of *othama* is the illusion that life will be made carefree or stable as a result. By escaping to the district capital, Jemusse and Fátima did not see themselves as transcending their problems but as simply affording themselves new terrain on which to confront them. Life is made viable through these small rebirths, these everyday acts of natality, the latest (and surely not the last) for Jemusse being that of our conversation that day—his off-loading of worries onto me and my little notebook.

CHAPTER 2

Between the River and the Road

While Pastor Simões saw fit to censure Jemusse's and Fátima's departure from the countryside, a different set of actors in the district capital would have likely looked on with favor. These are the Maúa district officers who affiliate today, as the postindependence state always has, with the Mozambican Liberation Front (Frelimo). Although originally an adversary of the Portuguese regime, Frelimo as a party-state has—from the perspective of many I spoke with—only replicated earlier colonizers' mania for confiscating lands and concentrating people. In shifting attention from Pentecostal evangelization to Frelimo sedentarization, this chapter explores the political conflicts that emerge out of efforts to manage a population whom Maúa's district administrator once described to me as "too mobile." The Makhuwa propensity for mobility has long frustrated state builders' efforts to settle their intended subjects. It is also, I argue, what stifles church planters' efforts to do the same.

Lightly on the Land

Local storytellers recount that when their earliest ancestors descended Mount Namuli, different lineage groups dispersed widely enough to remain independent of centralizing chiefdoms and kingdoms. This posed a challenge to invaders bent on ruling the land. Unlike the sixteenth-century Spaniards who came upon territorialized sovereignties in Aztec and Inca capitals, the Portuguese in central Africa encountered only small and scattered chieftaincies. With no large armies for them to defeat and no major battles for them to win, they were forced into warfare with no endgame. African polities' seeming disorder thus rendered them resilient to European invaders in a way that, ironically, the sophisticated imperial states of the Americas were not (Newitt 1995: 58). This strategic advantage may have been enough to motivate the Makhuwa to live, as they long have, in a diffuse and fragmented manner. Political considerations of this sort are the main subject of this chapter. These, however, are inseparable from more foundational factors to be examined first, factors pointing to what is until today a common Makhuwa assumption about land occupancy—about the impermanent, indeterminate relationship between individuals and the ground on which they stand.

Of greatest significance is the sheer vastness of the terrain across which groups could move. With a mere eleven persons per square kilometer in the year that I lived there, Niassa Province—one of four the Makhuwa inhabit—is the least densely populated of Mozambique.[1] A recent report from a foreign news source put it vividly: "Bright snaking dirt tracks mark the roads and slivers of green trees line the rivers, but there is an overwhelming sense of emptiness about the Niassan countryside. The towns are scarcely different" (Casey 2015). Little has changed, apparently, since the late nineteenth century, when one of the first Europeans to pass through what he called Makua Land declared it "bare and uninteresting, monotonous and dreary" (Maples 1882: 86). Dreariness, however, is not without its advantages, for the local populace, at least. Primary among them is the option of escape whenever rulers and settlers encroach. Vast and land-rich frontiers have long served in this way to underwrite popular freedom (Scott 2009: 4).

Specifically Makhuwa conceptions of the land further foster such centrifugal possibilities. According to Makhuwa norms of matrilineal inheritance, land always passes through the mother's clan, thereby remaining under local control (Newitt 1995: 64). Moreover, Makhuwa economics is marked by an absence of inheritable goods and a closely linked lack of attachment to specific tracts of land. This may owe to the fact that, while the Makhuwa have been farming for centuries, they subsisted on hunting long after their neighbors turned to settled agriculture (Alpers 1975: 8–10). The resulting tendency toward territorial nonattachment finds expression in the premium placed on being "light-footed" (*oveya metto*). Whenever I asked about this notion, interlocutors explained it not with words, but with gestures—soft, fluid, and usually barefoot treading on the brown soil beneath us.

A suspicion toward acquisition and an embrace of mobility were widespread among those I came to know in Maúa's outlying villages. In defiance of their critics in town, they viewed their transience as a reasonable adaptation to a land predictable only in its unpredictability. Historian Malyn Newitt describes an early nineteenth-century period of persistent instability, known as the great Mozambique drought, as possibly the severest rain shortage on record. It was far from the only one. Some years of drought are expected to punctuate every person's lifespan. As recently as 2003, rains failed to fall in Maúa, forcing kin groups to activate coping strategies honed over centuries: first intensifying hunting and trading, then searching out and moving communally to more fertile regions (Newitt 1995: 253–54).

On a smaller scale, the same mobility transpires, even when the vagaries of drought and famine do not threaten. The Makhuwa of rural Niassa practice what is known as shifting cultivation. Rather than rotating crops within a single field, farmers rotate fields, relocating to a new area every year to preserve soil fecundity. One village elder spontaneously offered this as his example when I asked about the word *othama* (to move): "*Othama* is very important," he said. "The population stays in one place for a time and the land becomes tired. It goes to a new site, and later thinks of returning because the land recovered." This rotational method is sometimes called "slash and burn," though this term may be less than helpful due to its disparaging connotation when used by people presuming to speak for modern scientific efficiency (see Cairns 2007). For others, interested less in dominating the land than in caring for it, and receiving its care in return, shifting agriculture has proven effective in adapting to the uncertainties of the physical climate. It is likewise a time-honored response to uncertain political climates (Scott 2009: 178–219). It facilitates flight in case of such unwelcome intrusions as enslavement and war (explored in Chapter 1) or taxation and conscription (to be explored here). Given these advantages, it is perhaps unsurprising that the Makhuwa language has developed entirely different words to distinguish an abandoned crop field (*mathala*) from a new one (*mathatu*): an illustration of the many possibilities for talking about, akin to the many possibilities for bringing about, new beginnings in new locations.

The State Against the Peasantry

The characteristic mobility of the Makhuwa runs diametrically counter to the administrative logic of their would-be rulers. Managing a population requires first locating it in place, making it accountable by rendering it legible. Nomadic, fugitive, and maroon communities have therefore always posed a challenge to the state in its function as an "apparatus of capture" (Deleuze and Guattari 1987: 424–73). In her historical ethnography based in southern Mozambique, Merle Bowen (2000) refers to this in conflictual terms, as "the state against the peasantry." Bowen's is one of numerous Mozambican studies to chronicle the failure of state-engineered "development" policies to grasp the complexities of local conditions, let alone to promote economic growth. This conflict between state and peasantry is ultimately a conflict between two ways of being-in-the-world: fixity and containment versus mobility and the refusal to be contained (see Bertelsen 2016). Here I trace this particular dimension of the conflict across three major periods of Mozambique's recent past: the colonial, the postcolonial/socialist, and the postsocialist (during which my fieldwork took place).

Although Vasco da Gama first reached the coast of Mozambique in 1498 and Portuguese political rule commenced shortly thereafter, it was many centuries before Europeans ventured inland to regions such as that now known as Niassa. Only from the late nineteenth century did the Portuguese colonial regime exert dominion over the entirety of Mozambique, doing so through the concessionary companies to which it granted administrative and productive rights. Northern Mozambique was administered through the Nyassa Company (Companhia do Niassa), which, heedless of preexisting territorial patterns, imposed well-defined circumscriptions to advance its commercial ends—chiefly that of producing cotton and exporting it to Europe's textile markets (Medeiros 2000). Historians Allen Isaacman (1996) and Eric Allina (2012), among others, have meticulously documented the devastating effects of forced cotton cultivation on the everyday lives of ordinary Mozambicans, the brutal working conditions this brought upon them. The Nyassa Company compelled farmers to prioritize its export crop over their staple crops. What little the local inhabitants were compensated was subject to wage theft. Resistance was met with vicious beatings by company police. Under this system, concessionary companies and their managerial elite prospered and the Portuguese imperial project was buttressed. But peasants suffered grievously; some experienced an entire lifetime of hardship and hunger. It would be no stretch to describe this condition, as Allina in fact does, as slavery by another name.

Yet it was not without resistance, everyday practices that permitted peasants at least partial autonomy amid alienating circumstances. Acts of noncompliance included illegal intercropping, slowdowns, and sabotage. It was, however, through flight that peasants most effectively withheld their labor.[2] A famous instance, from the mid-twentieth century, took place in a district of Niassa Province proximate to Maúa. There, as Isaacman narrates, Makhuwa dissidents "fled to the Mutuene mountains to avoid labor obligations and taxes. They lived by eating bananas and herding goats. The Mutuene community became a symbol of defiance and a beacon for other runaways. As a result, colonial officials tried in vain to destroy it" (1996: 213). Peasants confounded colonial rule through numerous such acts of withdrawal, whether to inaccessible mountains or to neighboring British colonies with favorable labor conditions.[3]

The point of highlighting these withdrawal strategies is not to minimize the brutality of the Portuguese regime and its concessionary companies, whose reason for being was exploitation of the land and its inhabitants. As destructive and degrading as colonial rule was, however, it never robbed Makhuwa peasants of their agency, of their ability to improvise according to both situational needs and cultural logics. Portuguese domination would thus always remain more rhetorical than real, more aspirational than actual.

The end of Portuguese rule in 1975 brought political freedom to the nation as a whole. It failed, however, to bring meaningful change to the lives of peasants. In fact, many among whom I lived regarded the postindependence party-state, Frelimo, as even more hostile to their interests than the Portuguese colonial regime had been. Surprising though this may be, it is perhaps understandable given Frelimo's extraordinary distance from the lived experience of the populace. Its disproportionately southern, urban, and male leadership contrasted and still contrasts with the demographic profile of the predominantly northern, rural, and matricentric Makhuwa.

The politics around resettlement clearly indicate this contrast. The Frelimo program of forced "villagization," begun soon after independence and inspired by Tanzania's *ujamaa* villages, aimed to concentrate rural populations in *aldeias comunais* (communal villages). Ostensibly the reason was to centralize and collectivize agricultural production. Also promised was increased access to schools, clinics, and clean water. Yet, as anthropologist Christian Geffray argues, communal villages were never for rural development so much as for the state apparatus to establish its presence in the peripheries (1990a: 191). Behind the laudable objectives of collectivizing goods and improving living conditions lay something decidedly more suspect: the attempt to rein in and monitor recalcitrant subjects.[4]

Concentrating otherwise mobile and dispersed populations has long been a strategy of states. Before Frelimo, the Portuguese regime forcibly relocated rural inhabitants onto planned settlements known as *aldeamentos*, the better to tax and conscript them. Thus, the *aldeias comunais* of the postindependence period did not arise in a vacuum. They were literally grafted onto a preexisting colonial structure (Newitt 1995: 472–73).[5] The Frelimo state did, however, intensify previous efforts. It did so by fortifying and militarizing the settlements, surrounding them with land mines, barbed wire, and troops (Lubkemann 2008: 194). The aim in this was to prevent peasants from collaborating with the Mozambican National Resistance (Resistência Nacional Moçambicana) in the run-up to civil war. Frelimo also brought to these settlements a high modernist agenda, rooted in an ideology of state socialism that sought to ban customary practice, deemed "obscurantist," whenever it conflicted with the managerial priorities of the state (Isaacman and Isaacman 2013: 152–55).

Political scientist James Scott describes well the contrast between high modernist planning and local considerations in his observation that Tanzanian *ujamaa* entailed "essentially a point-by-point negation of existing rural practice, which included shifting cultivation and pastoralism; polycropping; living well off the main roads; kinship and lineage authority; small, scattered settlements with houses built higgledy-piggledy; and production that was dispersed and opaque to the state" (1998: 238). So all-encompassing a negation would explain why Makhuwa elders recalled for me their feelings of despair at Frelimo's villagization campaign. They reported being told how and how large to build their homes (six meters in length, five meters in width), how even to arrange them (in straight rows along a Cartesian grid).[6] The location was always far from their own plots of land, far from the rivers on which their subsistence depended.

As in the colonial era, however, peasants managed to find ways of subverting sedentarization, limited though their options were. Throughout Mozambique, they deployed the same agricultural pluralism that informed their shifting cultivation techniques. While contributing to state farms adjacent to the communal village, farmers clandestinely returned to their own plots and cultivated unclaimed lands beyond the jurisdiction of village authorities.[7]

One might guess that, if not the earlier transition from colonialism to independence, then the early 1990s transition from a state-based to a market-based economy would bring an end to large-scale social engineering. Such was not the case (Bowen 2000: 185–210; Pitcher 2002).[8] When the civil war ended in 1992, the current inhabitants of Kaveya village returned to the countryside: not to the roadside communal villages, but to the rivers from which they were first expelled. But beginning in the mid-2000s, administrators of Maúa district revived efforts to return them to the wide, laterite byways on which the district's few motor vehicles travel. This time, resettlement was administered in the name of poverty alleviation. More than once, in his tile-floored office, the then district administrator announced to me his intent to meet the United Nations Millennium Development Goals.[9] Careful to use neither the colonialist language of *aldeamentos* nor the socialist language of *aldeias comunais*, he referred to the project currently under way as one of *agrupamento* (grouping). Though the policy was drawn up in the district headquarters with support from the national government, the administrator regularly traveled to the countryside to urge his constituents to conglomerate in roadside residential blocks. Always through a translator—not being Makhuwa himself—he promised to those willing to do so the prospect of a modern life.

During the year of my fieldwork I observed many leaving the rivers for the road. Few, however, stayed there. The administrator correctly diagnosed what he saw as the problem when he confided to me that the local population is "*móvel demais*" (too mobile) to take advantage of all that *agrupamento* has to offer. He recognized that people were eager to embrace opportunities for new beginnings. But he lamented that they did so on terms he could not comprehend. Rather than replacing their homes in the bush with new ones by the road, they maintained two distinct residences—many kilometers apart—and circulated between them: rainy seasons far from the road, dry seasons (after harvest) alongside it.

From the villagers' perspective, this dual residency afforded them the best of both worlds: near the road, they had schools, water pumps, and transport to the district hospital; in the bush, they had fertile land for cultivating. From the administrator's perspective, it bespoke an incapacity for progress and change. He insisted at every public address to villagers that moving permanently would only serve their interests. It would grant them access to government services that would reduce rates of poverty, prolong life expectancy, and integrate them with the national economy. The prospects were enticing, but their oral delivery was unconvincing. In Mozambique, the informal nature of bureaucratic practice has made governance more about control over the timing of policy implementation than about the efficacy of policy implementation (Gonçalves 2013). Many villagers thus came to expect that promises made will be promises delayed.

They remained indifferent to what were presented as the obvious benefits of permanent resettlement. They also worried that they were seeing in *agrupamento* a replay of the sedentarization and forced-labor programs of earlier times. Their driving desire was to remain invisible to the array of forces that have long sought to manage their and their forebears' lives. This strategy required distance from the main roads on which they could be easily reached and easily monitored. Yet while Maúa's district administrator readily admitted wanting peasants to resettle there, he never wavered in insisting that it was only for the sake of bettering their lives. Nor did he waver in declaring *agrupamento* distinct from compulsory campaigns of the past. "Today is the era of democracy," he said. "We cannot force people to move against their will."

Of Elephants and Governance

Coercion, indeed, was not overt. Yet many still felt they were being flushed to the roads from their riverine homes, and others, similarly, to the district capital from the countryside. Their suspicions owed to a history of being denied various forms of state support, such as proper funding of village health clinics.[10] They also owed to the state's handling of human-wildlife conflicts, particularly those involving the animal so grand it is said to carry all other animals within it.

That is the African bush elephant, considered by conservationists to be at high risk of endangerment, though many in northern Mozambique would have a hard time believing that. One of the promises made in the early years of the *agrupamento* campaign was protection from the beasts who, with increasing frequency, were raiding crop fields and granaries, threatening lives and ruining livelihoods.[11] As Chief Kaveya explained, "The government said: 'Go to the road and we will make a reserve and the elephants won't invade your land.'" The benefit of clustering along the road made sense, but the idea of animal reserves held special appeal. These would have created boundaries to keep elephants apart from humans. Of course, the human costs of such conservation efforts are well known. Conservation has historically functioned as much to evict native peoples as to protect native wildlife (Neumann 1998). Nevertheless, the local population responded enthusiastically.

But the promises of protection, and of roadside schools and services, scarcely materialized. "At first, my people were animated to move from the bush to the road," Chief Kaveya said, "but now we feel deceived." No reserves were formed and so elephants continued to roam. This posed a mortal threat, not only to human sustenance—the bananas, beans, and corn that villagers cultivate and elephants plunder—but to human bodies as well. Numerous nights during my stays in Kaveya village, in the compound of Jemusse and Fátima, we were awakened by the slow, heavy gait of elephants traversing the woodlands nearby. Residents of surrounding compounds would wake up panicked and rush toward the intruders with fire torches and shrill voices. During the harvest season, men would take turns on watch, staying awake in lookout structures atop nearby hills from which their cries of "*Itthepo!*" (Elephants!) stirred villagers to rise and assume their paltry defenses.

One morning we woke to the news that a man had died—had been killed—fifteen kilometers up the road, in the village of Lioma. The local chief was indignant. "We are told that if we cluster our homes on the roads the elephants won't attack, but look at what happened!" he said. In fact, the victim resided along the road and met his end when the elephant he thought he had turned away doubled back and charged. It trampled him underfoot before goring him with his tusks and grinding him into the earth. His wife could do nothing but wait in horror for the beast to be finally turned back—at which point she and others went out to salvage what remained of the man with whom she had just been asleep.

It happened that the governor of Niassa Province was to pass through Lioma village the following week. It was part of a preplanned tour through the towns and larger villages of Maúa district. Yet the governor came with no intention of addressing the attack. Approaching the crowd waiting by the road, he stopped with his entourage, took a few steps from his Land Cruiser, chanted Frelimo's rallying cry, and delivered a five-minute speech reiterating the district administrator's pleas to resettle along the roadside. He then bid farewell and left. Kicking up dust as his convoy sped away, the governor hastened to the district capital, where on Independence Plaza a large public rally awaited him. To fanfare and applause, he told the gathering there that twenty years have passed since Mozambique's brutal civil war. There must be no return to conflict, he said. All must unite as Mozambicans, join forces against the scourges that remain—none greater than that of poverty. "And so," he declared, "we have come here to say once more:

in this country there will be no more war. The war we now have? To eat. For our bellies to become big. This is the war we now have." The governor patted his own somewhat elephantine gut as he said this, inviting and receiving gleeful cheers from the crowd.

Back in Lioma, meanwhile, those who had spent the morning awaiting their honored guest returned to their compounds. Most had already resolved to take the day off from the fields. It was supposed to be a historic visit. The governor's curt appearance, though, left everyone dispirited, more than the elephant attack already had.

"For a person to feel content," Chief Lioma told me, "he should speak and what he speaks should receive a response. He can then inform what he feels in his heart. We could have told the governor that here in our village, this happens, and this and this and this. But on that day, he came, spoke, and left." A true leader abides by the Makhuwa proverb that Chief Lioma said he himself strives to uphold: to be chief is to walk among the people (*Okhala mwene wettá n'atthu*). The governor's willingness to drive up to, but not walk among, the inhabitants of Lioma was further proof that the state does not care to notice them, to understand their problems or to bother with their solutions.

The solution villagers most often proffered for the human-elephant conflict was a return to policies of the colonial period. Then, as one man told me, antelopes, impalas, monkeys, and boars were all part of people's daily lives, "but all the colonists needed to hear is that someone saw elephant tracks and they would go after it until they found it. Many cars would come from town to go and kill the elephants there." Moreover, local hunters had greater means by which to take matters into their own hands, via the makeshift firearms acquired back in the slave trade era.

Mozambique's law criminalizing wildlife hunting passed in 1999.[12] During the year of my fieldwork, possession of firearms was itself illegal in Maúa, except for those few granted special authorization: state police and trophy hunters. Such was the case since the end of the civil war, when the United Nations led a countrywide disarmament campaign, ostensibly to protect the local population from bandits in their midst. The cost of greater protection from insiders, however, was greater vulnerability to outsiders. No longer subject to regular hunting, elephants felt less compelled to keep a distance. What compelled them, rather, was hunger, and it led them to the crop fields and fruit trees near population clusters. As a result, I was told, "it used to be that a child became adult without knowing an elephant. Today, a child of only two years will know what an elephant is."

I met with Maúa's district administrator to hear his side, to understand why villagers are not permitted firearms. Would this not help them defend themselves against elephant invasions? I asked. He mentioned the concern over public safety, but dwelled at greatest length on the cause of wildlife conservation. Allowing villagers to hunt elephants, he said, would pose a grave threat to what remains of Africa's biodiversity. He spoke movingly of what a loss to the world it would be if Africa's majestic megafauna were suddenly allowed to vanish.

He also noted an economic benefit in fostering elephants' reappearance: the thousands of dollars of licensing fees paid by trophy hunters, white men with deep pockets from South Africa and the United States. Their money, he said, promotes conservation efforts and benefits local communities. The presence, and increasingly the omnipresence, of elephants made Maúa attractive to these foreigners in search of "pristine" wildlands where elephants still roam. As reported in a wildlife management working paper of 2005, "The opportunity to hunt a problem elephant in Mozambique is being advertised in the USA at a trophy fee of $10,000 for the elephant" (Anderson and Pariela 2005: 42). By policy of Mozambique's National Directorate of Forestry and Wildlife, 20 percent of such fees must redound to the local communities in which the hunting takes place (DNFFB 1999). But loopholes of various sorts keep such benefits from trickling down.[13] In the year of my fieldwork, the best villagers could hope for was an ever-steadier stream of fortified jeeps carrying trophy hunters. Villagers cheered whenever these sped by; a successful hunt meant one less threat to their lives. It also, of course, meant weeks of high-protein meals. The hunters were gracious enough to leave carcasses behind.[14]

Architectural Circularity

Those constructing second homes along the road not only refuse to settle permanently, they also seem little interested in building what government agents and development workers alike call *casas amelhoradas* (improved homes). These are modern constructions that use durable materials like baked bricks and corrugated zinc. Rather, for many, simple abodes made of mud, bamboo, and thatch seem to serve just fine.[15] Mud huts, of course, easily succumb to the rains and must be continually abandoned or refurbished. But that may just be the point. Unlike *casas amelhoradas*, these dwellings are easy to construct. And because the sunk costs of doing so are negligible, they are not only quickly built but also painlessly abandoned: architecture for the light-footed (*oveya metto*).

The wisdom behind this preference occurred to me soon after Kalinka and I moved to Jemusse's and Fátima's compound, into the mud hut Jemusse built for us in only a matter of days. The following month, our hosts opened the *muttheko* (open-air shed) of their compound to yet another guest: an acquaintance from the large northern city of Nampula. Apparently this man came for a few weeks every year to purchase local farmers' surplus corn. He gathered the produce into large polyethylene sacks that he would later load onto a truck and transport for resale back in Nampula. I respected the entrepreneurialism that brought this man to those he was now living among but found myself endlessly irritated by his inability to say a kind word about them. He derided the Makhuwa of Niassa Province—different from him and other Makhuwa of coastal Nampula—as weak-willed for not openly protesting the district government's prejudicial policies, as effeminate for persisting in matrilocal residence patterns, and as backwards for not possessing national identification cards. "What would you do if you are stopped by police on the road?" he asked of people who sought to stay off policed roads in the first place.

He also never missed an opportunity to switch from Makhuwa to Portuguese, a language he seemed exceedingly proud to speak as well as "*os brancos*" (the whites) also living at the compound. My desire to carry out conversations in the vernacular struck him as laughable and retrograde. But I learned something important from my annoyance with this man. I learned just how wrong his criticisms were: mobility is not, as he saw it, a sign of primitivism but an adaptive strategy for dealing with unfavorable situations. Kalinka and I had just laid down roots, of a sort, by asking Jemusse to construct the first home we would ever call our own. Yet no sooner was it built that circumstances changed and we rued the self-inflicted difficulty of moving immediately away.[16]

Beyond their substitutability, the greater significance of mud huts rests in their traditional circularity. Conical-shaped structures, particularly the *muttheko* used for receiving visitors and seeking shade, are still prominent in the northern Mozambique countryside. Circularity in general is salient among the Makhuwa.[17] In his masterful study of

Makhuwa weaving traditions, mathematician Paulus Gerdes (2010) delineates the predominance of the curvilinear—in baskets and mats, in the spiral patterns woven into winnowing trays, even in Makhuwa fishermen's practice of drying fish by placing them in a circle around a fire. Equally of note are the peaks of Mount Namuli: the sacred mountain believed to be replicated by the termite mounds that dot the landscape, the *makeya* offerings poured for ancestors, and the pits into which the dead historically were buried. All these are curved or rounded in shape. Yet today, many homes, particularly the *casas amelhoradas*, are rectilinear and flat roofed. This architectural transformation is not new. As far as two generations back, people began building four-cornered homes because "this is what you [foreigners] came here and taught us," one elder told me.

Squaring the architectural circle was a key aspect of the European civilizing and Christianizing mission (Comaroff and Comaroff 1997: 274–322), a way of ordering otherwise "savage" domestic space, though rectangularity possibly spread in East Africa first through Arabic influences (Soares 2009: 62). Either way, it would be wrong to see exogenous architecture as replacing, wholesale, that which came before. Referring to African architectural forms generally, Claudia Zaslavsky observes that "not all Islamized folk gave up their traditional circular houses. Today one may find both the circle and the square in the same village, and even in the same compound" (1973: 166).[18] Indeed, among the Makhuwa (and in the home, pictured below, being built by Jemusse) one finds such architectural hybridity even in the same structure. While a home's base and walls are four-cornered, semicircular overhangs often cover side verandas, while pliable bamboo poles are made to curve into Namuli-like roofs.[19]

What this comingling of shapes demonstrates is a principle of openness to the new, but not in a way that completely breaks with the old. Perhaps nothing represents this principle better than the circle itself. Unlike the rectangle, which has a limited number of right-angled corners, the circle requires with every step around it a change in direction, but an incremental one: *vakhani vakhani ntoko namanriya* (step by step, like the chameleon). One might say that the circular structures so prominent in the landscape—from residential constructions to Mount Namuli itself—express this kind of incremental, yet revolutionary, mobility. The idea of "incremental revolutions" describes not only architectural shifts but also migration patterns such as those addressed in this chapter and the last. The Makhuwa are not

Figure 4. Architectural hybridity in construction of a new home, Kaveya village.

averse to change and to movement; these have long been both unexceptional and reversible. Hence their long history of not just mobility, but mobility of the circular kind: between the living and the dead, between the home and the refugee camp, between the river and the road.

Mobile Roots

Along the same roads to which the district government was promoting *agrupamento*, Pentecostal churches have been slowly appearing; the Kaveya congregation of the African Assembly of God (Assembléia de Deus Africana, or ADA) is but one example. This coincidence derives from a number of factors. According to the district administrator, while the official policy of the state is one of secularism, the pluralization of religious options is a positive boon for the populace. This openness contrasts sharply with Frelimo's earlier hostility toward religion. Its fight against Catholicism, Islam, and other forms of "obscurantism" was inspired by a secular Marxist ideology that saw religion as antithetical to progress. With the disavowal of socialism that accompanied the collapse of the Soviet Union, tolerance for new religious movements became state policy.[20] In this context, many new Pentecostal churches entered the country. They were not just welcomed but encouraged through financial incentives (Freston 2005: 55). In Maúa, one Frelimo party member and leader of a rapidly developing *agrupamento* remarked that he hopes to attract Pentecostal evangelists because they often build their churches in the modern style of the *casa amelhorada*. Their presence, he imagined, would inspire leaders of the Catholic chapel and of the Islamic mosque in his village to follow suit, replacing their thatched roofs with zinc and their mud walls with brick. "People will really say that we are developing," he said, "because all our buildings will have zinc roofs."

There is another level of consonance between political administrators' efforts to draw people to the roadsides and religious evangelists' efforts to draw them to churches. Despite their common rhetoric of change, both are in fact interested in making people more settled or sedentary than they have customarily been. Newitt argues for seeing Frelimo's *aldeias comunais* as modeled not only on the colonial-era *aldeamento* but also on the older Iberian tradition of the planned Jesuit settlement, best known by its Spanish term, *reducción* (1995: 549). The *reducción* facilitated agricultural production, but it especially aided Catholic instruction by minimizing indigenous peoples' contacts with ancestral spirits and engagements with ancestral rituals. Throughout colonial east Africa, mission stations allowed for the provision of services—food, shelter, hospitals, schools, and opportunities for employment (Green 2003: 39–45). It was, however, their ability to confine people so as to enforce orthodoxy that led planners to arrange mission stations as grid-like enclosures (Kollman 2005).

Pentecostal evangelists' project of making people "permanent Christians," of affixing to them an eternal Christian identity, should thus not be seen as unique to Pentecostalism. However, as I discuss in Chapter 4, the missiological approach of the Catholic Church underwent a tremendous shift around the mid-twentieth century. It came to promote "inculturation" and dialogue over earlier attempts at unsettling local traditions by resettling local populations. Pentecostalism, in more recent years, echoes the earlier period of Catholic missionary practice. In describing Pentecostal and charismatic churches' "rather merciless attitude toward local cultural traditions," anthropologist Birgit Meyer points to the tendency of Pentecostals "to critique mainline [e.g., Catholic] churches for seeking to accommodate local culture through Africanization" (2004: 456). Numerous Pentecostal sermons I heard teemed with chastisements of worshippers' deviations into ancestral religious practice, and of the willingness of Catholic clergy to countenance such deviations.

Pentecostal leaders explicitly denounced people's seeming inability to embrace the singular identity or set of practices required of authentic converts—a charge of indecisiveness not unlike the district administrator's lament of people's "too mobile" manner of being, their inability to embrace fully the modern lifestyle awaiting them on the roadside. In fact, the villagers I observed displayed little aversion to either form of change. Many were moving, and among those who did, many were converting. However, to the consternation of Pentecostal evangelists and government agents alike, few did either with any sense of permanence.

Pastor Simões, Maúa's district-level ADA leader, once described this as a constitutional defect of "us black people" as opposed to "you white people." Unlike in the multiethnic urban settings of northern Mozambique, where Pastor Simões has also ministered, "here things are different. People abandon their homes, even new homes, go to another place, construct again. The government builds schools and people still leave for other places. This doesn't help. It's so much better for a person to organize his life in a single place, build a modern home [*casa amelhorada*], dig a good latrine, plant an orange tree, whatever, and say, '*Pronto*. Here we will remain, here itself.'" This is, of course, the same preference for sedentarism expressed by the district administrator. Where Pastor Simões went beyond was in connecting the problem of geographic nomadism to the backsliding (*voltando atrás*) he constantly had to police in the district's congregations. Even those who participate in his churches fervently, he admitted, still habitually consult with diviners, visit with healers, and make offerings to ancestors.

"The problem is that people here are too rooted in tradition," Pastor Simões told me one day. It was a suggestive claim because of how often I heard it among Pentecostal preachers—also because if there is one thing that any newcomer to village Mozambique learns immediately, it is the importance of roots. Literally. Roots are essential components of the medicines prepared by healers, and root crops, particularly manioc, are the most common gifts with which strangers are sent off after a visit. They are also a prime nutritional source for people who prize their mobility. Scott describes manioc, yams, and potatoes as the ultimate "escape crops."

Unlike grains, they grow underground, invisible to tax collectors; and they can remain safely there for up to two years, to be dug up piecemeal as needed. They are illegible to state powers, just as the people who grow them aspire to be (2009: 195–96).

It was in conversation with Paulino, one of my research assistants, that I learned these properties of roots. Sensing Paulino had more to say, I asked a question that I hoped would shed light on the pastors' complaints. "But what is it that roots us?" I asked. "Do we need to be rooted the way trees and plants do?"

"Of course," he replied without pause, "which is why we also have roots!" He grabbed his forearm, and I looked at him quizzically. "Here," he said, pointing to his veins. "These are our roots."

While the Makhuwa language has a word for veins (*misempha*), these are described as performing the function of roots (*mikakari*). In one sense, of course, veins are decidedly not roots: my veins run through my body; they do not anchor it to the ground.[21] Yet in another sense, recognized in the Makhuwa metaphor, our veins do exactly what the roots of a plant do. They are the channels through which flow the sources of our vitality: lifeblood for us, soil nutrients for plants.[22]

Continuing his lesson, Paulino said, "*Mikakari sahu* [our veins/roots] make our blood to circulate." Then, dramatically bounding to his feet: "And that makes *us* to circulate!"

Of concern for Pentecostal evangelists in northern Mozambique is not that people do not participate, but that they selectively participate. They move into the new churches, but they also move out, and when new needs arise they move back in. If they do this because they are "too rooted in tradition," it is not in Pastor Simões's sense of roots that stabilize, but in Paulino's sense of roots that mobilize.

Life Within Limits

For the Makhuwa, religious conversion is conceived less as a change in one's heart than as a change in one's body. To convert, in effect, is to move (*othama*). Thus, the goal of this chapter and the last has been to understand the Makhuwa propensity for religious mobility in terms of the Makhuwa propensity for geographic mobility.[23] Significantly, both processes are not only regular; they are reversible. They entail regress as much as egress—

circular mobilities that disrupt linear teleologies. During the time of my work in Maúa, both state builders and church planters attempted to reform local inhabitants by sedentarizing them—settling them in planned villages and urban settlements, or in an eternally Christian identity. Deploying their historical proclivity for mobility, those among whom I lived appeared simultaneously eager to partake in such resettlement schemes and reluctant to remain settled by them.

Having made this point, I hasten now to qualify it. In the first place, not everyone moves, at least not physically. Likewise, even with the proliferation of new religious options, not everyone converts. I came to know Diniz, a sugar cane harvester in a village halfway between Kaveya and Lioma, after word got around that the very night he made an offering of *otheka* (sorghum beer) to his ancestors, elephants got into his crops. I immediately sought out this man, expressed sympathy for his loss, and asked how he planned to respond. He restated what I often heard, that the only solution is firearms—unfortunately, the solution expressly banned by the authorities.

"So what can you do now?" I asked.

"I am planting for next season," he said. "I don't stop. Each moment I have to plant."

I asked about relocation. Could he not move to a different locale?

"No," he said, "elephants are in every corner."

Well, then, could he not turn to a different religion, take his pleas for protection to powers other than the ancestors who, he himself said, failed him on this occasion?

"I haven't thought of moving religion either," he said. "Now it's just doing many crop fields. A person cannot trust [*ororomela*] in just one thing. At the river, I will try sugar cane again, here I will produce cotton. I can't trust in the river alone. One of the things will pay off."

I was impressed with Diniz's resolve to diversify agriculturally, finding his statement that "a person cannot trust in one thing" consistent with the experimentalism I had seen elsewhere. Nevertheless, I still wondered why this did not impel him to think more ambitiously, to experiment more widely. How would simply varying his crops protect him from elephant raids? And if it is true that one cannot trust in only one crop, then why trust in only the ancestors? Why trust in only this place?

"We will stay here. We see no place to go," he said. "There is no place without elephants. There is no other possibility."

"How can you say that?" I insisted, finding his attitude deeply unsatisfying. "If the elephants keep invading your crops, your children will die of hunger."

As if to mock my evident desperation, he gave his answer with a smile: "Then my children will die of hunger."

I was floored. His acquiescence contrasted starkly with what I had become used to seeing elsewhere: people courageous and pragmatic enough to flee, whether to new physical terrains or new spiritual ones. One could argue that times are changing—that unlike in the past when governing powers did not control the peripheries, there is today an increasing parceling of all land, a closing off of the frontier.[24] Yet surely Diniz knew of towns like the district capital and cities like Cuamba that are considerably safer from elephant invasions. Why, I struggled to understand, could Diniz not even consider moving to such places?

I only came to an answer when I learned that the Makhuwa word *erima* has two meanings: patience, but also courage. Patience and acceptance of one's limits suggests something less active than flight, certainly less so than fight. But was there not also courage, perhaps even agency, in Diniz's patience, his persistence in doing what he knew to do—maintaining faith in the ancestors despite his doubts, maintaining his agricultural practice despite his defeats?

Suggested in Diniz's response is the kind of bounded freedom Michel de Certeau theorized as tactics, those everyday practices that express the refusal of actors to be defined by circumstances upon which they are nonetheless dependent. De Certeau may as well have been describing Diniz when he wrote, "Without leaving the place where he has no choice but to live and which lays down its law for him, he establishes within it a degree of *plurality* and creativity" (1984: 30). In his own polycropping techniques, in his micromaneuvers within an externally imposed order, Diniz seemed to find a means of turning that which could not be radically changed into that which could be meaningfully endured. Perhaps, after all, changing one's viewpoint need not require changing one's standpoint.

Yet even for the many I observed moving around regularly—across regions and across religions—it is crucially important that they sought neither transcendence of their situation nor a linear rupture from their past. Though transcendence is a central trope in Christian thought and practice, something quite different appears to be at stake for the Makhuwa, even for

Makhuwa Christians. Their movements are not about escaping what came before but about displacing it.

"Leaving here behind is not leaving death behind because every place has death," Chief Kaveya once told me. His view conveyed a realism born of life amid scarcity and adversity. No single geographic location or religious tradition can remove one from the human condition. The best one can do is maneuver well within the limits of life.

Yet even those who revolt through escape—through migration or through conversion—do so, one might say, in the manner more of Sisyphus than of Icarus: fully attuned to how modest, momentary, and therefore multiple such revolts must be. The goal, thus, in *othama* (migration/conversion) is less that of attaining immortality than of attaining a fresh start, of carrying on despite the absurdity of a world where death lurks, like elephants, "in every corner."

PART II

Ohiya ni Ovolowa—
To Leave and to Enter

CHAPTER 3

Border Crossings

Previous chapters have presented religious conversion among the Makhuwa as a spatial phenomenon, a matter less of the heart's transformation than of the body's transportation. If the alternative to *opittukuxa murima* (to change heart) was *othama* (to move) in Part I of this book, in Part II it is another phrase commonly used to reference conversion: *ohiya ettini ekina, orowa ettini ekina* (to leave one religion and enter another). The language of leaving and entering (*ohiya ni ovolowa*) arises also in numerous everyday affairs: leaving the village and entering the bush, abandoning one crop field and rotating to another, moving into and out of the spaces of ritual. One ritual, that of initiation, is the subject of this chapter. It illustrates not only how perennial are patterns of motion, but also how predicated these are on bordered spaces and bounded domains. This carries implications for how religions are experienced, at least to the extent they too are conceived as bounded. Those implications will be addressed in Chapter 4, but to understand how boundaries function between Christianity and what has come to be called ancestral religion (*ettini ya makholo*), it would help first to clarify how boundaries function in the latter.

Florêncio

Initiation rites reach back to the time of the ancestors, say Makhuwa elders. Even when outlawed by the postindependence government of the Mozambican Liberation Front (Frelimo) in its campaign against "obscurantism," these rites took place, only clandestinely and for shorter lengths of time (Pitcher 2002: 99). Largely owing to decades of prohibition, the rite has lost significance among some; the transition to adulthood nowadays occurs more in the classroom than in the bush. Yet many expressed disappointment that village chiefs were no longer exerting themselves to conduct the ceremonies as they used to. When, in 2009, Chief Kaveya organized a male initiation ceremony (*olukhu*), older men and women especially embraced the opportunity to put their progeny through what had been so formative for them.

One of the boys participating that year, Florêncio, was already well into his teenage years. The nephew of a village counselor (*namiruku*), Florêncio had found his way into Kaveya's African Assembly of God (Assembléia de Deus Africana, or ADA) congregation while still a child. He was following age-mates into the small Pentecostal community but soon became so involved that he earned the title of *maestro*, responsible for leading the dances and music. From his uncle, Florêncio received strong support to participate in Kaveya's initiation ceremony. From his Pentecostal church, predictably, he faced strong opposition. The ADA prohibited participation in initiation rites, sporadically organized though they had become. The objection was not to circumcision per se. When done in biomedical facilities, this was acceptable. The church in fact encouraged it as a substitute for the bush ceremony and all related happenings: ancestral teachings, sacrificial offerings, the consumption of traditional medicines.

"I was in Cuamba that year, helping my father sell tobacco," Florêncio told me. "When I returned, I heard that others in the church had gone to the hospital, finished it off, so the only option was to do it here, by the Nakukula River. I tried to do it secretly. Only Mamã and Papá knew. The church, no."

Yet Florêncio did involve the church in other ways. Two other young members of the congregation accompanied him (namely Jemusse and Abílio, whose stories appear elsewhere in this book). Both had already undergone the hospital circumcision but wanted to be with their spiritual brother at this pivotal moment in his life. Additionally, the three of them carried off the church's *nlapa* drum. Since the ceremony was to last less than a week, they thought they could get away with pinching the drum. They planned to return it before the church elder could know it was missing.

They were not so lucky. The elder got wind of the boys' transgression and immediately reported it to the district head of the ADA, Pastor Simões's predecessor. Shortly after the ceremony ended, the pastor arrived and issued the three young men a reprimand, the church's standard punishment for behavioral violations (what it calls "sins"). The sanction was set for two months, during which the wrongdoers were directed to attend services but without participating. No singing, no clapping, no preaching, no dancing. They would only sit silently and solemnly while others moved and shouted. This was a severe punishment particularly for Florêncio, accustomed as *maestro* to not just enjoying but generating the church's lively worship experience.

After hearing Florêncio describe all this, I broached the possibility, then before him, of leaving the church altogether.

"My uncle told me to," he said. "But me? No way. I said to myself that I will withstand the reprimand for the two months."

"Was that difficult?"

"It was very difficult. We had to arrive on Sundays and just sit there, silent, until the end of the service, every Sunday like that." He paused as a thought formed in his mind. "But after a week in the bush it wasn't so bad," he said.

Florêncio ticked off all the ordeals of initiation: receiving lashings, sleeping unclothed, eating unseasoned dishes, and, of course, undergoing circumcision. Yet, as undesirable as all of that was, there were also benefits. Besides camaraderie with his fellow neophytes, entrée into Makhuwa personhood, and the acquisition of ancestral wisdom, Florêncio said he was also able to cultivate *erima*—the Makhuwa word for both patience and courage. This virtue had immediate applicability: it helped him cope with the punishment awaiting him from his church.

"In the end, the reprimand was nothing," he said. "It was just arriving at church, staying seated and quiet. No one was beating us. And, after those two months, we could return to playing the drums and singing."

Enclosures

Florêncio's participation in the initiation ceremony, in spite of his Pentecostal affiliation, exemplifies the same ease with mobility and multiplicity seen earlier in Jemusse's and Fátima's response to the death of their daughter. That mobility is key to understanding religious conversion was argued in foregoing chapters with reference to Makhuwa myth and history. It would be easy to come away from those examples with the impression that, for those I worked with, it is mobility all the way down, that fluidity exists without friction. Even the caveat introduced through the example of Diniz—that some people sometimes find it best to accept the limits of their possibilities and do well within them—may not have reduced the sense that when people go on the move they stay on the move.

Undoubtedly, the vogue of fluidities and flows in contemporary theory would offer solid intellectual ground for making mobility the final word, for coming to rest in the phenomenon of flux. The only constant is change, says a line of thinkers stretching from Heraclitus to Henri Bergson, and including such recent philosophers as Gilles Deleuze and Rosi Braidotti.[1] There is no doubt great value in their challenge to theoretical reason's tendency to freeze and fetishize conceptual constructs. "The essence of life is its continuously changing character," writes William James in an appreciative essay on Bergson (James 1909: 253). Yet is that always how life is experienced?

In the contemporary, hypermobile world, border regimes have only intensified, electrifying their fences, fortifying their control.[2] This geopolitics of enclosure should keep us from overstating or unduly romanticizing mobility, fluidity, and flux (Cunningham 2004). James provides resources for understanding this philosophically, radicalizing Bergson's empiricism by noting that time is not always and only sensed as flowing; it also "comes in drops" (1909: 232). Discrete moments sometimes matter, and lived experience comprises both the intellect and intuition. This insight leads James to attend equally to continuities and discontinuities, conjunctions and disjunctions. Consciousness is like a bird's life, he writes, "made of an alternation of flights and perchings" (1950: 243).[3]

Mobility is not about movement per se. It is about the oscillations one makes between periods of movement and periods of stasis, between motion and rest, between crossing and dwelling.[4] These distinct but complementary ways of inhabiting the world conjoin in the most everyday of journeys Makhuwa men and women take: the journey from village to bush and back. The alterity of the bush is essential for the vitality of the community. It is not only where initiation rites are performed and where healing substances are sought, but also where fields are cleared, animals are hunted, and firewood is collected. As commonplace as many of these activities are, one never undertakes them lightly. The bush demands respect: *Nthupi khannayeva, onayeva onètta* (The bush is not small; small is the one who walks in it). The crossing point is always acknowledged with a pause and a plea that ancestors "open the path." Such care is needed because the energies of the bush may, in excess, threaten the stability of the village. It is in the bush, after all, that animals, bush spirits, and shape-shifters hold sway. Imperative for existential vitality, then, is not the absolute severing of village and bush but the effective management of their interface.[5]

The significance of boundaries to the ongoing dialectic between openness and closure is best illustrated in their ceremonial creation and re-creation. One such ceremony, known as *ovirela elapo* (literally, "enclose the village"), is performed in times of crisis to defend the community against unwelcome intruders—invasive animals, sorcerers, epidemic diseases. It was organized numerous times during my fieldwork year, including in Lioma village soon after the elephant violated village space by killing a man within it (see Chapter 2). Beginning at night, all members of the village extinguished the fires at their compounds and carried both firestones and split wood to the river. There a *namuku* (healer) waited at a fresh fire he himself started without the aid of matches or petroleum. Villagers acquired from that fire a new flame, then returned with it to their homes to reignite their hearths. They then remained in a proscribed state of dormancy—no talking, no pounding grain, no intercourse—while the village leaders together with the *namuku* began the rite's second stage. This involved a slow circumambulation of the village, laying down flour offerings along its edges, all the while praying for protection from further intrusions. Taken together, the two phases of the ceremony demonstrate the mutual entailment of enclosure and renewal; the renovating of fires, and thereby of lives, requires the securing of a spiritual boundary. Yet the duality guarantees that *ovirela elapo*, while intended to minimize exogenous dangers, never seals one off from the sources of regeneration that lie beyond the mundane. While boundaries made are understood to be real, they are also understood to be porous, at least potentially so. Overly insulating oneself invites death every bit as much as overly exposing oneself does. The aim is not to eliminate but to manage vulnerability, to see that it be admitted in tolerable degrees, whenever the commonweal so demands (van de Port 2015).

While *ovirela elapo* rituals, without forsaking receptivity, privilege enclosure and boundedness, initiation rituals emphasize openness—at least in the scholarly literature. In *Les rites de passage*, Arnold van Gennep ([1909] 1960) set the course for initiation studies by documenting the ritual's tripartite structure: separation, transition, incorporation. The most influential anthropological elaboration of this process is Victor Turner's extensive work on male initiation among the Ndembu of central Africa. In one summation, Turner writes, "the boys are removed from their homes in the villages, circumcised, secluded for a period during which they are subject to special rules and interdictions, and returned to their villages as men" (1962: 124). The purpose and trajectory of the sequence, from separation to incorporation, from removal to return, is the transformation of boys into men. This passage—signaled in the phrase *rites of passage*—is the overarching focus of scholarship on initiation.

The exact moment of passage is associated with the liminal phase, the second and, for Turner, the essential part of the ritual process (1967: 93–111; 1969: 94–130). It is marked by the suspension of structures and boundaries, and the amorphous state of the neophytes transiting through it. Given its inherent ambiguities, there is a certain irony in the impression Turner gives of liminality as a singularity, unified and coherent. He does note that the liminal period is broken into different events but gives little sense of these events transpiring at different times or in different places. In a sentence whose main purpose is to describe the role of the novice's guardian, for example, Turner notes it is he "who carries the novice from the circumcision site to the *ifwilu* or 'site of dying,' where the novice sits until his wound stops bleeding" (1967: 194). Of the next locational shift, from the *ifwilu* to the seclusion lodge, Turner has nothing to note beyond this: "The lodge was built immediately in front of the dying-place which it concealed from the view of anyone going along the old path" (1967: 224). Concealed from readers is any sense of neophytes going along any paths whatsoever. Perhaps, in the Ndembu context, they simply did not. It is also possible that Turner's failure to remark in any detail on differentiated sites or the nature of movements between them reflects his own theoretical concern to explicate, if not celebrate, liminality as antistructure—a place free of the boundaries and distinctions marking quotidian social life. As a zone "betwixt and between the positions assigned and arrayed by law, custom, convention, and ceremonial" (1969: 95), the liminal zone is important precisely because of its indeterminacy, a most fitting setting for the equally indeterminate beings—not still boys and not yet men—progressing through it.

Since the work of Turner and others, anthropological studies of initiation have largely fallen out of fashion. This may owe, sensibly enough, to the ritual's largely diminished prevalence in Africa and, indeed, throughout the world. In Mozambique, confiscatory pressures from mid-twentieth-century Catholic evangelists and postindependence Frelimo modernizers nearly ensured the rite's eradication. However, as Eduardo Medeiros notes in his exhaustive ethnography of Makhuwa initiation, a combination of factors has coalesced over recent decades to spur revitalization. These factors include the efforts among some Catholic leaders to bring initiation under the church's domain (Medeiros 2007: 36).[6] Thus it was that during the school vacation period of the 2012 dry season, a male initiation took place under the auspices of Maúa district's Catholic parish church. I was privileged to be permitted to attend.

A Rite of Passages

It was a chilly start to the day. Inside Maúa's main Catholic church, near the center of town, thirty-six boys were gathered. Each one, between the ages of eight and fourteen, stood beside an adult male relative who would serve as the boy's guardian for the duration of the rite. Padre Giuseppe Frizzi—the Italian, Makhuwa-speaking leader of Maúa's Catholic community—led all gathered in a Mass. Prayers to God and Jesus, Mary and the saints, officially opened the initiation period, just as they have every year since 1989, when the Frelimo government softened its opposition to what it called "obscurantism." Padre Frizzi took this as an opportunity to resurrect, as he put it, the initiation rites that had become nearly obsolete. He insisted on the rites proceeding collaboratively, involving both Makhuwa catechists of the Catholic church and Makhuwa ritual leaders. That is why, when the Mass ended, the boys and their guardians, along with the boys' mothers and other kin, processed from the compound of the church to the compound of the *régulo* (paramount chief) just on the outskirts of town.

There a *makeya* offering took place, though not at the base of the *mutholo* tree, as usual, but atop the clean-shaven heads of the initiates. The millet flour formed as a mound—a simulacrum of Mount Namuli—and white particles sprinkled down onto the boys' faces and bare chests. The neophytes stood still throughout, even when the adults around them broke into dance and drumming. Then came the departure for the bush, a place of regeneration but also of danger—hence, the *makeya* ceremony with pleas for protection. The boys walked the entire time in silence, heads bowed reverently. Even the adults, previously boisterous, sobered up for this border crossing.

We stopped when we reached the first encampment. Called *nipantta*, this was a clearing around a *mutholo* tree, situated a short distance from a small stream. It was late afternoon. We laid down reed mats and fired up cooking vats, and the festivities resumed. Dances associated specifically with the initiation rite went through the evening and into the night. *Otheka* (sorghum beer) was consumed liberally, passed around in calabash bowls. All of this, again, was done by the men and women gathered. The boys sat in a circle around the fire, legs extended and heads down, straight-faced and straight-backed, as if oblivious to the ongoing festivities. The principle was already set. There would be physical action and bodily motion throughout the rite, but only on the part of adults. The boys themselves were to behave stoically, Apollonian contrasts to the Dionysian dynamics around them. The remaining days would regularly reprise this juxtaposition of stasis and mobility, equanimity and agitation.

At no moment was poise more called for, or more tested, than at what followed the next afternoon: the circumcision. Just beforehand, the master of ceremonies—Kayaya, whose name means "bush spirit"—again gathered the neophytes around the *mutholo* tree. Seated on the ground, they were hand-fed a special concoction of chicken morsels, corn porridge, and ingredients that I had observed Kayaya earlier pounding in a mortar: medication that gives "forces to procreate." Along with the feeding came speeches, from Kayaya but also from the *régulo* and other elders, on the significance of the transformation set to occur. The boys were told they will soon be fit to bring new life into the world and help the deceased take leave of it—fit, in other words, for marrying and for burying. Kayaya also gave special instructions to the mothers. Until their sons' wounds heal, they must abide by strict taboos: no salt in their cooking, no bathing, no intercourse.

The speeches concluded, each guardian then led his neophyte away from the *nipantta* clearing. Mothers yelled out ebulliently as the proceedings left them behind. Down the hill, toward the stream, the initiates lined up in single file. They were instructed to strip off their shorts. Drums frenetically beat at the head of the line, where the circumciser knelt on the ground. The Catholic catechist crouched beside the circumciser, a bag full of individually wrapped razor blades in hand. One step at a time, each novice approached the decisive moment. His eyes covered, he was likely clueless as to whether his turn was next but surely noticed the drums' increasing volume with each step forward. He only knew it was his turn

Figure 5. Receiving instructions at the *nipantta* site, outside Maúa town.

when a ritual assistant grabbed his legs and dropped him to his back. Guardians tried to soften the fall even while keeping their hands over the boys' eyes. The catechist handed a razor to the circumciser, who sliced down swiftly and surely. The initiate was then yanked back to his feet, led over the small stream and up the opposite embankment.

After all the boys had been cut, the circumciser's aide returned to the mothers to report that their sons were now men. Ululations resounded as far away as the stream where I stood, audible even over the drums that still beat. The mothers could now return home, not to see their sons until their return from the bush. The action was now up the hill at a site called *namuhakwa*. The boys sat in a dirt clearing, their knees bent to keep their penises from grazing the ground. The guardians stomped and clapped in front of them, kicking up dust as they chanted: "The vagina has opened! The vagina has opened!" The dust's astringent properties served to staunch the bleeding.

After an hour or so at the *namuhakwa* site came yet another decampment, this time to a site requiring nearly a half-hour walk through dense woodlands. Beside a river, this site was referred to as *nvera*, also the word for the seclusion lodge that the guardians were tasked with erecting. The lodge was constructed of chopped tree limbs and bundles of thatch laid upon the roof and draped along the sides. The only two openings were in the middle of the long side walls. Bisecting the hut's interior was a *khanyipu* tree log, called the *ekuluwe* (wild pig). Initiates were under strict orders to treat this as a dividing line. Until their wounds fully cicatrized, they were to occupy only one side of it: the same side from which they entered the encampment. During the time it would take the scars to heal, they would only play and at night sleep—shoulder to shoulder—on that side of the *ekuluwe*.

On the third evening, the catechist, who with a small medical kit in hand monitored each boy's healing, declared it time for the next set of ceremonial acts. At sunrise the next day, the initiates lined up outside the primary entrance of the lodge. They were ordered to rush into it, one at a time. As each entered, his guardian handed him a spear (*nivaka*) carved from bamboo in the preceding days. Inside the lodge, the initiate used the spear to stab the *ekuluwe* log, then for the first time crossed that line and exited the opposite passageway. He continued running down the short path straight into the river. The "wild pig" log and its slaying were of great significance.[7] It served as a border drawn so as to demarcate distinct zones, and then as a border crossed so as to generate new life—yet another example of the vital interplay of closure and openness.

The boys stood half submerged in the river, shivering but basking—not in the sun, which was yet fully to rise, but in the cheers of their guardians on the riverbanks. The guardians egged the boys on, pushing them to brave the frigid water and plunge headfirst. When the first one did so, the guardians howled with delight. The other boys then followed suit. When they eventually climbed out, each guardian greeted his charge with sheets and shorts. For the first time in three days, the neophytes were permitted to dress. From this point on, the initiates would only play and sleep on the river side of the *ekuluwe* log. It is also on that side where they would receive their instructions, both Catholic and ancestral.

The instructions went on for five days, at which time yet another shift occurred. The *nvera* site was abandoned. In fact, the *nvera* itself was set ablaze. Even more quickly than the lodge was constructed, it was destroyed. We were back on a footpath, heading in the direction of the *nipantta* site from two weeks back. It was at this final site, called *mpandamo*, that the last set of rituals would be performed before reentry into town.

The following day, the borderline between bush and town was recrossed. The neophytes were covered up by tall sheaves of grass, unable to see or be seen. This scarcely reduced the jubilation of their mothers, who greeted the procession at a major crossroad leading into town, at exactly the hour of dusk. From there the procession continued, with singing and dancing, to a compound adjacent to the Catholic church but presided over by the *régulo*. There the final, all-night session of ancestral teachings took place. The initiates were exhausted and were fighting off sleep; one man walked around the circle with a calabash, flicking water from it onto anyone seen dozing off.[8] The following morning, a Sunday, the initiates were led to a river where they took their final baths and donned the finest clothes their families could afford. Some were given new shoes. Along with the female initiates, whose own rite was timed to end the same day, they were honored at that morning's Catholic Mass—an especially celebratory one—as new, adult members of the community.

According to a Makhuwa proverb, initiation links a person to his or her land (*wineliwa onampharela mutthu elapo awe*). As the details of this section reveal, however, that land is highly marked: each ritual moment transpires at its own site. Medeiros refers to the "subspaces" that divide up the liminal zone, subspaces that remain well defined and well preserved even in the face of colonial and postcolonial pressures to shorten the rite's duration (2007: 289–303; translation mine). Not only are the sites differentiated from each other, but also the grounds of the Catholic church are differentiated from the grounds of the *régulo*'s abode, the town is differentiated from the bush, and the near side of the *ekuluwe* log is differentiated from its far side. Initiation studies in the tradition of van Gennep and Turner focus on the demarcation between the normative and the liminal space. Yet of importance for the Makhuwa is not only the grand space of structure in relation to the grand space of antistructure. Betwixt and between are many more betwixts and betweens. The rite of passage is more properly a rite of passages.

A Rite of Return

The rite of passage is also a rite of return. Vincent Crapanzano (1981) coined this phrase to characterize the male circumcision rite of Moroccan Arabs. In what he observed, Crapanzano found the idea of passage, of a unilinear movement from dependence to adulthood, to be illusory. After being taken from their mothers and paraded to the local mosque or saint's sanctuary, initiates were returned home, where the circumcision itself occurred. Following the operation, initiates (in this case aged between three and six) were swaddled in cloth and placed on the backs of their mothers, who danced until the crying stopped. The women then collectively tended to the boys' wounds. Given the "intensely feminine atmosphere" of these proceedings, Crapanzano claims they actually renewed rather than severed the maternal bond (1981: 127). The contrast with other African initiation rites is striking. Following van Gennep's paradigm, these emphasize what T. O. Beidelman calls the "journey" from childhood to adulthood (1965: 145).[9]

Makhuwa initiation is frequently spoken of as a maturation or growing (*wunnuwa*) and is filled with instructions pertaining to the neophytes' impending adult responsibilities. Yet this scarcely diminishes the centrality of maternal return. On the morning after the night of "strong teachings," the initiates were joined by their mothers for a ritual known as *othanla manawo* (discover the feet). They sat arrayed from head to ankle in *capulana* (printed cloth) garments. After the paramount chief greeted each novice, opening the cloths only enough to glimpse each boy's face, he stepped aside and signaled for the mothers to approach. They rushed toward their sons, whose feet were the only visible parts of their bodies. Each mother's task was to inspect the feet and identify those belonging to her son. None had trouble doing so. Each rejoiced at the sight of her child and sang in celebration. Though the initiates remained motionless as ever, one can only imagine them content—maybe smiling, maybe crying—under their wraps. Having passed the two most consequential and possibly most demanding weeks of their lives without them, they were at least for a moment back again with their mothers.

Among the Ndembu, the reunion of mother and child also entailed disguise: "The significance of the disguise must be mystical—for their mothers they are changed persons, they are no longer children, they have entered the adult male moral community" (Turner 1967: 255). This interpretation may apply as well to the Makhuwa case, but it would be incomplete. While Turner acknowledges that mothers still recognized their children despite the disguise, he leaves open whether the recognition made any difference. What I heard in the mothers' spirited response to the sight of nothing more than feet left no doubt: a Makhuwa initiate may be a changed person, a newly conferred member of the adult male moral community, but he does not for that reason cease to be his mother's child.[10]

On the very last day of the two-week period, following the closing Catholic Mass, the newly initiated men and women returned to the natal home. Dancing, drinking, and feasting lasted from midday to sunrise the following morning. Although a Monday, nobody went to the fields. The children remained home from school, and most market stalls stayed closed. There is much more that could be said about this homecoming, but I have already reported more than most do. Following meticulous details of the initiation rite itself, Turner pivots away from it by writing, "All that remained was for the boys to go home with their guardians to their respective villages, where a further celebration awaited them" (1967: 260). For Turner, the crux of the rite is its liminal stage. Without negating the importance of the threshold, I follow Crapanzano in regarding as no less essential the neophyte's return to his mother's embrace.[11]

Furthermore, the rite itself is laden with themes of maternity and femininity. One of Medeiros's crucial insights into Makhuwa initiation is that circumcision is a symbolic menstruation, a ritualized menarche performed at approximately the same age that girls undergo physiological menarche (2007: 327–36). Because virility and fertility do not come naturally to males, boys need circumcision and medication to obtain the reproductive capacity (*oyara*) so central to Makhuwa personhood and society.[12] Medeiros's analysis differs markedly from the Freudian view of circumcision as castration, inflicted upon boys by adult males who regard their offspring as threats. An alternate psychoanalytic theory views circumcision as resulting from womb envy, the unconscious desire of males to identify with females, thereby claiming some of their regenerative powers (Bettelheim 1954). Circumcision, on this reading, is not castration but menstruation.

Across a variety of cultures, studies of initiation make this connection.[13] The dominant interpretation, however, suggests the opposite. Rather than as a way of approximating female natality, circumcision serves to negate femininity. Beidelman, for example, notes that for the Kaguru, "the uncircumcised, moist penis makes a male unclean because this makes boys resemble women, whose moist genitals, especially during menstruation, are sources of pollution" (1997: 117). Circumcision therefore allows boys to discard all the polluting elements of womanhood. Likewise, among the Ndembu, Turner reports that the prepuce is thought to be " 'like the labia' of a woman. The boys are being 'made pure' by the removal of their feminine attributes" (1962: 161). Such understandings befit Beidelman's and Turner's reliance on van Gennep's trope of passage: from a childhood of amorphous sexuality to an adulthood of strict masculinity. Yet Turner at one point does acknowledge a connection between the color red in certain liminal rituals and the color red in menstrual rituals. In these cases, Turner notes, "the novices are implicitly treated like brides at their first menstruation" (1962: 152).

What Turner finds to be implicit is strikingly explicit among the Makhuwa. Except where influenced by coastal Islam, Makhuwa male circumcision has not entailed and, in its revived form under Catholic sponsorship, does not entail the removal of foreskin, but rather a slit across the top of it (Medeiros 2007: 329–30). It is more an incision (*opopha*) than a circumcision (*etxantto*). The result is a looser foreskin more easily pulled back over the glans as opposed to an excised foreskin that leaves the glans exposed. What matters for the rite, therefore, is not the removal of any symbolic female genitalia but the blood drawn by the cut, whatever the cut. Whether the foreskin is removed or slit, blood flows. Menarche is realized.

That circumcision serves as a mimesis of menstruation is illustrated in numerous other ways. As noted earlier, immediately following the operation, guardians regaled the novices with chants of "The vagina has opened! The vagina has opened!" This is a reference to the boys' symbolic vagina. Shouting over the chanting, one elder explained: "We crossed from there to here, to the other riverbank. There we came upon the menstruation of your mother, growing up like you are in the vagina of your mother. Everyone salivates because I said vagina. In the beginning, your mother released blood in the vagina for you to be born. From there on the other riverbank [where the operation occurred] you are imitating [*otakiha*] your mother." Initiates also approximate womanhood by adhering to the taboos in place for menstruating women: against having sex, bathing, and consuming or cooking with salt. Until the initiates' wounds heal—that is to say, until the bleeding stops—both they and their mothers accept the same prohibitions. That which the mother undergoes is undergone by her child as well. This may be seen negatively, as irksome restrictions to be endured, as in Florêncio's listing of unseasoned dishes as one among many ordeals of his own initiation. However, as posited in an important volume on the anthropology of menstruation, taboos may serve less to shield society from polluting women than "to protect the perceived creative spirituality of menstruous women from the influence of others in a more neutral state" (Buckley and Gottlieb 1988: 7). Menstruation, on this count, is not viewed negatively as dangerous or defiling but positively as the source of life.[14]

Multiple stories and song-riddles recited throughout the instructional period referred, sometimes graphically, to female reproductive organs and processes. I asked one of the storytellers why. He reaffirmed what I had heard in all my queries about Makhuwa values. "We speak of the vagina," he said, "because all life comes from there. For our culture, the principal point is regeneration [*oyara*]. All of us come from the vagina, so we have to respect it." Respect for female fertility, the capacity to bring newness into the world, may be only one aspect. Vicarious experience of it seems to be another. Through this mimesis of menstruation, the neophyte undergoes a *turning into woman* not entirely disconnected from his end-of-rite *returning to woman*—the woman who birthed him for the first time. If initiation is meant to differentiate men from women, it ironically does this by transforming men into women (see Silverman 2003).

Gender boundaries are thus simultaneously constructed and traversed, much like the spatial boundaries of the initiation grounds that also seem made to be crossed. What Crapanzano writes of the Moroccan case—"there is no transition, only repetition and return" (1981: 129)—aptly describes what I observed of the Makhuwa. An even better description relies on a likely etymology for the mountain where humanity originated (see Chapter 1). Namuli, the name of that mountain, comes from the verb *wula* (to menstruate, specifically for the first time), such that *nam-uli* could grammatically signify "she who menstruates."[15] In this light, the clearest statement that passage to manhood is inseparable from (re)turn to womanhood is that most familiar of Makhuwa proverbs: From Namuli we come, to Namuli we return.

Role-Playing

Initiation into adulthood involves the same kinetic qualities, the same dialectic of egress and regress, discussed in Part I of this book. Yet, more than merely expressing the Makhuwa disposition toward mobility, initiation rites in fact help cultivate it. Movement and migration are not only, as previous chapters may have suggested, a calculated response to turbulent histories. James Scott, in his otherwise commendable efforts to highlight everyday forms of resistance, gives at times the impression that peasants do little more than subvert authority through meticulously crafted strategies of evasion.[16]

It is to Pierre Bourdieu (1977, 1990) that anthropology owes the insight that dispositions often bypass consciousness, that human action traces as much from embodied habituations as from careful deliberations. His concept of the *habitus* conveys his refusal of the Cartesian mind-body split and his understanding that social conditions come to be expressed through prediscursive practices. The Makhuwa proclivity for dispersal and flight would accordingly be seen not only as a conscious, considered response to external pressures, but also as a mode of being-in-the-world. It is an unreflective dynamism—a protean propensity inscribed onto the body through such ritual means as those discussed in this chapter.[17]

In his study of Kuranko initiation, anthropologist Michael Jackson notes the prevalence of role reversals and identity alterations among adult participants. During the ritual period, women freely parade outside the home, don men's clothes, and carry men's weapons. This activation of role-playing possibilities is, however, a reactivation, for Kuranko children also "enjoy a free run of house and village space, unconfined by the conventional rules that strictly separate male and female domains" (Jackson 1989: 129). Kuranko children are thus sexually indeterminate, as I also found Makhuwa children to be, bound neither to the male side nor the female side of churches, mosques, and *mutholo* shrines. Whether a boy or a girl, the child's side is always the mother's side. Thus, what Jackson calls initiation rites' "disruption in the *habitus*" through acts of role-playing is the disruption of a specifically adult *habitus*. The disruption, moreover, is by way of return—to the transitory "modes of comportment and opposite sex patterns instilled in the somatic unconscious" of children (1989: 129).

Role reversals and identity play were also prominent at the rite I observed—among adults, that is.[18] As early as the first ritual meal, one especially tall, gangly man squatted between two of the novices as Kayaya went around the circle hand-feeding each boy a helping of medicinally leavened cornmeal. When it came to the man's turn, he licked his lips and extended his tongue as far as he could. The master obliged and fed him a scoop, eliciting uproarious laughter from all of us onlookers—though, as usual, not from the initiates. Of course, no one finds it particularly funny or even noteworthy when, in everyday life, children inhabit multiple roles and spaces. Humorous about the man's playfulness on this occasion was the fact that roles are defined for him in a way they are not for children. Women are not supposed to act like men and men are not supposed to act like boys. The mobility of adults across age and gender spectrums is comical in a way that the mobility of children is not.

From where, then, does the sense of defined roles and bounded domains come? Among the Makhuwa, at least, it comes largely from the initiation rite itself. For while adult participants play with their roles and identities, the initiates themselves remain still and stoic. They are expected not only to maintain composure throughout, including during their operation. They must also restrain their pleasure while the adults around them clown and jest.[19] Initiates must monitor their emotions as carefully as they monitor their movements. Many other distinctions come to consciousness during the ritual process: the bush is rendered clearly distinct from the town, as is one encampment from another, and the *ekuluwe* log's near side from its far side. After the rite, initiates emerge as men distinct from women, as adults distinct from children. Thus, "the conventional rules that strictly separate male and female domains" (Jackson 1989: 129)—along with other domains of adult life—are actually made conventional by the initiation rite itself. While adults engage in a disruption in the *habitus*, returning to their preadult boundlessness, initiates themselves undergo a similarly significant disruption of the only *habitus* they had hitherto known. They emerge from a sense of fluidity and freedom to an awareness of propriety and bounds.

Yet if, at initiation rites, distinctions and classifications are instituted (Bourdieu 1991), they are just as importantly transgressed. The initiates themselves perform such transgressions insofar as becoming men requires that they pass through womanhood, and insofar as becoming adults coincides with returning to mothers. But the permeability of borders finds greatest expression in the adults' role reversals. These serve not just a cathartic but a pedagogical role. Although initiates must feign indifference to the adults' border crossings, as well as to their dancing and bantering, no initiate I spoke to afterward denied noticing—and enjoying—any of this. What they observed, and arguably what they learned, is that though their lives are becoming ordered, they are not becoming fixed. Makhuwa adulthood has to do with bounded domains, but no less with movement between them. It has to do with roles, but no less with their reversals.

Dispositions Toward Discontinuity

My argument is not that initiation erases the early childhood *habitus* of movement and flux, only that it adds a new element: border consciousness. Among the initiated, mobility is not so much diminished as framed. What was in childhood a *habitus* of open-ended flux becomes in adulthood a *habitus* of border-crossing flux. The disposition toward mobility without bounds becomes a disposition toward mobility across bounds. I call this a disposition toward discontinuity.

By conjoining, paradoxically, "disposition" and "discontinuity," I position myself against the conservatism—the assumption of continuity—in Bourdieu's theory of *habitus*. Despite allowing social actors a "margin of freedom" (2000: 234–36), Bourdieu comes close to a stance of structural determinism. According to Michel de Certeau, Bourdieu's dispositions "have no movement of their own. They are the place in which structures are inscribed, the marble on which their history is engraved. Nothing happens in them that is not the result of their exteriority. As in the traditional image of primitive or peasant societies, nothing moves, there is no history other than that written on them by an alien order" (1984: 57). This image of primitives and peasants appears classically in Hegel's remark that Africa has "no movement or development to exhibit" ([1837] 1956: 99). More recently, it appears in anthropological studies of Pentecostalism that presume rupture and radical change to be uniquely introduced by the "alien order" (to use de Certeau's term) of Pentecostalism.

If a disposition toward discontinuity is internal to Makhuwa frameworks, then fidelity to Makhuwa tradition may not guarantee stability. It may actually invite change. What Bourdieu calls "durable dispositions" could just as well be called malleable dispositions or dispositions toward malleability. These dispositions promote not stasis and conservation but motion and experimentation. On this reading, structure and agency, continuity and change, conservation and innovation are bound together, and moving beyond one's conditioning coheres with being true to it. Roberto Mangabeira Unger posits this possibility in his political philosophy—the possibility of paradigms that collapse the distinction between the routine and the revolutionary, wherein movements within paradigms are continuous with movements between them. These would be frameworks "so arranged as to facilitate and to organize their own piecemeal, experimental revision," structures that render transformations banal extensions of everyday life (2007: 7, 57).

What Unger outlines speculatively I have observed empirically. The Makhuwa self is a shape-shifting self whose "essence" is mobility and mutability. Changes and movements occur endogenously, with no necessary dependence on crisis or catastrophe.[20] This explains why it seems so easy for people like Florêncio to join Pentecostal churches, despite their demand of discontinuity. It also explains why it seems so easy for people to slip out of Pentecostal churches, despite their demand of discontinuity, as Florêncio also did when he partook in the prohibited initiation rite.

What prevents most scholars of Pentecostalism from noticing, let alone documenting, such transgressive moves is the tendency to view processes of conversion as van Gennep views rites of passage: as singular, momentous, and once and for all. Studies of initiation readily refer to boys "converting" (Beidelman 2005: 1799) or who "are converted" (Turner 1967: 265) from partially feminized youths into purified adult males. There is nothing wrong with conversion as a metaphor for initiatory transformation. The problem is that the kind of conversion assumed here is that expected by elites of religious traditions and recorded by scholars of religious traditions, but not necessarily adhered to by followers of religious traditions.

This chapter's aim has been to sketch a Makhuwa model of conversion on the basis of a Makhuwa rite of passage. To the point already made that conversion for the Makhuwa is a spatial affair, this chapter adds that space is not homogeneous. The site of initiation is full of discontinuous and noncontiguous domains; and thus the sense of self formed through initiation is full of discontinuous and noncontiguous identities. Yet because boundedness coexists with mobility, rupture—such as that demanded by Pentecostalism—is not a one-off event. Rupture is routine—repeatable and, indeed, reversible.

Florêncio was so easily able to break from church teachings and undergo initiation because his religious conversion was not singular, momentous, and irreversible—just as "conversion" to Makhuwa adulthood is not. His crossing from Pentecostalism back to "tradition" is best seen in light of exactly what transpired at the initiation itself: not just a rite of passage but a rite of passages, and not just a rite of passages but a rite of return.

CHAPTER 4

Two Feet In, Two Feet Out

From the perspective of Pentecostal leaders, what I have been calling a Makhuwa disposition toward mobility is less a capacity than a defect: the defect of having "one foot in the church and one foot in tradition." Assumed in this complaint is a dividing line across which true converts must definitively cross. In northern Mozambique, the idea of religion—any religion—as a bounded entity arrived through the work of foreign actors. Yet, over time, many members of the local population have come to accept that idea. The central question of this chapter, then, is not whether the category of religion is relevant for the Makhuwa; as Chapter 5 will show, the answer depends on whom you ask. The question, rather, is how those who have received it have refashioned it. I argue that the view of religions as mutually exclusive does little to displace the nomadic properties of Makhuwa selfhood so far explored. Dividing lines meant to be barriers can be made into bridges. Of crucial importance is that crossing over and fully engaging what is on the far side need not preclude crossing back to engage, just as fully, what is near.

Religions and Their Borders

As previously noted, scholars of Pentecostalism have placed great emphasis on the disjunctive dimensions of the faith, the predication of conversion as rupture on an opposition between Christianity and non-Christian religions. Significantly, however, Makhuwa has no native term for religion.[1] What it has is *ettini*, a loanword from the Swahili *dini*, itself derived from the Arabic *dīn*. Religion, or at least the word for that complex of things so called, came to inland Makhuwa populations only in the nineteenth century when they were incorporated into oceanic trade networks and, thus, into the broader Swahili and Arab worlds.[2]

Yet the Arabic *dīn* has often meant something different from the Latin *religio* as it developed in the modern West. The difference is that *dīn* was never so easily reified and systematized; in its earliest Arabic meaning, it could not be rendered in the plural (Smith 1963: 98–102). These features are evident in Makhuwa terms for Islam. These include *esilamu*, a verbal noun that (like the Arabic "Islam") names an act of submission, and *emaka*, from the Arabic pronunciation of "Mecca." In these cases, the name refers not to a reified essence, but to devotional acts and sacred lands. Likewise, the Makhuwa word for the Islamic place of worship (*ejuma*) derives from the Arabic *jumu'ah*, the Friday prayer ceremony. Here, also, the relevant point is not institutional structure but pious practice.

In 1926, mostly Italian missionaries of the Roman Catholic Consolata order arrived in Niassa Province.[3] Wherever they settled, they drew converts, and wherever they drew converts, they drew boundaries. These boundaries functioned symbolically to separate the holy from the profane, but they took the material form of walls: walls enclosing the spaces of Catholic churches, mission stations, schools, and hospitals (cf. Comaroff and Comaroff 1997; Hovland 2013). The word *ettini* became conflated with *ekereja* (church, from the Portuguese *igreja*) and *ekapela* (chapel, from the Portuguese *capela*). Correspondingly, in the Islamic *ettini*, the term *musikitti* (mosque, from the Portuguese *mesquita*) came to complement, if not replace, *ejuma*.[4] Now, to involve oneself with a religion meant less to submit to God or perform the prayers than to place oneself within a bounded space, a sanctuary set apart. In this shift from practice-based to place-based terminology, the space of the church became clearly differentiated from the space of the mosque. Interreligious borders became important in a way hitherto not the case. Christianity and Islam were now the two available *ittini* (plural of *ettini*): noncontiguous "religions" whose conceptual and spatial separation was assured by the borders around their sacred spaces.

The most significant border, however, is that which came to divide the church and the mosque from ancestral ritual grounds. Conceptually, this is the divide that emerged between each *ettini* and the newly conceived *ettini ya makholo* (religion of the ancestors). Importantly, until today only certain sectors of the local population—those more likely to have attended school and to speak Portuguese—nominalize ancestral practices and beliefs as a "religion." More commonly, the predicate is conveyed not with a noun but with a verb: *ettini ahu ti omuhela makeya* (our religion is to offer *makeya*). Religion, in other words, is not a substance but an action, the action of laying down *makeya* offerings to ancestors. Yet the concept of *ettini* still gets applied to ancestor-based traditions, at least by some. Insofar as it does, ancestral religion stands as one more *ettini* alongside Christianity and Islam.

Indeed, it stands not only alongside but also apart from them—a development owing largely to the proselytizing efforts of the earliest Consolata missionaries. Whereas Islam's spread among the Makhuwa entailed "the partial Islamization of pre-Islamic religious practices" (Alpers 2000: 313), Consolata evangelists mandated that indigenous religious practices be simply renounced. Practitioners of divination, traditional healing, and ancestor veneration would not be accepted into the Catholic fold unless they first set aside those practices considered heathen and demonic. Studies from surrounding regions confirm the commonality of colonial-era Catholic attacks on what was deemed incommensurable with Christianity (e.g., Green 2003; West 2005: 109–19). Yet the impact of this stance went far beyond the realm of cultural politics. At an epistemological register, it further threw into relief a wide and heterogeneous range of indigenous practices and beliefs, shaping them into a reified unit: an ancestral set of customs conceived as external to both the Christian *ettini* and the Islamic *ettini*.

The global gathering of Roman Catholic bishops known as the Second Vatican Council (1962–65) helped reorient Catholic missionary practice toward greater acceptance of and tolerance toward that which missionaries previously labored to obliterate. One sees this changed outlook in the ministry of such missionary anthropologists as Giuseppe Frizzi, Elia Ciscato, Francisco Lerma Martínez, and Simona Brambilla. All four are Catholic leaders originally from Europe who have lived at length among the Makhuwa—in most cases, for many decades. All dedicated themselves to studying and understanding Makhuwa dialects and cultural traditions.[5] Though they did so for broader evangelistic aims, their writings nonetheless exude respect and even admiration for a people prone to being dismissed as irreverent and irrelevant by the intended readers of those writings. My own entrée into the Makhuwa lifeworld was facilitated greatly by conversations with Padres Frizzi, Ciscato, and Lerma Martínez, each of whom worked in a different area of northern Mozambique during my research year (Sister Brambilla no longer worked in Mozambique at the time). Each is regarded as an elder by the local Makhuwa population, even by non-Catholics.

Lerma Martínez, a Spanish-born Consolata missionary who has lived with the Makhuwa since 1971, offers helpful insight into the Catholic Church's changing relationship to what he calls "African religions." In a book titled *Religiões Africanas Hoje* (African Religions Today), he writes of his intent to "read and discover the 'seeds of the Word' and the signs of truth and grace present in these religions" (2009: 13; translations mine). The phrase "these religions" refers to those indigenous to Africa, each such religion tied to one specific ethnolinguistic group.[6] In a pointed critique of earlier missionaries' view of Christianity as the only valid religion, Lerma Martínez writes that "one cannot talk of religion in the singular" and that "anthropology confirms that there is no people, however ancient, without religion" (2009: 16–17). Collectively, the missionary anthropologists' driving contention has been that what preceded and persisted through European contact merits study and appreciation, not dismissal and derogation.

Ironically, however, by promoting "the genuine encounter of Christianity with the ancient African tradition" (Lerma Martínez 1989: 19; translation mine), the epistemological divide introduced by earlier triumphalist missionaries remained firmly intact. The move from denunciation to dialogue did little to diminish the sense of two "religions": distinct, discrete, and dichotomous. For missionaries, no less than for explorers and anthropologists, sorting hitherto fluid and polymorphous humans into separate groupings helped to render Africa's diversity less bewildering, to order it by imposing a taxonomic grid over it. More perniciously, classification regimes helped advance colonizers' administrative ambitions. Conceptual containment served the end of political containment (Ranger 1993; Chidester 1996). The clearest instance of this is European imperialists' partitioning of the African continent into nonoverlapping nation-states, within which populations accustomed to migration and exchange could be controlled, regulated, and surveilled.[7]

Indeed, postcolonial authorities, no less than their colonial counterparts, found it expedient to organize fluid and open lifeworlds into hermetically sealed abstractions. Following independence in 1975, the party-state of the Mozambican Liberation Front (Frelimo) engaged in just this kind of reduction. In line with its project of socialist modernization, it constructed an opposition between "science" and "obscurantism," both understood to be discrete entities, the former to be promoted and the latter expunged.[8]

By grouping a complex of customary practices—practices as varied as initiation, divination, and polygyny—as "obscurantism," Frelimo smoothed a path toward managing and modernizing the population. Ironically, the Frelimo state, born of anti-imperial struggle, based this classificatory scheme on a modernist imaginary originating in imperial Europe. This is the worldview common to the motley array of outsiders—Portuguese colonizers, Catholic missionaries, Frelimo socialists—that have descended on the people who today self-identify (largely because of those outsiders' interventions) as Makhuwa.

Yet recognition that such systematic divisions are foreign to a given context—that there is an invented quality to them (Hobsbawm and Ranger 1992)—should not lead us to miss where and when they are nonetheless salient. While "religion" in the sense of an integrated "belief system" is peculiarly and parochially a remnant of European intellectual history (Smith 1963; Asad 1993), it and similar categories have nevertheless "been let out of the bag, and we are hardly in a position to scoop them back up again" (Keane 2007: 86).[9] Second-order abstractions may not always have organized people's perceptions of the world around them, but for many in postcolonial societies, today they do. Even when able to resist "conversion" to Christianity, the targets of evangelistic campaigns still find themselves drawn into Eurocentric frameworks. If we take seriously this "colonization of consciousness" (Comaroff and Comaroff 1991), then the postcolonial celebration of hybridity, like the postmodern championing of flux, should come in for greater scrutiny than it hitherto has. Definitive borders around this or that ethnicity or this or that religion may be fabrications, but fabrications are real—as much for the colonized as the colonizer, for the evangelized as the evangelizer.[10]

Polyontological Mobility

In conversations with me, Pentecostal leaders frequently expressed disdain for Maúa's Catholic church, mainly for what they saw as its inadequate evangelization of the Makhuwa people. Locals are not easy to save, they complained, because the Catholic church has misled them into thinking reverence for Jesus and reverence for ancestors are mutually compatible. The Pentecostal pastors' concern was that people had "one foot in the church and one foot in tradition." This illegitimate blending of Christianity and "tradition" tarnished the sanctity of the former with the profanity of the latter.

However one may view this charge, its characterization is not quite right. In broad strokes, one might see the phenomenon of baptized Catholics consulting diviners, imbibing traditional medicines, and offering *makeya* as evidence for the fusion of religious worlds. But the broad strokes miss what is evident up close: that ancestors are rarely brought into the churches and that the apostles, saints, and Virgin Mary never appear at ancestral shrines. One does not invoke Catholic intercessors at home, one informant told me, because there it is only one's family, including one's ancestors, "who know my environment, my suffering, my life." The popular Catholicism of the Makhuwa differs in this sense from that of other parts of the world where distinctions between the "popular" and the "official" go unheeded, and hybridized rituals are performed "as if [they] were unitary—fully Christian and fully indigenous" (McGuire 2008: 197).[11] In Maúa district, rather than such fusion, one sees an acceptance of disparate zones, of pluralism left as pluralism.

Compartmentalization of this sort was clear in the male initiation ceremony I observed in 2012. As mentioned in Chapter 3, the Italian priest Giuseppe Frizzi has helped organize such rites in the district capital every year since 1989. Seventy years of age during the year of my fieldwork, Padre Frizzi was easily the most well-known individual in Maúa, recognizable to all as the white-skinned, Makhuwa-speaking, bicycle-riding leader of the district's Catholic community. He was known, and respected, for his linguistic expertise—his encyclopedic knowledge of the local language—as well as for his long-standing commitment to the district. People especially appreciated the affirming stance Padre Frizzi took toward Makhuwa "tradition" in the wake of earlier efforts, by the state and by the church, to eradicate such things as healing, divination, and initiation rites. Catholic sponsorship of initiation, of the kind seen in Chapter 3, is not uncommon in the wider region. These days, in Maúa, it is only under Catholic sponsorship that the rites take place with anything like the regularity and on anything like the scale of times past.[12]

Yet while Padre Frizzi speaks of this as the "Christianizing" of the ritual, something far subtler comes into view, again, when seen up close. For both the male and female ceremonies, Padre Frizzi invites Makhuwa ritual specialists and sages (*anamiruku*) to participate. They are invited to do so, though, not *for* the Catholic church but alongside it. At the *nvera* site of the boys' initiation, I witnessed both church catechists and Makhuwa *anamiruku* offering their wisdom teachings (*ikano*) to the neophytes. Their teachings were imparted, however, not simultaneously but alternately. During the daylight hours, initiates heard biblical narratives, partook in a midweek Mass, and made confessions to Padre Frizzi. Nights, however, belonged to the *anamiruku*. Against the flickering of firelight, Makhuwa elders instructed—through chants and drums, with stomping and dancing—on proper ways of burying the dead, relating to ancestors, respecting elders, and bearing new life.

Church catechists were present and participated in these nocturnal proceedings; likewise, the *anamiruku* were involved during the day. Significantly, though, a strict dichotomy was maintained: I heard no reference to ancestors during the day and no reference to Jesus at night. Distinct yet complementary—like day and night, man and woman, town and bush—the two traditions or, as one increasingly hears, the two *ittini* coexist without one subsuming the other. Padre Frizzi, despite his "Christianizing" of the rite, actually insisted that it be run this way, in accordance with what he (in a personal conversation) astutely described as the Makhuwa principle of "duality without dualism."

This is not to say Padre Frizzi has at all times resisted greater integration. A few years before I carried out fieldwork, he brought to his catechists the idea of creating within the parish church a commission of traditional healers (*anamuku*). A diligent ethnographer of Makhuwa healing traditions, Padre Frizzi saw no reason to exclude the forms of bodily healing offered outside the church from the spiritual salvation offered within.[13] One can readily appreciate how distant this approach was from that of early Catholic missionaries (and contemporary Pentecostal ones), who deemed traditional healers agents of the devil and refused to legitimize them outside the church, let alone inside it. The kind of "inculturated Christianity" Padre Frizzi proposed, however, was in this case rejected by his own church council, a group comprising Maúa-born and Makhuwa-speaking catechists. It was not that they devalued customary healing practices; most considered them necessary for their own well-being. Rather, they could not accept Padre Frizzi's proposal to meld them with affairs of the church. They could not accept it, one of them told me, because the earliest Catholic missionaries taught them these disparate worlds simply did not mix. They are separate, converts were told, and consciousness of that separation has over time been internalized.

Extraordinarily attuned though Padre Frizzi is to the particularities of Makhuwa language and culture, his search for singularity in his proposal for "Catholic *anamuku*" suggests at least one point of disconnect. Western scholars, not least anthropologists, have long viewed religions as systems of belief: ordered, coherent, and logically consistent. Both the theological category of inculturation and the anthropological category of syncretism disrupt assumptions of religious purity and homogeneity. Ultimately, however, they too manifest the bias toward wholeness. Syncretism is, after all, yet another "ism," a totalizing construct no less than "Hinduism" and "Judaism."

In her study of Islam among the Giriama of Kenya, Janet McIntosh (2009) observed a model of multiplicity that, she argues, is captured poorly by "syncretism" and "hybridity." She proposes, as a conceptual alternative, polyontology.[14] Eschewing the need for overarching coherence, polyontology holds open plurality and fluidity without discarding the sense of distinct, compartmentalized essences. Religious plurality, McIntosh writes, "is not about reconciling Islam and Giriama Traditionalism into a new, systemic whole, but about drawing on both religions while continuing to mark them as distinct. More than one religion may be used, but they are juxtaposed rather than blended" (2009: 188). The multiplicity of states, identities, or positionalities one might assume in this model is not a simultaneous multiplicity but a serial one, akin to what computer scientists call toggling or multitasking, what linguists call code switching, and what psychologists call cognitive shifts.[15]

Combining the modernist (but also now Makhuwa) sense of distinct "religions" with the long-standing Makhuwa disposition toward mobility brings us to what I call, building off McIntosh, polyontological mobility. People have by and large accepted the epistemology of nonoverlapping "religions," but not its implications for identity.[16] Thus, while borders between religions are real—they have become social facts—what a mobile people brings to borders is neither an acceptance of confinement nor a refusal of acknowledgement. They bring a facility of transgression.[17] Offering praise to Jesus and offering *makeya* to ancestors are neither mutually incompatible nor simultaneously compatible. They are *serially* compatible.

Anthropologists working in southern Africa have amply documented such oscillatory modes of religious practice. Thomas Kirsch (2004) argues that while his Zambian informants view genuine belief as necessary for a practice to have effect, this does not impede them from switching, pragmatically, between disparate religious options. What matters for them is "believing" at a particular moment, not "belief" as a perpetual state. Similarly, Michael Lambek (1993) finds that those he studied in Mayotte juggled three traditions: Islam, cosmology, and spirit possession. While these are regarded as incommensurable with one another, shifts between them were normal, each brought into play according to the dictates of circumstance. Alcinda Honwana, working in southern Mozambique, likewise contends that while there is no contradiction between being Christian and accepting ancestral spirits, these domains remain distinct (2002: 160–62). What brings them together is not mixture but movement.

Writing about the presumed antagonism of religion and science in Western societies, philosopher William James asks, "Why, after all, may not the world be so complex as to consist of many interpenetrating spheres of reality, which we can thus approach in alternation by using different conceptions and assuming different attitudes?" (1985: 122–23). For the Makhuwa, the alternating approach to discrete religious spheres translates into a sense that commitment to Christianity at one time and place need not preclude commitment to ancestral religion in another. The Makhuwa see no need to equate fidelity with exclusivity or sincerity with singularity. Fausto, one of my research assistants and a self-described Catholic, made the point perfectly in a discussion about Pentecostal pastors' complaint. "It's not that we have one foot in the church and one foot in tradition," Fausto said, "but both feet in the church *when we're there*, and both feet on the ancestral grounds *when we're there*."

Heaven Below

I posed this "two feet in, two feet out" principle to Abílio, the secretary of Kaveya's Pentecostal congregation, to see whether it resonated beyond the local Catholic population. He said that while not everyone would be willing to admit it, this does in fact describe the nature of most Pentecostals' participation. As an example, he recalled the conversation he and I had soon after Pastor Simões delivered the funeral address for Luisinha (see Chapter 1). Pastor Simões did there what the first Catholic missionaries did nearly a century earlier: insist on a new conception of the afterlife, one involving ascent to and permanent rest in a place called heaven. This celestial conception was meant to replace the Makhuwa view that the deceased return to Mount Namuli and, from Namuli, circulate back to the living. The

Makhuwa term for heaven, though, ended up doing more to preserve than supplant the Makhuwa understanding. The word used is *erimu*, whose suffix, *mu*, connotes interiority, depth, and profundity, as opposed to *osulú*, the word for sky, which the early missionaries first proposed. According to Padre Frizzi, the Makhuwa preference for the former illustrates nothing less than a conscious rejection of a central Western construct. Suggested by *erimu* is that, after death, one does not withdraw from the world but continues to engage it, maintaining a presence among the living, fortifying rather than severing relationships. Hence, chiefs in particular were customarily buried under termite mounds, those simulacra of Mount Namuli considered subterranean passageways to the sacred mountain. Likewise, argues Padre Frizzi, what is important about mountains (Namuli and others) is not their majestic heights but their hidden depths—the grottos and caves out of which medicinal roots are extracted and within which humans have long sought shelter.

The Makhuwa aversion to verticality also came out clearly in conversation with Hariwa, a Lioma village *namiruku* (sage), who explained that the most important thing about rain is not its fall from the sky but its rise from the ground. The earliest signal that rains are approaching, he said, are visible below—in the sprouting of herbs, the changing of leaves, the appearance of particular insects, and the presence of moist soil below the surface. "When the rainy season approaches," he said, "a person should pay attention to the earth. We are mistaken to think that it begins up there. Everything begins here."

I recalled from grade-school science class that water vapor condenses in clouds and forms raindrops that fall to the earth, after which the water transforms again to vapor, light enough to rise again to the sky. This process is, properly speaking, a cycle. But in the way I learned it, the starting point was the sky. The Makhuwa, by contrast, prioritize events not up above, but down below. The water cycle's generative step is not precipitation but evaporation—not the falling of rain, but the rising of vapor.

"Do you see people walking there, planting cassava there, building houses there?" Hariwa asked, gesturing to the sky. "No, all our life is here on earth. And it is here on earth that Muluku laid the path to Namuli."

Emphasizing immersive depths over transcendent heights, Makhuwa sensibilities are plainly existential in the sense conveyed by Friedrich Nietzsche's injunction: "Stay true to the earth" (2005: 66). Theirs is not an abstract metaphysics that privileges heavens and peaks, but a concrete

Figure 6. *Namiruku* Hariwa, Lioma village.

existence grounded in the lived world. In an essay on the origins of existentialism, Herbert Dreyfus (2009) contrasts the Greek philosophical ideal of detached objectivity—of knowledge gained (as in Plato's famous allegory) through escape from caves—with the other of Western civilization's great inheritances: the Judeo-Christian tradition. The latter emphasizes the local and historical over the universal and the eternal. Its approach to knowledge is not detached and objective but immersive and involved. According to Dreyfus, it is the Judeo-Christian model (albeit not always in theistic terms) that nineteenth- and twentieth-century existentialists attempted to reclaim from the underside of Enlightenment rationalism.

In the oppositional terms laid out by Dreyfus, African traditional cultures (broadly speaking) could be said to approximate the Judeo-Christian pole, having largely bypassed the Greek philosophical predilection for essences and abstractions (Hood 1990). In most African cosmologies, for example, spirits are far more consequential than the Supreme Being, whom one rarely summons or bothers with daily affairs. Much early scholarship on African cosmologies missed this basic point due to the tendency to interpret African deities through Greek metaphysical frameworks (p'Bitek 2011). Among the Makhuwa, ancestral spirits (*minepa*) not only interact more with humans than does Muluku, the Supreme Being; their reality is inseparable from those interactions. As the anthropologist Godfrey Lienhardt argues in his work on the Dinka, divinities and powers "cannot be understood by us if they are regarded as referring to theoretical 'beings' whose existence is posited, as it were, before the human experience to which they correspond" (1961: 169). Existence, in other words, precedes essence.

Most significant about this existential orientation is the pluralistic disposition to which it leads. When I asked Abílio what he thought of Pastor Simões's homily—specifically, its emphasis on heaven as a place to which the soul ascends for eternal rest—Abílio said this point is indisputable. But it is not what he imparts to his children at night around the fire of the family compound.

"There, I tell them we go to Namuli, where our ancestors came from," Abílio said.

"And when you're at the church, with Pastor Simões?" I asked.

Abílio smiled and said, "There, I say we go to heaven."

"Can you have two answers like that?" I asked. "With both being correct?"

"For the ancestors, yes, it is correct. Inside the religion, yes, it is correct."

Imperative for the Makhuwa is not logical coherence and correspondence with reality, but community and context. Time and again, I was impressed by the Makhuwa elevation of relationality over rationality, of people over principles. I asked the missionary anthropologist Elia Ciscato, who has lived since 1967 among the Makhuwa, about the curious tendency of people to say "Yes, yes, that's it" in response to one proposition and "Yes, yes, that's it" in response to its opposite. He explained it well: "The priority is not the truth. The truth passes through relationship." In other words, less important than grasping and conveying truth to one's interlocutors is *being* true to them. Similarly, Padre Frizzi has also argued that of cardinal importance to the Makhuwa "is not speculative and abstract knowledge but life in its concreteness, plenitude, and abundance" (Frizzi 2009; translation mine). True knowledge, presumed in Greek metaphysics to transcend history, is nothing if not grounded. It is in the spaces within (*mu*) that life transpires—within the immediate world that surrounds us and the intersubjective world that sustains us.

The Makhuwa imperative of intersubjectivity—*okhalano* (to be with)—is the organizing motif of Part III of this book. But *okhalano* is underwritten by the pluralistic epistemology at issue here. Makhuwa ways of knowing open up to the Makhuwa knowing of ways—many ways, many paths, many truths. This pluralism, however, is no sign of insincerity. As discussed in the Introduction, relationality, when understood existentially, presupposes commitment—indeed, an unconditional commitment (Kierkegaard 1985). But the plenitude of that commitment refers to its intensity, not to its duration.[18] One can be unconditionally committed to one thing and unconditionally committed to another—both feet in *and* both feet out, ancestors in heaven *and* in Namuli.

My argument here is that the Makhuwa ability to abide in contradiction has everything to do with the Makhuwa conception of heaven. *Erimu* is below. It is grounded and existential. Yet insofar as the afterlife entails not transcendence but immersion, not eternal rest but continual passage (from Namuli, to Namuli), it is not just a matter of existentialism but of existential mobility. And insofar as existential mobility involves both pluralism *and* commitment, it is mobility, most specifically, of the polyontological kind.

Continuities of Conversion

Religious conversion premised on polyontology is not incompatible with the direction in which Joel Robbins, in his defining work for an anthropology of Christianity, has led the field. It in fact affirms his insistence on viewing Pentecostal conversion in terms of rupture and discontinuity, in terms of the "radical change" required by acts of border crossing (Robbins 2007). In my conception of polyontological mobility, however, the demand for rupture is not a demand for definitiveness. Discontinuity is a continuous affair, a series of oscillations and alternations, a bidirectional process rather than a one-off event. Problematic about Robbins's formulation is his acceptance of official Pentecostal views that there is something incomplete about conversions made for pragmatic reasons. Such conversions have only reached the first stage of what Robbins delineates as a two-stage process: the first characterized by utilitarian poaching, and the second, by intellectual assent (2004: 84–88).

Elsewhere, Robbins accuses anthropologists of operating with an implicit model of "crypto-religion" when they discredit Christian converts' claims to have disconnected from traditional religion. A typical anthropological account, according to Robbins, holds that such people "have managed to preserve their religious consciousness largely intact and thus should not be counted as Christians" (2011: 412). The task Robbins sets for himself is to understand why, in cases usually ignored by anthropologists, "people stay with the new religion and come to engage it deeply" (2004: 87). This requires positing a second stage—the intellectualist stage—of conversion, which moves converts beyond crypto-religious utilitarianism to full-fledged Christianity.[19] But what is implied by pairing the idea of *staying with* a new religion with that of *engaging* it deeply? Is duration necessary for depth? Is temporariness necessarily superficial?

Robbins's theory of Pentecostal conversion deserves credit for taking native exegesis into account (Chua 2012: 16–18). But which natives are granted exegetical authority? In Robbins's case, it appears to be the Christians any outside observer would be most prone to hearing: converts offering their testimonies in church and leaders instructing on authentic conversion. In making these the Christians whose views should be heard, Robbins ends up basing his conclusion on an assumption that effectively predetermines it. He assumes that those authorized to define conversion are only those who have already arrived at an intellectual relationship with

Christianity—at Robbins's second stage. But what of the perspective of ordinary practitioners, those guided by "mere" utilitarianism, those who are likely as irreducible to ascribed identities as they are to the tidy stages of theoretical models? Such people are easily missed or dismissed, guided as they are by something other than intellectuals' predilection for "intellectualism" (Bourdieu 2000). Thus, when Robbins writes that one advantage of his two-stage theory is that "it hypothesizes that what can look like chaotic processes of change actually have a structure" (2004: 87), one wonders who really needs that structure: the convert or the anthropologist, the practitioner or the theorist?[20]

James Scott writes that what strikes observers as "a series of abrupt, wrenching changes" in nomadic peoples' ethnic self-identification may be experienced by those accustomed to mobility as "a gradual and imperceptible process" (2009: 273). In other words, shifts in ethnicity, location, or religion may be discontinuous, but discontinuity may be a way of life. Scott adds, "If we can imagine this ethnic succession as a relatively seamless affair, then it follows that it could be just as seamless when the direction is reversed. . . . The way to the valley state was a two-way street and leaving need be no more jarring or traumatic than entering" (2009: 273). For the Makhuwa, leaving and entering (*ohiya ni ovolowa*) discrete traditions—like moving between river and road, village and bush—is similarly neither jarring nor traumatic. Nor is it irreversible.

In Search of Life

Of the two Pentecostal churches in Maúa town, the Evangelical Assembly of God (Evangélica Assembléia de Deus, or EAD) comprised primarily *vientes* (newcomers), relatively well-off and formally educated individuals who came from elsewhere to take up one of the district's few salaried jobs. Unlike at the African Assembly of God (Assembléia de Deus Africana, or ADA), dress at the EAD was formal—the fact that worshippers wore shoes was alone enough to deter many locals—and the language of worship was Portuguese. Only two people born and raised in the district regularly attended EAD services in the year of my fieldwork.

One of them was Raimundo, a young man who drew my attention because his uncle held a prominent leadership position in the district's

Catholic church. As the lead catechist and chief aide to Padre Frizzi, Raimundo's uncle was well known and well respected. He not only officiated at many of the Catholic parish masses, he was also the man called by government officials to give the Christian invocation at public assemblies. That Raimundo broke from the Catholicism of so prominent a family seemed to exemplify the narratives on which much attention in Pentecostal studies has focused—narratives of defection not only from kin networks to church networks but also from Catholicism to Pentecostalism.

I asked Raimundo how he came to participate in the Pentecostal church. He was following a friend, he said. I discerned quickly, though, that this friend was more of a benefactor, a man for whom Raimundo had initially done menial tasks, but later relied on for financial gifts. Raimundo did not speak of it as a relationship of patronage or employment, but it certainly was one of dependence. In return for this support, Raimundo did his best to reciprocate with what little he had. He accepted the man's invitation to visit his church. After attending once, Raimundo found it hard to stop. He knew that his patron received accolades from Pastor Manuel for bringing in a new member, particularly one from the local population. Raimundo liked that he could pay back the support of his "friend" by granting him, through steadfast church attendance, the reward of spiritual blessings. Thus Raimundo remained in good standing with the church, and thereby in good standing with the man.

Enmeshment in relations of dependency was not unusual for Raimundo. As a child, when his mother was transported to Cuamba due to a severe illness, Raimundo found a way to follow her, taking advantage of his youth to hitch a ride on a Red Cross plane (during the civil war, this was the only viable means of long-distance travel). After his mother recovered, Raimundo set off once again, following a friend to another town nearby. There he put himself at the service of various employers, washing plates and cleaning patios, only to find himself in one abusive situation after another: accused of stealing, robbed of wages, beaten. One year later he decamped again—for Lichinga, the provincial capital, where a restaurant owner took him in. Raimundo spent mornings hauling crates of beer atop his head; the rest of the day he labored in the kitchen. His compensation was food and a bed.

The conditions to which Raimundo submitted himself throughout this time seemed to me deplorable. It was the kind of hierarchical arrangement that unsettles those of us brought up with what anthropologist James

Ferguson calls the emancipatory liberal mind. But, as Ferguson argues, relations of obligation have long been part of what it means to be a person in southern Africa. Rather than to autonomy—a Western ideal—aspirations are to "a plurality of opportunities for dependence" (2013: 226). That very plurality serves as a check against abuse, since exit is always an option. This, it turns out, has long been Raimundo's modus vivendi: escape in times of hardship, even if only to another situation of subordination.

When Raimundo could no longer bear the work in Lichinga he returned to his natal Maúa. That is where he met the man who called him to join his Pentecostal church. That Raimundo entered the church in pursuit of one man's support may make his conversion seem insincere or inauthentic. Yet such judgments fail to account for the field of impoverished alternatives in which his actions were set, the limits on the scope of his agency. Moreover, it should be noted, within weeks of entering the EAD, Raimundo found himself caught up in forces of attraction internal to church life itself. He appreciated the camaraderie, support, and mutual respect exhibited by members of this community. He also felt the connection to God to be more intense and intimate than he had experienced elsewhere. By the time I met Raimundo, on my first visit to the EAD, he was a fervent worshipper, articulate when called on to pray and boisterous in call-and-response sequences. Not unlike everyone else I observed in both the EAD and the ADA, Raimundo related to Pentecostalism with passion and vigor.

Yet Raimundo's faith encompassed more than the church could contain. This became clear when he contracted an illness, a painful and disfiguring skin infection known locally as *munapheyo*. I received the news during a Sunday worship service at the EAD. Following the service, I walked with congregants across town to Maúa's district hospital, concerned just as all of them were about the condition of our friend. It was not good. We found him under the care of his aunt and mother (who had come in from Cuamba) inside one of the hospital rooms. It was a sparse, dank room, with nothing marking it as a place of healing other than an admonition tacked to a wall: "Beds are for patients, not for visitors."

Raimundo was on one of those beds, propped up on one side, head resting on rolled sheets. The exposed half of his face was discolored, covered with lesions and boils from the edge of his mouth to his forehead. That eye was completely shut, the skin around it puffy and purple. What little energy Raimundo seemed to have he spent swatting at flies swarming around his sores, taking care to swipe away from his face so as not to graze his open wounds.

As those of us from the church entered and greeted Raimundo, he did his best to open his mouth and speak. Nothing came out. We took turns approaching him, holding his hand, expressing words of encouragement. Most of the hour, though, we spent in silence—except of course when we prayed, which we repeatedly did. These were not the same demon-exorcizing prayers with which Pentecostal worship services are replete—the clapping, stomping, and screaming kind that were, anyway, more characteristic of the ADA than the relatively more staid EAD. They were, however, prayers that anticipated the miracle of healing:

> We give you thanks, all powerful Father Lord. Thank you, God. This afternoon, Holy Father, we come here before you. Our brother is suffering, our God. We ask, Father, for the Holy Spirit, King of Glory. We ask, Father, that you come to end this infirmity, our God. Because, Father, we place all our faith in you, Holy Father, dear Father. Pour out your Holy Spirit, King of Glory. Pour out your Holy Spirit, Father. Operate a miracle in this brother here, Raimundo, who is suffering. In the name of the Lord Jesus, we ask you and thank you this afternoon in the name of Jesus. Amen.

Leaving the hospital, the man who offered this prayer—a schoolteacher from the largest northern city of Nampula—told me it is prayers alone (*orações só*) that will heal Raimundo. The emphasis on "prayers *alone*" did not indicate opposition to hospital treatment. It was specifically a rebuke of "traditional" solutions: roots, herbs, ancestral offerings. "We place *all* our faith in you, Holy Father," went the prayer, for which Raimundo afterward exerted himself to thank us. He seemed also willing to put *all* his faith in God, in the healing technologies of the Pentecostal church.

But for Raimundo, it turned out, putting *all* his faith in God was not inconsistent with pursuing other avenues of healing, also with *all* his faith. He could commit wholeheartedly to prayers without committing wholeheartedly to prayers *alone*. Praying by itself, he told me after his discharge, would leave him helpless and inactive.

"Suppose you are hungry," he explained. "The church prays for you to be filled, but doesn't give you anything to eat. But God said that you have to eat something, anything. You don't eat, but someone prays for you. You won't be filled that way. You can die of hunger!"

The value of prayer is in its inducement of, not substitution for, further activity. Lienhardt observed something similar in Dinka ritual action, which, he writes, "is not a substitute for practical or technical action, but a complement to it and preparation for it." It is "a model of . . . desires and hopes, upon which to base renewed practical endeavour" (1961: 283). The consequent movement from passivity to activity is "the conversion of a situation of death into a situation of life" (1961: 296). This "conversion" is spoken of, among the Makhuwa, as *wasasa ekumi*, literally "the search for life." In that search, Raimundo never contented himself with deploying any one tactic, with taking any one route.[21]

It should come as no surprise then that, upon leaving the hospital, Raimundo had no trouble taking up residence at the compound of his aunt and uncle, despite church members urging him not to. They saw the home of his "pagan" relatives as "a house of lies." Raimundo, however, feared for his safety at his own home. If this had been a normal illness—an "illness from God" (*eretta ya Muluku*)—the hospital would have cured it. It did not. Immediately after leaving the hospital, Raimundo consulted with diviners to ascertain his ailment's true cause.

Raimundo learned that his illness came about through a sorcery attack committed by envious neighbors—envious, Raimundo speculated, of his having an influential uncle and a rich benefactor. So identifying the cause of the problem opened the path toward a solution, the consumption of *murette* (traditional medicine). "Yes, I had to take *murette* after praying," he said. "A person has to do something, has to ask God for something to do, anything." He spent the rest of his convalescence in the compound of his aunt and uncle, where he continued to receive prayerful visits from EAD congregants during the day, and where he continued to receive *murette* from his aunt at night.

The final time I saw Raimundo was at that compound. He was preparing to travel back to Cuamba, to return to his mother's home and continue his recovery there. He would be able to receive more extensive hospital treatment at that city's superior medical facility, but it was also where one of his trusted diviners lived. He was not going to close off any options: wherever the destination, whatever the tradition, whoever the healer.

A few days before his departure, Raimundo paid a visit to Pastor Manuel. In the pastor's telling: "Raimundo came and said to me, 'Well, I won't try to hide that I tried everything: the way of traditional medicine, the way of the hospital. But I am not finding a solution. I see now that the solution is with God alone.' I said to him, 'This is all that has been lacking. If you had decided this awhile back, you would already be well. God is not a person who promises and does nothing. He is the master.'" Raimundo requested forgiveness and prayers, both of which he received on the spot. He followed up those requests with one for a stamped transfer letter that would grant him welcome at the Cuamba congregation of the EAD. Pastor Manuel was happy to oblige. The next day, Raimundo caught a microbus to Cuamba. At service the next Sunday, Pastor Manuel seemed only too glad to tell the story of Raimundo's repentance, triumphantly announcing to cheers from his congregants: "He has returned!"

But, in fact, Raimundo was already back on the move—regionally and, I suspect, religiously as well. Not unlike in his adolescence, he was again on the road, in pursuit of whichever path enhanced his share of health, wealth, and well-being. He was back, once again, in search of life.

Side-Stepping

This chapter began by recognizing the reality of "religions"—including *ettini ya makholo* (ancestral religion)—in the Makhuwa context, religions understood as bounded, coherent, and discrete. This epistemology owes largely, but not exclusively, to nearly two centuries of influence from the two self-conscious religions: Islam and (Catholic) Christianity. Research on world religions in local contexts emphasizes how the religions come to be indigenized, appropriated according to local logics and made to serve local needs. This chapter has taken a different approach, emphasizing less the indigenizing of one or another religion than the indigenizing of "religion" itself, the way in which the category and its attendant assumptions have been appropriated according to local logics and made to serve local needs. These are, most prominently, what previous chapters have already explored in depth: the Makhuwa logic of mobility and aversion to fixity. Thus, what is notable about the relation of people like Raimundo to the newest religion on the scene, Pentecostalism, is not so much the epistemological divide between it on the one hand and the *ettini ya makholo* on the other. What matters is that, despite the distinct domains, people move bidirectionally between them, and that they do so with nimbleness and ease.

The everyday experience of the Makhuwa is replete with such opportunistic oscillations, with what philosopher John Dewey (1929) refers to as an experimental, as opposed to dogmatic, habit of mind. This pragmatic attitude, evident in the way people like Raimundo relate to novelties like Pentecostalism, is not unique or exceptional to the Makhuwa. Throughout Africa, pragmatism characterizes people's pursuits of health, security, and prosperity. This is certainly true regarding religious practice in multireligious milieus.[22] Especially in situations of scarcity, no single approach is granted the status of finality. If one measure of rationality is ideological consistency and logical coherence, it has almost always been reasonable for the Makhuwa to be "irrational." In this regard, Raimundo's and others' passing and partial participation in the newly arrived Pentecostal churches is a contemporary variation on a perennial theme. In becoming Pentecostal, they may (temporarily) abandon Makhuwa traditions like healing and initiation rites, but they do not abandon the experimentalism and pragmatism of the Makhuwa way of being.[23] Conversion out of "traditional religion" is an extension of ordinary conversions within it, and regress is as likely as egress.

Such words as pragmatism and opportunism may worry those who, for good reason, wish not to see Africans portrayed as they long have been: as irrational primitives incapable of engaging, other than superficially, such "civilizational" markers as monotheistic world religions, centralized state centers, and permanent residential structures. However, when those among whom I lived do such things as rotate from one crop field to another, or consult with multiple diviners before laying out a further course of action, they do so far from superficially. They do so as if their lives depend on it. Quite often, their lives do.

Raimundo always struck me as exceedingly engaged in his Pentecostal devotion: passionate in his prayers, enthusiastic in his gestures, full-throated in his singing. Yet the plenitude of his devotions inside the church did not interfere with the plenitude of his devotions outside. This manner of polyontological mobility—of relating to multiple traditions in a serial and juxtaposed, rather than a simultaneous and blended, manner—is entirely consistent with engaging "deeply" either (or each) of the traditions involved. That in his search for life (*wasasa ekumi*) Raimundo entered the Pentecostal church (*ovolowa*), left it (*ohiya*), and then entered it again (*ovolowa*) may make his participation temporary. But it is not, for that reason, superficial.

Regarding religious conversion, William James writes: "That it should for even a short time show a human being what the high-water mark of his spiritual capacity is, this is what constitutes its importance,—an importance which backsliding cannot diminish" (1985: 257). I share James's view that intensity matters at least as much as duration, though this vital point may be better made without reference to "backsliding." Suggested by "back" is a fall from some advanced state; conveyed in "sliding" is a continuum rather than a division between traditions, as well as a passive rather than agentive relation to them.

The better alternative to "backsliding," if one were needed, would be "side-stepping." This is not to be confused with "sidestepping," an evasive move, for the polyontological mobility of those I knew is certainly not an evasion of their circumstances. It is a confrontation of them through all avenues available. It is a pragmatism that is not idle but involved, a mobility that is not escapist but existential.

PART III

Okhalano—To Be With

CHAPTER 5

A Religion of Her Own?

Thus far I have presented Makhuwa border crossing not only as a strategic response to calamity, but also as an embodied disposition, a modus vivendi. It would be a mistake, however, to consider mobility an end in itself. In these final two chapters, I contend that mobility, of the religious kind in particular, is a means toward an end—that of connection and coexistence. Modern possessive individualism entails having a singular self, a stable identity. Key for this chapter is the foreignness to the Makhuwa context of having anything at all: "to have" is literally "to be with" (*okhalano*). Owing largely to their exclusion from processes of modernization, Makhuwa women, better than men, preserve this long-standing ethic of commensality and care. Focused on gender relations and their shifts over time, this chapter discloses how religion and religious identities have served (and, for some, still serve) not as objects of acquisition but as avenues for "being-with." They meet the human need not to possess but to partake.

"Makhuwa Women Have No Religion"

Not long into my fieldwork year it struck me that I was failing to get female perspectives on my research questions. Men exerted tight control over women's lives, and it was difficult to gain the trust of most men to talk directly with the women they saw themselves as responsible for if not sovereign over. Nonetheless, women quite frequently came up in my queries about why and when people change religions. It is really only women who do so, I was told, and that is because "Makhuwa women have no religion." They are never the ones to determine their own affiliations or practices. Girls follow the religion of their maternal uncles; wives follow the religion of their husbands. Religious conversion most often occurs when a woman marries, leaves a marriage (through divorce or widowhood), or remarries. Not surprisingly, it was men who most often told me this.

Yet as jarring as it was to hear it from men, even more so was hearing it from women, which I frequently did. I wondered, should I enlighten these women by sharing how differently we do things in my society, indeed in my marriage? I tried this once, telling one, whose schooling in the provincial capital led me to think she would see things differently, that my wife Kalinka and I are happily married, though we are not of the same religion. "Then that is not marriage!" she said.

It would not be wrong to connect the adage "Makhuwa women have no religion" to male chauvinism, to the same patriarchal forces that made it so rare for me to interact directly with women. Yet when an opportunity to do so finally did arise, it forced me to think the issue through anew. It raised the question of whether something other than internalized oppression may be at play in women's willing elision of religion.

Neuza

I first learned of Neuza from Paulino. He was telling me about the people he knew to be former participants of Kaveya village's African Assembly of God (Assembléia de Deus Africana, or ADA) congregation. Apparently, Neuza had been active there for a full two years before returning to the Catholic church in which she was raised, and in which Paulino had served as catechist. Intrigued by the longevity of Neuza's Pentecostal involvement, I jumped at Paulino's offer to introduce me.

On a cool but sunny morning, Paulino and I wandered down a footpath off the main road, asking farmers along the way if they could direct us to the fields where Neuza was working. When we reached her, she appeared younger than I expected, probably in her late teens. Though clearly engrossed in her work, tilling soil and scattering seed, she seemed happy to see her former catechist Paulino. On the strength of that familiarity, Neuza accepted my request, conveyed through Paulino, that we sit down and talk. Appropriately, she suggested we do so in the presence of her elders. Gathering her hoe and seed bag, she led us on a footpath back toward her family compound.

There, seated on reed mats in the shade of the *muttheko* shed, were two women, both aunts of Neuza's, and one man, Neuza's *tata* (maternal uncle). I bent low and greeted each in turn, touching my hands to theirs and then to my head and chest. There was no need for lengthy introductions since they knew me from my occasional visits to Kaveya's Catholic church. I sat down and, after some minutes of small talk, turned my attention to Neuza. A list of questions had already piled high in my head. What drew her to the ADA? What did she gain from participating in it? What led her eventually to leave? She began telling her story, but did not seem entirely at ease. Before long, she was interrupted.

"It was all a big lie," her *tata* said.

I looked back to Neuza. She had been talking of how she fell ill after nearly two years in the Pentecostal church. ADA leaders came to her family compound to offer prayers for healing. That is where they noticed *murette* (traditional medicine) laid out on a reed mat, likely the same mat on which we were sitting just then.

"People in the Assembléia speak badly of *murette*," Neuza's *tata* said.

"But it was me who was using it," interjected one of the women. "I was also ill at the time."

The *tata* took this as his cue to launch a tirade against the ADA. He said their leaders are all liars and deceivers for condemning Neuza over traditional medicines she had not been using. Neuza kept quiet as her *tata* spoke, building in volume and vigor as he went on.

It became clear this interview would not yield what I had hoped. Sensing my disappointment, Paulino suggested to our hosts that we would understand Neuza's story better if we had the chance to sit with her alone. It was a request I would not myself have made, but I was grateful to Paulino for doing so, trading in the social capital he enjoyed as a respected figure in Kaveya's Catholic community. One of the older women supported Paulino's idea, voicing aloud what was on my mind: "Neuza is not speaking what she wants to." Indeed, Neuza was no longer speaking at all. Her aunt suggested we move to the Catholic compound along the main road. It was only a few hundred meters away. To my relief, Neuza's *tata* consented. So did Neuza.

Paulino and I took to tracing Neuza's steps again, this time to the Catholic compound whose entrance off the path was just beyond earshot of Neuza's family. Marking the long, mud-walled structure before us as a Catholic chapel was nothing more than the modest, curvilinear wooden crucifix atop it.[1] In front of the chapel was the *muttheko* shed one finds on every village compound, though this was larger than most, and it had a sturdy clay bench lining its circumference. On that bench we sat and resumed our conversation.

Neuza still spoke softly but seemed less hesitant than before. She started the story again. It was her brother, now living in Maúa town, who had introduced her to the ADA. Whenever she attended, she felt better. Her relationship with the church—and with Jesus and the Holy Spirit—helped her resolve many of her ailments over those years, indeed not only her ailments but also those of her family, on whose behalf she never ceased praying.

Neuza then broached the circumstances around her departure. Soon after the incident involving the *murette*, the ADA issued Neuza a formal reprimand—a prolonged period of probation, though with the expectation of continued attendance. Her attendance itself only ceased because of her *tata*, who then, as now, wanted his family to have nothing to do with the Pentecostal church. He channeled his anger over Neuza's wrongful indictment onto Neuza herself, banning her from returning to the Pentecostal church that she had slowly come to enjoy and that he suddenly came to revile.

Neuza's split from Pentecostalism was thus not of her choosing. But, she said, she had no regrets—neither about returning to Catholicism nor about resuming consumption of the *murette* that the Pentecostal (but not the Catholic) church barred.

"My heart is still with the Assembléia, but it [*murette*] is good for the body," she said.

"So when you are sick now, what do you do?" I asked.

"I take *murette*," she replied. "And I do *makeya* [ancestral offerings]. But I also do prayers."

"In the Catholic church?" I asked.

She glanced back toward the compound from which we had just come, then leaned in. Sometimes, she said, when her suffering is severe, she goes into the woods by herself. There she prays as she had only ever prayed among Pentecostals.

"No one in the Catholic church prays like that," she said.

"Like how?" I asked.

She closed her eyes and pressed her right hand on the crown of her head, a gesture indeed distinctive of a particular kind of Pentecostal intercession. These are the prayers for exorcising demons. Preachers and other church officials would place their hands atop prayer recipients and yell to the demons within: "This body does not belong to you! Remove this sickness! Take it from here!" They would then scream in rapid succession—"Out! Out! Out!"—thrusting their hands upward with each exclamation, hastening the demon's departure.

Following her split with the ADA, Neuza's ailments worsened. But with no one to help her expel what she saw as their demonic causes, she devised a way to do so herself. She would retreat alone into the bush, as far back as necessary to give full voice to her Pentecostal prayers—forceful and hortatory as they are, never hushed or subdued. She had to distance herself from her *tata*, just as we now had to as well.[2]

I had never before heard a story like this—of a person simultaneously punished by her church and barred from it by her family, yet a person nevertheless resourceful enough to turn her double marginalization into a position of privilege. She had devised a way both to perform the Pentecostal prayers prohibited by her family *and* to partake in the traditional remedies prohibited by Pentecostalism.

This improvisational skill, it turns out, was not unique to Neuza. It was especially apparent among women—women who, forced by the men in their lives to renounce some element in their religious repertoires, found creative ways to respond. Belinha, one of Kalinka's close friends in Maúa town, was very young when her parents died; she was raised by missionary sisters of the Catholic parish church. But at the age of fifteen, her extended relatives married her off to someone she had no say in choosing. He was a Muslim, and so Belinha became one as well. She attended the mosque faithfully and strove to abide by Qur'anic teachings. Never, however, did she cease singing to herself the hymns still dear from her Catholic upbringing. She turned to those hymns especially when her husband (now former husband) turned abusive—ordering her to serve him, beating her when she did not, and prohibiting her from leaving the compound unaccompanied. The hymn Belinha found most consoling spoke directly to her situation: "Alleluia / Alleluia / Alleluia / Alleluia / I am a slave / A slave to God the Father / May he do with me his will." The decidedly illiberal declaration of enslavement—to God—may seem alarming in light of her very real subservience to the man she had married. Yet there is something telling about this paradox. She found subjection of this sort to be not just meaningful but uplifting, which is why this hymn in particular came to her in those darkest moments.[3] She found a sense of freedom in them, she said—in her ability (imaginatively, at least) to choose her master, likewise in her ability (privately, at least) to connect with the faith she converted from but never left behind.

What lies behind these stories of religious resilience under situations of duress? How can we assess these women's ability to be religious in institutionally structured ways even when barred from institutional religious structures? What, if anything, might this have to do with their willingness to claim no religion of their own?

Gender Politics

These questions are best explored against the backdrop of Makhuwa gender relations more generally. Not unlike the similarly marginal hill peoples of southeast Asia, Makhuwa societies have long been marked by "a rough egalitarianism, which, not incidentally, includes a relatively higher status for women than in the valleys" (Scott 2009: 19). The notion that distance from civilizational centers could correlate with greater gender parity is surely counterintuitive for those brought up with what anthropologist Eleanor Leacock (1981) calls "myths of male dominance" that assume patriarchy to be normative in "traditional" societies. Later in this chapter, I draw on Leacock and others to argue that gender inequality among the Makhuwa is actually a recent development, brought about largely by colonial-era shifts toward centralized authority in virtually every social sphere. Most consequential have been the introduction of world religions, the standardization of education, and the infusion of market economies. Yet even in the aftermath of such modernizing trends, evidence available to me as late as 2012 disclosed the kinds of female power and presence that were once far more common.

Descent and social structure throughout the interiors of northern Mozambique—different from in the south, central, and coastal regions—have been and continue until the present to be matrilineal (Sheldon 2002: 5–15). Matrilineal social organization privileges mothers and their children over fathers and their children, thus recognizing as well as favoring the personal and social power of women (Poewe 1981). Further, among the Makhuwa specifically, residence patterns are matrilocal.[4] Ifi Amadiume, theorizing African feminism from an array of evidence across the continent, refers to these factors as promoting matricentric production units and matriarchic ideologies (1997: 71–88). Of course, female-based social organization alone does not translate into women's economic or political power. Suggesting a degree of female authority in Makhuwa politics is the unique institution of the *apwiyamwene*. Frequently translated into Portuguese as *rainha* (queen), the *apwiyamwene* is in fact not the spouse of the chief (*mwene*) but a member of his matriline. The most powerful woman of a clan or village, she functions as the *mwene*'s principal counselor on matters of governance, administration, and succession. Rare are the occasions when a *mwene* acts without first consulting the *apwiyamwene*. It is also she who officiates at such public rites as female initiation and community *makeya* offerings.[5]

With the national government's postsocialist efforts to formalize customary authority, the local chief attained the status of sole recognized authority, thereby reducing some of the *apwiyamwene*'s standing. Yet, remarkably, these local chiefs are sometimes women (Pitcher 1996a: 28). That such women are only appointed in the absence of male successors hardly diminishes what must still be considered the impressive standing of women in Makhuwa polities.[6]

Similarly, in the domestic sphere, women have long inherited and controlled both land and household. At the conclusion of most visits to family compounds, I would offer a token of gratitude for my hosts' time and hospitality, usually a bag of salt or a bar of soap. (To villagers at a distance from markets and lacking money to spend at them anyway, these gifts were always appreciated.) Most times I would hand it to my interlocutor—a male occupant of the compound—who would then call his wife close and hand it off to her. This was not initially surprising; I could understand why males not responsible for cooking and cleaning would pass what I had to give onto the person who was. Unexpected were the occasions when I had already exhausted my supply of gifts, when I could only offer a crude quantity of cash, and yet the same handoff occurred. Just as before, my conversation partner would receive my offering and immediately call over his wife. She, in turn, would pocket the coins or bills in a small cloth pouch tucked into her *capulana* (printed cloth) garment.[7]

Paulino told me that the same transaction occurred at his home with what I paid him for his research assistance. His wife, he told me, is the *capitaz* of the compound: "She controls everything. The man brings home fish or cloth or whatever, and hands it over to the woman." Paulino's use of particularly colonial terminology—*capitazes* were the Portuguese overseers of concessionary companies (Isaacman 1996: 55–58)—was striking. It showed that, at least in some cases, even where colonial influence is pronounced, precolonial understandings persist.

According to the missionary anthropologist Giuseppe Frizzi (2014), the elevated standing of women in both domestic and village affairs is grounded in Makhuwa cosmological principles that honor the feminine. The Supreme Being (Muluku) is conceived of in feminine terms. As such, the feminine is irreducible to Catholicism, Islam, or any other *ettini* (religion). As one proverb declares: *Muluku muthiyana khaettini, ti ettini enene* (Muluku, like woman, has no religion but is religion itself). Applying a structural analysis to gender relations, Padre Frizzi described for me the moon and night as paradigmatic symbols of womanhood. The lunar cycle, also the menstrual cycle, is how time is measured among the Makhuwa. One speaks of the rains coming in three moons, *mweri* being the Makhuwa word for both "month" and "moon." Additionally, the time of the moon is the time of contact with ancestral spirits, therefore also the time of healing. While the principal work of men—clearing land, building homes, hunting animals—and the manual labor of women transpire between sunrise and sunset, it is exclusively women who, as healers, lead and carry out the nocturnal rites (Arnfred 2011: 137–216).

At my first all-night *matxini* ceremony, for the expulsion of djinn spirits from an afflicted woman, nearly a dozen women followed the female *namuku* (healer) into the healing hut shortly after sunset. The few men present remained outside, and I sat with them around fires throughout the night.[8] Knowing something of my research objectives, they urged me to join the women inside the hut, to observe the proceedings up close. When the husband of the *namuku* offered to accompany me, I finally entered, but in my initial reluctance to violate the gendered divide, my friend and assistant Leonardo took the opportunity to tease me.

"What's the matter, afraid of women?" he asked to uproarious laughter from the other men gathered.

"*Anyi*," I said, playing along. "*Athiyana annalipa.*" (Yes, the women are strong.) The men hooted with joy and nodded with delight, impressed less with my Makhuwa, I think, than with my arrival at an important truth.

Rematriations

It is during the nocturnal period of male initiation ceremonies that ancestral wisdom is conveyed. Among those wisdom teachings, none is more

Figure 7. Singing in the first light of a new day, at the end of a *matxini* ceremony, Kaveya village.

emphasized than the sacred power of female fertility, a lesson not just verbalized but embodied in the mimesis of menstruation that male circumcision is understood to be (see Chapter 3). The myth of Namuli, recited and reenacted in a wide range of rituals, similarly highlights the procreative principle of *oyara*, identified by my interlocutors as one of two Makhuwa pillars. Not only is the name Namuli etymologically suggestive of female menstruation, the narrative of the myth makes life itself contingent on the primordial flow of blood (see Chapter 1). Thus, the proverb "From Namuli we come, to Namuli we return" indicates that each human not only originates from and returns to the sacred mountain but also originates from and returns to woman.

Rematriations (to play on a term) recur throughout the life cycle. Immediately following birth and throughout infancy, small children are tucked into *capulana* slings on their mothers' backs. Childbirth is thus a repositioning more than a rupture, with little loss of intimate contact in the transfer from inside the mother's body to outside. In the crucial transition from childhood to adulthood, return to the mother's embrace is consistent with, even crucial to, the growth of boys into men (see Chapter 3). At life's end, the body of the deceased was historically laid to rest in a curved rather than rectangular pit, and in a seated rather than supine posture (Macaire 1996: 285; Ciscato 2012: 92–93). Burial pits were symbolic wombs that the body reentered just as the spirit (*munepa*) once occupying that body rematriated to Mount Namuli.

Marriage, to take one last example, reprises the theme of religious change. When a young man marries and goes to live with his new wife's clan, as matrilocal residency requires, this does not prevent him from returning regularly to visit his own matriline. He does so to escape conflicts on the marital compound, to tend to health problems in his natal family, and to help venerate and supplicate the ancestors he grew up with. Whenever a ceremony occurs in his natal home or village, he returns with contributions—of flour, of meat, of time and presence—to help ensure its success.

Yet the male whose proper abode is now on his wife's compound is equally obligated to *her* family's ancestors. Without renouncing his natal line, he has entered into what Padre Frizzi, in a personal conversation, called the "domestic religion" of his wife. "So much so," Padre Frizzi said, "that in the ancestral celebrations that occur, the man must contribute. The future of the marriage depends on this fact."

The consequent cosmological oscillations—the polyontological pattern of conversions and reversions explored in Chapter 4—occur regularly in the rural villages of Maúa district, where matrilocality remains much the norm.[9] In the realm of domestic cults, then, it is not the wife who follows the "religion" of the husband but exactly the opposite. Bound as much to the matriline he was born into as to the matriline he marries into, one could say in this case that it is the Makhuwa man, in fact, who has no religion of his own.

The Elision of Religion

But to what extent are the domestic ancestral cults "religions"? A primary objective of Islamic clerics in the nineteenth century, and of their Catholic counterparts in the twentieth, was to displace ancestor-based traditions by either incorporating or prohibiting them. Missionaries deemed these traditions incompatible with devotional practices properly conducted inside the mosque or the church by the class of clerics authorized to stand front and center in them. Those clerics were, and until today remain, exclusively male. Meanwhile, the disparaged indigenous traditions were, and until today remain, precisely those in which women carry influence and authority. The male priest and male imam came to assume much of what was previously reserved for the female *namuku* and female *apwiyamwene*.[10]

Along with a patriarchal authority structure, Islam brought and Catholicism shaped yet another novelty: the category of religion (*ettini*). As discussed in Chapter 4, Islam and Catholicism were, during my fieldwork year, universally regarded as "religions," even though this is not an originally Makhuwa concept. "In the time of our ancestors, we did not know religion," I was told by one elder. There is still considerable resistance among ordinary men and women to systematizing indigenous, ancestor-based practices and beliefs. These are increasingly, but still only occasionally, assimilated to the Arabic-derived *ettini* or the Portuguese *religião*.

In Pentecostal practices and beliefs, one finds the same reluctance to nominalize. I frequently heard Pentecostal preachers distinguish themselves and their followers from Catholics by declaring, "We are not *religiosos*, we are *crentes*." The word *religioso* could be rendered "adherent to a religion," while the word *crente* signifies a believer, one who puts his or her faith or trust (*ororomela*) in someone or something else. A common mantra in evangelical (including Pentecostal) parlance holds that "Christianity is not a religion but a relationship," implying that this particular kind of faith can be neither compartmentalized into its own sphere of life nor equated with formal liturgy or tradition (McBride 2012: 220n2). In this self-understanding, African Pentecostalism shares something in common with African indigeneity as I have described it throughout this book: both resist capture by the reified construct of "religion."

Pentecostalism also shares with indigenous traditions their affirmation of women. In Pentecostal churches throughout the world, women vastly outnumber men. That is largely because these churches recognize, even esteem, women's charismatic powers. The only requirement for spiritual authority is that one manifest such gifts of the spirit as speaking in tongues. Numerous studies have shown how the Pentecostal stress on equal access to authority and, indeed, to salvation has opened for women a space to negotiate and reinterpret gender values. It has provided an empowering alternative to non-Pentecostal religions and cultures, particularly those premised on male prestige.[11] The Pentecostal services I attended frequently featured women in positions of authority: preaching, healing, prophesying, and leading praise music. In fact, the Evangelical Assembly of God (Evangélica Assembléia de Deus) in Maúa, one of the district's two Pentecostal ministries, is known (proudly, by its members) as the church plant of a female Brazilian missionary. On both matters, then—status as "religion" and status of women—Pentecostalism shares with indigenous traditions qualities that differentiate both from Islam and Catholicism, the two self-conscious *ittini* (plural of *ettini*).

I learned to appreciate this distinction one morning in a greatly embarrassing visit to my first *makeya* ceremony. When I arrived at the shrine, at a clearing deep within the bush, proceedings had not yet begun, though most of the villagers were already gathered. Men were seated in a semicircular row on one side of the sacred *mutholo* tree, women on the other. This did not strike me as unusual; it was the same spatial divide evident in Sunday masses I had already attended at the Catholic church and in Friday prayers I had witnessed at the Islamic mosque. In the church, men sat together on the right side of the center aisle and women together on the left.[12] In the mosque, women sat not just apart from men but in a separate room behind them. It was only in Pentecostal services that I observed intermingling, as much an example of Pentecostals' flaunting of local customs as of the relative egalitarianism of their gatherings.

Assuming the norm to be not only separation but also isolation, I reasoned that morning that the same protocols of the Catholic church and the Islamic mosque apply to the *makeya* ceremony: men and women neither sitting among nor talking among each other. After removing my shoes at the edge of the clearing, I walked toward the row of seated men and proceeded to greet each of them—bending low to touch their hands, asking each one, "*Moxeleliwa*?" I then took my seat on a patch of ground at the end of the line, ready to observe unobtrusively the ceremony set to begin.

My plans were immediately thwarted when a woman yelled from the opposite side: "He didn't greet me!" Laughter erupted from both sides as I sheepishly rose again and made my way across the grounds. I extended my hands and my "*Moxeleliwa*?" to my good-natured heckler and the women beside her, offering an apologetic smile and two-armed wave to the remaining women. These same women I would soon observe standing up, one by one, approaching the winnowing basket at the base of the *mutholo* tree, collecting sorghum flour into their hands, kneeling down, and then sifting the flour through their fingers onto a growing Namuli-like mound. This is how *makeya* offerings are made, one person at a time "feeding the ancestors" (*otxihá minepa*) while vocalizing the community's pleas for well-being. Far different from the silence and seeming passivity women displayed in the *religious* contexts I had hitherto observed, here they articulated with verve their petitions to the ancestors, asserting their right to receive their blessings as resolutely as they had their right to receive my greetings.

If it is only in the spirit-based, healing-centered traditions—ancestral and Pentecostal—that women retain the voice, authority, and power that have customarily been theirs, and if these are the traditions that do not constitute "religions," as do Islam and Catholicism, might this be why women accede to "having no religion" of their own? To explain women's disproportionate populating of Pentecostal churches, researchers have focused on such factors as enhanced authority and autonomy within the church and improved relations at home (see Brusco 2010).[13] What my research offers is confirmation of the first point, though I cast it in different terms. In a context where religion and patriarchy are mutually reinforcing, Pentecostalism, to women, may be so attractive a religion expressly because it is *not* a religion.

Women have good reason to be indifferent to religion insofar as those things so called tamp their ritual authority, sideline their spiritual prestige, and generally keep them silent. In this sense, women's endorsement of the phrase "Makhuwa women have no religion" may in fact be quite the opposite of internalized oppression. Women may have no problem being without religion not because they see themselves as inferior to men but because those things they recognize as "religions" have not done much to recognize them.[14] Meanwhile, in the indigenous and Pentecostal traditions, which barely register as religions, women's presence is not only recognized; to a considerable degree, it is revered.

Even if women did enjoy more authority in the self-evident *ittini*, they may content themselves to leave these to the men. The *ittini* are highly relevant for engagements with state actors and regional partners, but not so much for engagements with ancestors, *djinn*, and, nowadays, the Holy Spirit—all of which are seen as the real governors of everyday affairs.[15] In a world where the state, market, and civil society are derelict at worst and unreliable at best, to be Muslim or to be Christian is to assume a primarily public identity that borders on irrelevant. On the other hand, in the pursuit of health, sustenance, and security for oneself and one's household—in fulfilling, in other words, the duty of *capitaz*—there are far more pressing concerns than that of which religion one does or does not have.

Modernization and Masculinization

With the world religions came not only the category of religion and the ideology of patriarchy but also the institutions of formal education. Nicodemus, an instructor in Maúa's top secondary school and a respected local intellectual, noted that the first generation of converts to Catholicism, of which there were many, came to the faith in schools run by the Catholic missions. The mutual arising of institutional religion and formal schooling is acknowledged to have occurred in colonial contexts throughout the world. The same elder who told me there was no religion in the time of the ancestors added, "And they didn't have school. The schools came with the religions and people saw that to read is good, to study is good, because something that is written is never forgotten." Islam and Catholicism are locally referred to not just as the two *ittini* (religions) but as the two *ilivuru* (books). That ancestral traditions and Pentecostalism fit so uneasily in the category of "religions" may owe to their being less textual than oral, less religions of the book than religions of the body.[16]

Different from rituals of initiation—which always include one for girls and one for boys—the educational programs of mission schools, as well as of Qur'anic schools and government schools, vastly favored boys. This gender imbalance is reflected in adult literacy rates. While only 26 percent of adult males in Maúa district could read or write in 1997, the last year of gender-specific census data, an astoundingly low 6 percent of adult females could (*Perfil do Distrito de Maúa* 2005: 12). Compared to Mozambique as a whole, whose adult literacy rate then stood at 40 percent, literacy rates were dismal in the district (Firmino 2001).[17] But if they were bad for men, they were even worse for women.

Given its privileging of boys, formal schooling joined institutional religions in elevating, whether intentionally or not, the status of men relative to women. As important as mission schools were for national politics—in helping foster decolonization movements in Mozambique as elsewhere

(Cruz e Silva 2001)—they were just as important for local and family politics, for reconfiguring relations between men and women. This is not to say that women failed to benefit from mission schools. Many mothers encouraged their sons to attend and exerted tremendous effort to make that possible. Furthermore, those few girls admitted to formal schools used their acquired skills to break out of gendered social expectations (Sheldon 2002: 79–113). None of this, however, diminishes the fact that vast disparities of opportunity have existed and, despite recent strides toward equity, persisted.

An argument can be made that girls' and women's lack of schooling points up not an absence but a presence, the presence of an alternative way of being and knowing. Formal and compulsory education is a contingent cultural invention with nothing necessary or natural about it (Harrison and Callari Galli 1971). Therefore, to normalize literacy, formal education's chief criterion of success, and to regard the absence of literacy as a negative (illiteracy) rather than an alternative (nonliteracy) is to commit an ethnocentric fallacy. Furthermore, there may exist positive motivations for placing oneself outside the reach of literacy. As Claude Lévi-Strauss has observed, "The only phenomenon with which writing has always been concomitant is the creation of cities and empires" with their attendant social hierarchies. Thus, writing "seems to have favoured the exploitation of human beings rather than their enlightenment" (1992: 299). For the hill people of southeast Asia, James Scott suggests that the rejection of literacy may have been strategic, a means of thwarting political authorities' efforts to know and control people through censuses, genealogies, tax records, and other indelible documents of statecraft (2009: 220–37).

Makhuwa women, largely excluded from schooling and literacy, are by means of that exclusion the more accomplished evaders of colonizers' and other modernizers' efforts at capture and assimilation. They, more than men, have managed to conserve Makhuwa oral traditions and histories, just as they, more than men, have always been the principal authorities in and on nontextual indigenous traditions. These oral narratives articulate at multiple registers the principle of Makhuwa mobility. They not only record stories and histories of movement and migration, they themselves are mobile—unfixed, unfinished, and open to alteration with every new telling. This openness and adaptability is the special reserve of women not only because of the prestige they enjoyed in bygone times but also because of, not in spite of, the prestige they "lack" today.

What makes it hard to see women's low rates of formal education as nevertheless a travesty is the fact that along with Western schools arrived an economic system based on wage labor for which those schools came to be gateways. Education went from a means of joining the local community to a means of joining the labor force.[18] "Education, yes," Nicodemus said, "but education that brings money, no? It is not education to be educated, because we have education in our initiation rites. It is education for a job." Indeed, vocational aspirations are the reasons many I spoke with gave for sending their children to school. Their hope was that their children would attain the qualifications to work as nurses, teachers, or government clerks.

In the contemporary, postsocialist era of Mozambican history, the value of a salaried profession has only increased, while money is an ever-expanding medium of everyday transactions. The shift from a gift-based to a cash-based economy began in the colonial period but never gained much traction, particularly in the rural north.[19] As late as 2012, very little money passed through the countryside where I worked; no banks operated even in the district capital. However, while the shift to a cash-based economy has been slow, it appears to be steady. This is evident not only in increasing enrollments in government schools, sometimes at the expense of initiation rites, but also in the increasing cultivation of cash crops, often at the expense of subsistence crops. Mozambique Tobacco Leaf Company (an affiliate of the United States–based Alliance One International) and other multinational corporations make their profits convincing subsistence farmers to dedicate large plots of land to the cultivation of tobacco. A price of twenty-five *meticais* (at the time, around forty US cents) per kilogram of produce was promised to Maúa's farmers in the year of my fieldwork. The payoff is enticing, but the downsides are many: few guarantees that after the work of cultivation the company will return to purchase the harvest or honor the quoted price, rapid depletion of the land due to the toxic properties of tobacco plants, and less land available for dietary staples such as corn and beans. One villager told me that "tobacco brings hunger," an echo of the phrase "cotton is the mother of poverty" spoken during the colonial era (Isaacman 1996). Yet anxieties over the need for cash in an increasingly monetized and decreasingly predictable world are palpable.

No less than with the world religions, the shift toward a formal market economy has helped tip the scale in men's favor. Boys, more than girls, are the ones put through school. As a result men, more than women, are the ones earning incomes. This has not wholly eviscerated the role of women as household managers, including money managers. The legacies of matrilineality and matrilocality are not so easily undone. Yet, tellingly, the displays of female authority I observed in my fieldwork were almost always in those villages least proximate to the district capital and least integrated with schools, markets, and religions. Given the common portrait of traditional African societies as hopelessly misogynistic, in need of rescue by Western ideals, it is ironic that gender egalitarianism among the Makhuwa has in fact diminished as a result of Eurocentric modernization.[20] As social status increasingly correlates with educational attainment and earning capacity, only certain sectors of the population stand to gain. These have been, and for the foreseeable future will remain, men.

Being With

It is of no small significance that the affairs of schools and markets are conducted entirely in the national language. The increasing infusion of Portuguese in a district where only a fraction of the population speaks it (14 percent of men and 5 percent of women) has significantly altered local understandings of economic relations.[21] For in the Makhuwa language, one of capitalism's foundational ideas, that of private ownership, does not exist. "To have" finds its nearest Makhuwa equivalent in the compound word *okhalano*, *okhala* meaning "to be" and *no* meaning "with." "To have" something, in the Makhuwa conception, is not to own or possess it, but "to be with" it, and "to be with" others through it.

As Nicodemus explained to me: "I have a corncob, some corn here. This corn is not mine. It is corn for all. This is Makhuwa economics. Whatever I have is not mine. The other also has needs. What I have is for all. It is different in the Western world: 'I have in order to possess.' This is capitalism. The Makhuwa is not a capitalist." I asked what this means for the function of money, to which most people nowadays aspire. "What is money?" he began his response. "If I have a good life, I will not need money. Money, the *metical*, is that object brought by the West. But do you think that before money I could not live? Where is my economy? The economy is all of life. I have food, I have clothes, I have medicine, *pronto*. If I have all of this, do you think I will need a job? I will not." He returned to his initial point: "The purpose of money is not to become more powerful. It is not, 'I have money to dominate others,' but 'I have money to maintain also the lives of others.' This is what a Makhuwa conception of money would be." Well-being, Nicodemus suggested, is measured not in the quantity of one's belongings but in the quality of one's relations.

This Makhuwa principle of symbiosis or coexistence presents a radical alternative to the increasing hegemony of neoliberal development models that reward autonomy and individual initiative. Anthropologists of Africa have long recognized that persons are inextricably tied to other persons and even experience their being through them.[22] The self, so understood, neither precedes nor possesses relationships; it is constituted by relationships. Agency and subjectivity, far from a matter of controlling ever richer resources, are about connecting with others in ever richer ways. These views are expressed by existentialist Gabriel Marcel (1951) in his argument about the limits of "having," the main limit being its occlusion of modes of "being." Even more clearly, one finds them in Martin Heidegger's coinage of a term for which he may as well have turned to the Makhuwa. *Mitsein* (being-with), Heidegger argues, is a defining quality of human existence—which is to say, of human *co*existence. It is marked by practical involvement with others "from whom, for the most part, one does *not* distinguish oneself—those among whom one is too" (1962: 154; emphasis in the original).

Among the Makhuwa, this intersubjective imperative—this ontology of interconnectedness—extends to relations between the living and the dead. The real owners of the land are the ancestors; the living are but temporary guests. For temporary guests, people on the move, accumulated wealth can be more a burden than a blessing. That is why, despite government and development workers' promotion of the *casa amelhorada* (modern home), villagers' own preference remains for fungible mud huts, those which can be quickly built and painlessly abandoned (see Chapter 2). Particularly in a world so fraught with uncertainty, the premium is always on being "light-footed" (*oveya metto*).

That ownership confers mobility rather than stability is further reflected in what are arguably the two material "possessions" most prized by the Makhuwa. The first is the chicken, described as both "one of the more valuable assets that virtually all the rural Makua possess" and as a "liquid" or "mobile" asset, chiefly because of its propensity to wander onto neighbors' lands (Kottak 2002: 28–31). It should also be noted that poultry is raised and kept not just for consumption but for distribution—as gifts, for example, offered at funerary rites to the close kin of the deceased. Another prized possession is the bicycle, one of the first purchases villagers make after a successful harvest sale. Though still a rarity—in some ways a luxury—the bicycle first appeared as far back as the colonial period, imported by migrant workers returning from South Africa and Southern Rhodesia. Distinctive about the bicycle is its facilitation of transport, the ease with which it allows one to relocate oneself and one's goods. Jemusse, on whose family's compound I stayed during my visits to Kaveya village, transported the doors and window frames he constructed all the way to the district capital on the back rack of his bicycle, a feat that never ceased to amaze me (cf. Mavhunga 2013: 262–64). The high value accorded these "mobile assets" illustrates that wealth is meant not to be hoarded but to be circulated, or to enable circulation. The Makhuwa economic ideal is not "having" but "being with," or "having" as a means of "being with." The real value of possessions is in their promotion of mobility, which is not an end in itself but a means of enhancing one's presence among, and interdependence with, others.

With the introduction of markets, this more traditional economics of commensality and connectivity has had to make way for an economics of acquisition and accumulation. However, the lexical preservation of "being-with" in the very translation into Makhuwa of "to have" suggests that the arrival of capitalism does not necessarily imply the success of its logic. The linguistic point is one that Nicodemus insists on conveying to his students and mentioned repeatedly to me. Despite working within the school system, Nicodemus often expressed misgivings for the way it promotes ideals of capitalist development, in the postsocialist era, without accounting for the particularities of local context. This serves to distance young people from their cultural roots. It "teaches them to become white," he said. By presenting Makhuwa history, traditions, and language as viable and indeed valuable, he aims to inspire his students to resist ceding Makhuwa traditions to Eurocentric modernization. He admitted, though, that his real hopes rest in the uneducated masses, the nonliterate peasants most marginal to formal society—to its markets, its schools, and its religions. They rest, in other words, with a large proportion of Maúa district's men, and with virtually all of its women.

From Identity to Mobility

If "to have" something is "to be with" it, then the idea of "having a religion" in the sense of possessing a religious identity or affiliation is incongruous with Makhuwa grammar, not to mention Makhuwa economics. Yet the proprietary sense is precisely what men express when they say that women convert so easily because they "*have* no religion." It also lies behind the expression *otxentxa ittini* (to change religions), one of the rare nonspatial phrases used to convey religious conversion. The verb *otxentxa* (to change) is a loanword from the English "to change" (*otxentxa* sounds like "o-chān-cha"). This derivation owes most likely to colonial-era labor migrations to neighboring British colonies. That the verb *otxentxa* is, still today, used primarily in the context of monetary transactions (exchanging cash, making change) helps explain why *otxentxa ittini* is itself used by only a small subset of the population: the formally educated and economically well-off. It is almost never spoken by people whose lives and livelihoods are still largely marginal to formal economies. It is for such people that the more commonplace metaphors for religious conversion apply: *othama* (to move) and *ohiya ni ovolowa* (to leave and to enter).

The migratory properties of these latter terms suggest that what matters in religious conversion, as in life, is not "having" but "being with." While "being with" others is predicated on the ability to move to where they are, "having" things tends to weigh one down, impeding rather than aiding motion. Thus, the religious mobility behind people's propensity to convert and, once converted, to convert again, is grounded in an ethic of commensality, (okhalano in the sense of "being with"), rather than of acquisition (okhalano in the sense of "having"). Most people I met during the course of my fieldwork were not concerned with possessing religions or religious identities. Their concern, instead, was with connecting and coexisting with others, be they people, spirits, or deities. Alice Walker (1983) gave expression to this outlook when she shifted Virginia Woolf's worry over obtaining "a room of one's own" to the struggle of black women to connect with their foremothers.[23]

It is no coincidence that in an increasingly male-centered milieu, women especially maintain this way of being religious, of being with others religiously. Exclusion from centers of power carries with it at least one collateral benefit: an ability to draw seamlessly from a variety of traditions, unburdened by the normative concerns of religious elites, unconstrained by the proprietary implications of religious "belonging" (Voss Roberts 2010). If this holds for people marginalized, so much more for people doubly marginalized. The African American women around whom Walker and others developed black feminist thought would be one example, confronted as they are with intersectional structures of racism *and* sexism (Collins 1990).[24] Neuza, discussed at the start of this chapter, would be another, confronted as she was with prohibitions from both family and church. In colonial and postcolonial Mozambique, the exclusions of women have been similarly multiple: from "religions" where men predominate, from schools where European languages predominate, and from markets where economies of acquisition predominate.

Makhuwa men have been the beneficiaries of these relative novelties. This of course is not true of all men, which is why what Gloria Anzaldúa calls "a tolerance for ambiguity" (1987: 101–2) is present in the narratives of many men documented throughout this book, men marginal to economic and religious power who also go about their lives indifferent to the idea of possessing religious identities. The few men who have indeed benefited from modernization have been able to attain power in what had been a traditionally matricentric society. Seen otherwise, however, these men have lost at least as much as they have gained.

For while women may not have benefited materially from the boons of modernization, for this very reason they have also avoided assimilating to the modernist drive toward categorization, classification, and containment. They have been able to sustain a relationship to religion predicated not on possession but on participation, not on identity but on mobility. If it is true that "Makhuwa women have no religion" and are therefore more likely than men to convert, this may have less to do with patriarchal subjugation than with particularly feminine, which is to say traditionally Makhuwa, capacities: to make moves (*othama*), to cross borders (*ohiya ni ovolowa*), and, thereby, to be with (*okhalano*).

CHAPTER 6

Moved by the Spirit

By attending to a part of the world where Pentecostalism has failed to grow explosively, we stand to learn something not only about that part of the world but also about Pentecostalism itself. Shifting this book's focus from the precedents to the particularities of Pentecostalism, I attend in this chapter to the question of what difference this form of Christianity makes for those who engage it, however fleetingly they do. I argue that a disposition toward mobility and mutability, presented so far as characteristically Makhuwa, is also fostered by and within Pentecostal churches. Notwithstanding its official discourse of rupture without return, Pentecostalism is better seen as restaging without displacing the Makhuwa propensity for ongoing change. No less than the indigenous material considered thus far, Pentecostal practice and thought suggest that "being with" (*okhalano*) a tradition may entail going beyond it as much as staying within it.

Binding the Unbound

On a Sunday morning, cool and dry as always in the month of June, I had my first opportunity to attend an *eyinlo*: a dance ceremony held to recall and honor one who has recently joined the ancestors. The person who had passed on, two years earlier, was remembered as loving *eyinlo* dances. Her favorite was *nakula*, performed bent at the waist, with arms swaying and feet stomping. Kaveya villagers were now gathered in wooded terrain behind a cluster of compounds to perform for her the dance she so enjoyed.[1] This particular *eyinlo* was carried out almost entirely by women, more than twenty of them, many with babies strapped to their backs. Men were also present, seated silently in the shade, watching and admiring. They would participate between the dances, singing invocations and pouring libations.

Each dance had its own choreography, but generic features united them all. The women would first gather on the footpath beyond the clearing, obscured behind tall elephant grass. A drummer at the center of the ritual grounds would then blow a whistle, and the beats would begin. In single file, the women would appear, shuffling slowly and deliberately in a synchronized pattern called *wina wettaka* (walking dance)—left foot out, back together with the right; right foot out, back together with the left. With these measured, lateral moves the women appeared to be drifting onto the ritual grounds, although there was nothing leisurely in the accompanying rhythms and ululations. When they had formed a circle around the drummers and the offerings in the center, the women would face inward and step sideways, heaving their bodies, gyrating their hips, stomping their feet. Although the *nakula* dance was unique, performed throughout with waist bent, all dances included such inclinations—a gesture of respect (*nttittimiho*) and of deference to the honored ancestor.

Not just bowed bodies but circular motions were key to every dance. One even added a figure-eight pattern (*eholi*): each woman circling the woman in front of her, then the woman behind her, all the while continuing to circumambulate. Periodically each woman would twist her torso, first to one side then the other, a move so common it had its own name: *opittukuxa* (to invert). In nearly every respect, the performance displayed circularity and redirection, turns and returns.

At the end of each dance another single-file *wina wettaka* was performed, back onto the outgoing footpath where the dancers would regroup and rest. Then they would enter again. These movements into and out of the ritual grounds seemed to be continuous with the circular movements within it. Indeed, the Namuli-like dialectic—coming from and returning to—was consistent with and appropriate for the occasion as well: a remembrance ceremony for an ancestor sent to Mount Namuli soon after her death, now being summoned back two years later.[2]

The *eyinlo* was remarkable for its festiveness, fueled no doubt by the pulsating drums and the plentiful *otheka* (sorghum beer). As we sat watching the dances, one man turned to me and asked, "In your land, do you have *eyinlo*?" I answered that we do not, that many would in fact consider it unseemly to dance and drink on occasions having to do with death. "Like in the Assembléia," he said, and others grunted their assent. The reference was to the African Assembly of God (Assembléia de Deus Africana, or ADA) church, which everyone knew to condemn ceremonies that honor the dead.[3] Everyone also knew this as the reason Jorge, one of the deceased woman's children, was nowhere to be seen. He was a kilometer away, at Kaveya's ADA congregation. It was Sunday, after all.

I knew Jorge well from my time spent in the ADA. He joined the small congregation after his wife, who at the time was deathly ill, recovered only through congregants' prayers. The two eventually became among the ADA's more active participants. Nothing displayed their devotion more than Jorge's willingness to forego his own mother's *eyinlo* for that morning's Sunday service. Jorge explained when we talked later that week: "We are prohibited from dancing *eyinlo* just as we are prohibited from eating *esataka*. We only help at the funeral, make our contributions while the dead person is still in the home, before going to the cemetery. But once the person is buried? No. We stay away from the ceremonies. It's not possible to eat *esataka* while the person is already dead and buried. He will not rise again and eat it. Why didn't you give while he was alive?" I had already heard Pastor Simões offer this line of reasoning but always thought that while issuing such prohibitions may be easy, abiding by them must be hard. I asked Jorge whether it was, especially given that this case involved his own mother. He answered by reciting a gospel story, the one in which Jesus as a young boy strayed from his parents. He was eventually found "in the temple, sitting among the teachers, listening to them and asking them questions" (Luke 2:46, New Revised Standard Version). When his mother demanded to know why he ran away from his family, Jesus responded, in Jorge's rendition, "My kin (*amusi*) are those with whom I sit, with whom I do prayers. The one who birthed me and who does not follow my teachings is not my kin."

I was thoroughly impressed, not only that Jorge could instantly select so apt a biblical parallel but also by the resoluteness conveyed by the selection. Jorge's willingness to condemn the rituals for his own mother suggests his conversion may very well take the form of a definitive, irreversible change—the kind I have been arguing is most unusual in Maúa, Mozambique. Not everybody involved with Pentecostalism, Jorge served to warn me, need be involved in the polyontologically mobile way that I had been hitherto observing. It is important to acknowledge this fact. As reductionist as it is to assume from Pentecostal rhetoric that all Pentecostals reject ancestral traditions, it would be equally reductionist to assume that *nobody* takes on a durably Pentecostal identity, that *nobody* refuses return to mother.

The Difference Pentecostalism Makes

To make sense of such apparently permanent Pentecostals, anthropologists of Christianity have organized their research around a simple but profound question, first posed by Fenella Cannell in the opening line of a field-defining volume: "What difference does Christianity make?" (2006: 1). Answers range across multiple registers: from personhood to media, from language to materiality, from economics to politics. While the answers are not internally consistent—sensibly enough due to the multiple kinds of Christianity and the multiple approaches one may take to studying them—the very pursuit of an answer presupposes something in common: the stability of Christian commitments, the idea that once one becomes Christian one stays Christian. Yet this is a particularly orthodox conception of religious conversion, orthodox by the lights of Western Christian norms.[4] This ideal, as Cannell herself notes, does not necessarily capture how Christianity plays out empirically. Not all who convert to Christianity convert to the Christian idea of conversion (Comaroff and Comaroff 1991: 248–51; Cannell 2006: 25–30).

Throughout preceding chapters this has been my argument, the implication of which is not that Makhuwa Christians are "superficial" or "inauthentic," but that the duration of their Christian engagements does not reflect the depth of those engagements. I am thus not inclined to judge Jorge—by virtue of his evidently durable conversion—as a "real" Pentecostal unlike, say, Jemusse, Fátima, Flôrencio, Raimundo, and Neuza. Nevertheless, Jorge does provide an invitation to broach questions not likely to be asked otherwise.[5] These include the question of Pentecostalism's particularities and the question of the difference these make.

I argue in this chapter that, whatever else it may be, Pentecostalism is a mobile tradition, "a religion made to travel" (Cox 1995: 102). This is clearest in terms of Pentecostalism's transnational scope. The presence of the ADA where I encountered it owes to a long chain of global links that connect Los Angeles to Cape Town, Cape Town to Salisbury (Harare), and Salisbury to Mozambique and other mission fields of the Zimbabwe Assemblies of God Africa (Maxwell 2006a). Transnational Pentecostal churches have also been seen to connect to people who are themselves socioeconomically mobile (van Dijk 2009; van de Kamp 2013). Yet my concern here is not with mobility at the level of institutions or of political economy, but with the micro-mobilities internal to the Pentecostal tradition itself. By these I mean, for example, the preponderance of kinesthetic movements within ritual spaces and the oscillations between sinfulness and sanctity that mark the project of Pentecostal piety. Of the many differences Pentecostalism can be said to make, these latter are what I consider most crucial for understanding its peculiarly unpronounced presence where I worked. Pentecostalism there and elsewhere is distinguished by its inbuilt instability, its structural antistructuralism.[6] It is a mobile tradition, but it is no less a tradition of mobility.

In this, Pentecostalism may differ from other forms of Christianity, but it resembles and restages the pre-Pentecostal lifeworld of the Makhuwa. Paradoxically, Pentecostalism sustains even when it supplants what came before. This is because what came before are flexibility, dynamism, and kinesis—features one finds in Pentecostalism as lived (even if not in Pentecostalism as preached). Thus, the old platitude that the more things change the more they stay the same does not exactly apply. It is not *despite* change but *through* change that continuity abides.

Firmness and Flexibility

The first time I met Pastor Manuel I was startled by the strength of his handshake. I had not grasped a hand so firmly and formally since leaving the United States. The considerably more supple Makhuwa style of greeting is to cup both hands slightly in front of the chest and clap lightly two or three times, then in a fluid motion draw both hands, palms inward, up to the head, down to the heart, and further down to the thighs, finally letting them drop and open toward the ground. Spoken of as a gesture of *oxukurela* (gratitude), this greeting—performed by both parties—conveys a meeting of two heads, hearts, and bodies in a gesture of conjoined circularity. Pastor Manuel's handshake was not unkind; through it, I sensed warmth and generosity, indicative of his unflagging willingness to talk with me and welcome me into the Evangelical Assembly of God (Evangélica Assembléia de Deus) church he led. But the gesture, a fully extended, tensely gripped, vigorously pumped handshake, seemed out of place—not with the Pentecostal subculture he and other evangelists sought to fashion, but with the cultural milieu out of which they sought to fashion it.

The handshake was just one aspect of the body *hexis*—the socially inculcated movements, gestures, and postures—that Pentecostal leaders expected of their followers.[7] In one sermon I recorded, at a Pentecostal church service in Lichinga, the preacher excoriated consultations with traditional healers (*curandeiros*): "When you go to the *curandeiro*, before you enter, what do you do? You remove your shoes. Then you enter, inclined [he bowed down at the waist, eliciting knowing laughter], bend your knees. This says a lot! When you enter already bent down at the knees you are saying that he is your lord. By then, it's over!" The only one before whom genuflection is acceptable, the preacher went on, is "our God, Jesus Christ," the result of which should be uprightness in all other encounters. Bowing down before God enables one to "stand up" to the devil: "The *curandeiro* wants you down on your mat, but to get to the altar of God you have to climb. The devil wants you to stay down but God wants you up high." As he said this, he extended his body and even leaped off his feet. The contrast with the bowed bodies I had witnessed at the *eyinlo* was stark. From such ceremonies, sturdy handshakes and straight postures were meant to instantiate rupture. They accompanied and accomplished the decisiveness of one's break with the past, the firmness with which one should assume one's new identity.

Leaders had reason to insist on this bodily reinforcement of rupture. Few congregants assumed a Pentecostal identity to their satisfaction—exclusively and exhaustively. Stories throughout this book have made that clear. Here I present one more, focusing less on the details of the transgression than on its consequences. These consequences reveal the importance of flexibility, even amid fixity, in Pentecostalism.

Not long before my wife and I took up residence in Kaveya, Abílio—a young member of the village's ADA congregation—used a microloan from the government to buy a diesel-powered grinding mill. For a part of the world still lacking electricity and running water, this was to be a significant technological advance. Soon after installing the mill, members of the ADA congregation came and blessed it, imploring Jesus Christ to keep away all evil spirits who would love to see Abílio's project fail.

Four days later, it failed.

The village chief told Abílio why: the recently deceased chief had not received the requisite sacrifices. Without delay, Abílio gathered a different group to re-inaugurate the mill, this time with a *makeya* offering to appease and beseech the aggrieved ancestor. News of this soon reached Pastor Simões, the district level leader of the ADA. The very next Sunday, he traveled to Kaveya and issued Abílio a reprimand (*repreensão*), an official church punishment that barred Abílio from participating in church services. He was instructed to continue attending but to do so without preaching, dancing, or singing.

As severe as the punishment was, it was also telling—suggestive of what really matters in the Pentecostal tradition. In mainline Christian churches, especially in the industrialized West, the norm is to sit still and, on occasion, stand still. In this case, stillness was a punishment. Pentecostal churches are most distinguished by their experiential, exuberant, and embodied forms of worship. Understood to be animated by the Holy Spirit, services are replete with dances, trances, and emotional catharses.[8] Of special importance is the charismatic gift of speaking in tongues, ecstatic utterance that exceeds linguistic intelligibility (Cox 1995: 81–97). Its potency rests not in semantic meaning but in spiritual in-filling, the intense and immediate union with God. Not only do worship services allow for the Holy Spirit to fill one's body; they allow for demonic spirits to vacate it. Furthermore, ritual exorcism comprises multiple embodied acts: walking forward to the altar, laying on of hands, violent shaking, and even physical sparring with the exorcising pastor.

Pentecostal prayers were never recited from one's seat, nor from a stationary standing position. They were recited, loudly and vociferously, while pacing back and forth—each person taking a few steps in one direction, then turning and looping back, only to begin again. Similar motions were evident in the period of singing and dancing that, for up to an hour, began each service. Worshippers divided into four groups: the *mamãs* (women), the *papás* (men), the children, and the youth. The order was never standardized, but each group presented its dances in turn. The first group would organize itself outside the back passageway, the drumming would begin, and the dancers would shuffle in using the same slow, swaying steps (*wina wettaka*) I had seen at the *eyinlo* ceremony. With dancing and singing already under way, it was clear that the groups did not enter to praise; they entered praising. Once at the front of the hall, they would sing two or three more songs, each with its own choreography of twirling foot patterns, steps forward and backward, loose arm swings, and twisting torsos. Afterward, the dancers would exit with the same *wina wettaka* motion through the center aisle and out the back. The worship leader would then yell out—"*Papás*!" for example—and the next group would rush to gather outside, organizing itself to enter once again.[9]

For the participants, both the perambulatory prayers and the entrance-exit dynamic expressed what Daniel Albrecht, in his theological assessment of Pentecostal ritual, calls "a spirituality that cooperates and participates in the movements of God" (Albrecht 1999: 148). They seemed to me equally cooperative and participatory in Namuli-like circularity. I was struck by the numerous parallels to what I had been observing in ancestral ceremonies. Either way, given the kinetic character of Pentecostal worship, Abílio's enforced silence and stillness were punishing indeed.

The commonalities between indigenous and Pentecostal rituals may not be surprising in light of one important strand feeding into the emergence of Pentecostalism. In the North American context, that would be the phenomenon of African religiosity, brought by slaves to the continent, that infused nineteenth- and twentieth-century Christian revival movements with such elements as spirit healing, polyrhythmic drumming, and divine immanence. In the African context, what makes the continent such fertile ground for the Pentecostalism imported from North America is Africa's repertoire of healing practices, spirit possession, dance traditions, and oral storytelling.[10] In both North America and Africa, it is Pentecostalism's indigenous roots that lend the tradition its "fundamental attitude of flexibility and openness" (Vondey 2010: 15), a characterization of global Pentecostalism no less befitting the Makhuwa traditions I have been describing throughout this book.

Yet there is a countercurrent in Pentecostalism, born of another of its inheritances: the holiness branch of European Protestantism. According to historian Allan Anderson, "These historical roots in the radical fringes of 'free church' Evangelicalism tend to create a certain fundamentalist rigidity" (2010: 22). As this coexists with the experiential branch, Pentecostalism cannot be equated with fundamentalism (Cox 2009: 199–202). The evangelical legacy nevertheless introduced such aspects as biblical literalism and moral asceticism, which find expression today in the primacy given to God's Word in scripture and the prohibitions regarding illicit substances, sexual misconduct, and the kind of "idolatry" for which Abílio had to be punished. Not flexibility and openness, but fixity and rigidness stem from

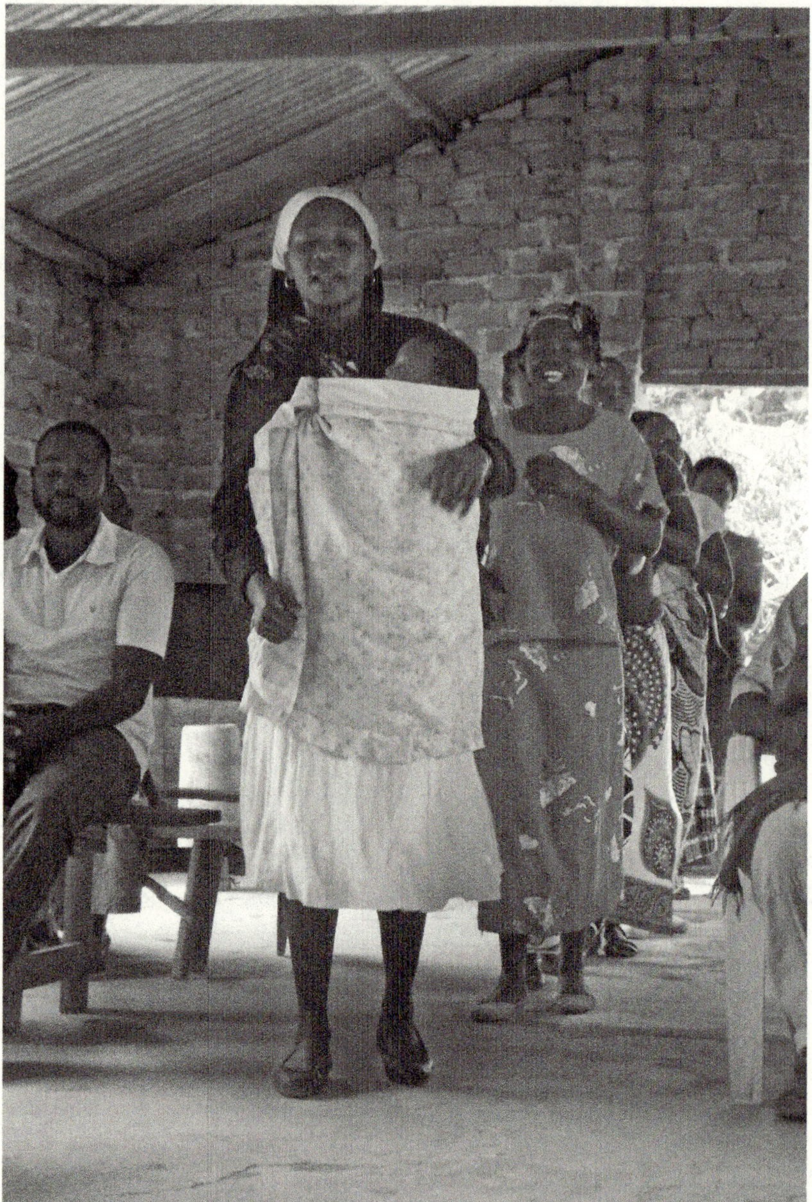

Figure 8. Entry of the *mamãs*, African Assembly of God church, Maúa town.

this inheritance. Pentecostal pastors—increasingly male, educated, and Bible-centered—tend to give it special emphasis, concerned as they are with placing discursive checks on their congregants' otherwise prediscursive practices. They want to ensure no mistaking of the Holy Spirit for an ancestral spirit, or of dances for Jesus for dances for ancestors. It is not that Pentecostal leaders neglect the body. As noted above, they are quite concerned to exhibit and encourage alterations of the body *hexis*. The aim of Pentecostal leaders, and the achievement of some of their followers, is the turning of inclined bows into straight-armed handshakes, of circularity into linearity, of moral laxity into moral rectitude.

But these intended transformations are perpetually undone by the ritual motions most important to ordinary Pentecostals. The same Sunday morning that villagers went to the woods to honor Jorge's mother with an *eyinlo* ceremony, Jorge went to the Pentecostal church: a far distance symbolically but not physically—and not phenomenologically. While the *eyinlo* dancers were entering and exiting their ritual grounds, shuffling their feet and twisting their torsos, Jorge was entering and exiting his ritual grounds, shuffling his feet and twisting his torso. He was not only replicating, in one space, the circumambulations of another. He was, through repeated patterns of entry and exit, performing a small-scale simulacrum of the kind of circulation I knew people like Abílio to make *between* those two spaces. If, as argued in Part I of this book, circular conversions are an expression of Makhuwa mobility (*othama*), then even *within* Pentecostalism conversions never cease.

Being and Becoming

The particularities of Pentecostal thought join those of Pentecostal practice in revealing the tradition's internal dynamism. They show that Pentecostalism is less an accomplished state than a project of perpetual renewal. Pentecostal theology shares with existential phenomenology (as discussed in the Introduction) an aversion to abstraction and systematization. It is nothing if not concrete, embodied, and engaged.

That is why the pastors I came to know disavowed the category of religion. They saw Pentecostalism as neither fixed nor rigid enough to be reducible to the term. Religions were seen to be the impersonal and thus inconsequential traditions of Catholicism and Islam. These are what should be abandoned, I once heard Pastor Manuel preach: "Leave behind tradition, leave behind culture, leave behind religion. Our only salvation is with Jesus." It is not the proper religion but the proper relation that matters in the Pentecostal framework. In this, as in the embodied rituals described above, Pentecostalism shares common ground with African indigenous traditions. These, likewise, emphasize the theoretical only insofar as it emerges from the practical, the abstract only insofar as it relates to the lived.[11]

Another injunction regularly preached in sermons—"Have faith, don't believe!" ("*Crer, não acreditar*!")—conveys this same existential orientation. Suggested by this is the kind of distinction Wilfred Cantwell Smith draws between rational and relational notions of belief. Prior to the Protestant Reformation, "belief" in the West had little to do with intellectual assent to propositional truths. To recite the Credo in medieval liturgies evoked "I believe" not in the sense of judging God to exist in the face of uncertainty but in a sense best revealed by its Latin etymology: "*Credo* literally means 'I set my heart' (from *cor, cordis*, heart). . . . This verb means to pledge allegiance, to commit oneself, to give one's loyalty" (Smith 1977: 41). Smith's compelling argument is that the universalizing of a parochial category has led outsiders to distort the religious worlds of people beyond the modern West. For them, belief is more like what Smith prefers to call faith, a performance of trust within a relation of intimacy.

This sense is preserved in Pentecostalism's urging to commit with the heart more than with the mind. The tradition's affective qualities have been amply documented: theologian Harvey Cox argues that Pentecostalism is "about the experience of God, not about abstract religious ideas" (1995: 5), and anthropologist George Saunders (2010) sees in Pentecostalism a critique of logocentric reason. Pentecostalism's irreducibility to rational beliefs corresponds to its refusal of reification.[12] Therefore, the fact that experiential truths count for more than propositional truths reinforces why Pentecostalism, like Makhuwa indigenous traditions, cannot easily be captured by discursive categories and pinned to conceptual frameworks.

Pentecostalism's de-emphasis on reason and intellect connects it not only to the existential but also to the pragmatic aspects of the Makhuwa lifeworld. By stressing, as they do, the therapeutic powers of Jesus, pastors present him as a new, but far more efficacious, *curandeiro*. I never heard a sermon encouraging listeners to "trust in Jesus" in spite of difficulties, but always to "have faith and be cured." This is a high-risk proposition, creating clear expectations that, in so medically perilous a context, cannot always be met. Thus, when miracle healings do not transpire, by the pastors' own logic one must try something else. Although rationalizations abound for why a prayer may go unanswered, people are less likely to detain themselves figuring out what they could have done differently than to avail themselves of something else in their repertoire. Thus, Pentecostalism becomes one more resource in an already plural medical field. People will consult with a healer—whether one *curandeiro*, another *curandeiro*, a biomedical physician, or Jesus—as long as he or she heals. When the healing stops, so too do the consultations. By presenting itself more as a solution to problems than as an ideology or identity, Pentecostalism fits seamlessly into the pragmatic outlook that the Makhuwa call *wasasa ekumi* (the search for life).[13]

I once heard Pastor Simões boast about baptizing, at a single all-night service, five people who had never before been "saved by the Spirit." It was an impressive claim, but one wonders about retention in such a case. Compared with Catholic churches (where years of catechesis precede full communion) and Islamic mosques (with their own Qur'anic schools), Pentecostal churches worry minimally if at all about intellectual formation and doctrinal instruction. As argued in Chapter 5, this is one of the reasons Pentecostalism attracts women as well as the unlettered and unprivileged. Such people can be not only baptized in the Holy Spirit but also empowered by it to preach and teach. Authority, like sanctity, is universally and almost instantly accessible, not the reserve of a specialized elite with formal credentials.[14]

Yet if the threshold of entrance into the church and the benchmark for advancement within it are low, so too must be the threshold of exit. The borders of the Pentecostal world, permeable as they are, do not displace but coexist with the pragmatic approach explored in this section as well as with the ritual movements explored above. The consequence of this coexistence for Pentecostalism as practiced, even if not for Pentecostalism as preached, is the same as that already argued in Chapter 4. It is a polyontological mobility, a border-crossing propensity, a capacity to leave matched only by a capacity to enter (*ohiya ni ovolowa*).

Even for those who, by all appearances, enter without leaving (people like Jorge), they too are offered opportunities—indeed they are required—to enact this interplay of entrances and exits, rises and falls. This interplay has been well documented by anthropologists working on Pentecostalism. Simon Coleman (2003) refers to it as "continuous conversion" and Diane Austin (1981) as being "born again . . . and again and again."

For Olivia Harris, the incompleteness of conversion is a general Christian motif, but it is especially in charismatic Christianity that "conversion is a permanent process, constantly renewed in ecstatic confession and renunciation of the Devil" (2006: 72).

This came across clearly in one Pentecostal service I attended, in Lichinga, where a preacher described the problems for which his listeners were seeking solutions: "Your health is not good, your finances are tight, your marriage is not going well." It struck me that these are effectively interminable problems of health, wealth, and well-being. One may achieve a temporary respite, but problems endemic to the human condition never cease. Despite Pentecostalism's ideology of a singular rupture point and its ideal of arrival at holiness and wholeness, much more at play are processual change and perpetual struggle. The closing prayer of that service included the line, "and may the evil spirits leave and never return." That the pastor followed his prayer with an announcement about the next scheduled meeting—"Come back on Wednesday at six!"—showed he had no expectation his prayer would actually be answered, no illusion that evil spirits could be banished once and for all. Damnation always follows on the heels of salvation, and spiritual warfare is an ongoing affair.

While certain aspects of Pentecostal theology encourage participants to relate to it pragmatically, others postulate salvation as provisional. In any case, committed Pentecostals find themselves in a state of perpetual oscillation: between an inside and an outside, between being and nothingness. It is in the interplay of these extremes that one may locate the dynamism of the tradition. *To be* Pentecostal is to engage the endless project of *becoming* Pentecostal.

Connection and Kinesis

Even though seven of its twenty lectures are devoted to conversion and its analogues, William James's 1901–2 Gifford lectures, published as *The Varieties of Religious Experience* (1985), have yet to be robustly taken up in anthropological studies of religious conversion. More commonly, James is dismissed as soon as he is mentioned. This may owe to James's (to some) unacceptably sympathetic stance toward religious practitioners and their theological claims, a stance born not of metaphysical certainty but of philosophical pragmatism. Explicitly, James is challenged for the inordinate attention he gives to inner experience and for the individualist thrust of his definition of religion: "the feelings, acts, and experiences of individual men in their solitude" (1985: 31). By making religion primarily a matter of the singular self, James leaves out the formative role of language and belief, of culture and history.

There is much that is valid in this critique, but it is useful to consider that the entirety of James's definition of religion refers not just to individuals in their solitude, but to individuals "in their solitude, so far as they apprehend themselves to stand in relation to whatever they may consider the divine" (1985: 31). Conversion is, for James, the shift of religious ideas previously peripheral in consciousness to the center (1985: 196). Foundational for James, then, is a view of human consciousness as embedded in wider fields, the center and periphery of which continually interchange. How we construe these fields—as the subconscious or the supernatural, the social or the extrasocial—is, to James, irrelevant. It matters little whether our language captures that which anyway lies beyond the reach of reason. Less important than the name, the source, or even the reality of that with which one connects is the connection itself: "Life is in the transitions as much as in the terms connected; often, indeed, it seems to be there more emphatically" (2003: 45).

Intrinsic to James's theory of conversion is his theory of connection—his philosophy of radical empiricism that seeks to accord what is elusive and transitive the same standing as what is stable and substantive. The implication of this philosophy, as summarized by anthropologist Michael Jackson, is that "one's well-being depends on one's relationships or connectedness to an 'elsewhere' or 'otherwise' that lies beyond the horizons of one's own immediate lifeworld" (2009: 7). James does not provide an explicitly *social* theory of intersubjectivity, but his view of conversion as connection, combined with his view of connection as of the essence, does not necessarily foreclose consideration of community and context.[15]

Concerns about James's hyperindividualism mirror claims about Pentecostalism's. At least one significant thrust of social scientific research casts Pentecostalism as a force of atomization and, thereby, of modernization. Sociologist Peter Berger, for example, connects Pentecostalism to the broader evangelical tradition's insistence on personal decision making. Thus, he argues, "the modernizing significance of Pentecostalism cannot be emphasized enough. . . . It provides a distinctive individualism" (2013: 254). Much research within the anthropology of Christianity generally has shown that the rupturing quality of conversion involves both a sociological break from kinship ties and a linguistic move toward individually centered speech. Yet, at the same time, other studies have called attention to how, after Pentecostal conversion, bonds are either maintained or made anew.[16] Anthropologist Mark Mosko (2010, 2015) even marshals such observations to argue for sociality as not just evident in but constitutive of the Christian self. Ilana van Wyk's (2014) study of the Universal Church of the Kingdom of God (UCKG) in South Africa is instructive on this point.[17] This is an anomalous Christian church insofar as communal bonds are actively discouraged: pastors transfer regularly between branches, worshippers attend services alone, and marriages go uncelebrated, sometimes even unannounced. Yet, van Wyk argues, this lack of sociality does not equate to modern individualism. This is, in part, because of Pentecostals' permeable conception of the body. It is also because prayers and sacrifices at the church are driven by concern for family beyond it.

In theological discourse, while the logic of singularity may appear on the surface, relationality reigns not far below. Elaborating a Pentecostal perspective on the doctrine of the Trinity, theologian Amos Yong brings a specifically pneumatological framework to bear (2002: 49–82).[18] He calls special attention to the capacity of the third element of the Trinity, the Holy Spirit, to serve as bridge between it and the other two. The Holy Spirit clarifies and instantiates the relational interplay of the Father, Son, and Holy Spirit, the unity obtained in diversity. Thus, the Trinitarian elements are not independent and autonomous. Each has its being in the others. This reciprocal understanding, termed perichoresis, is found in many schools of Christian theology. What Yong and the Pentecostal tradition add is that this Trinitarian interexistence owes to the fluidity and mobility of one particular element of the Trinity: the unconfined Holy Spirit.

Connectedness, in this understanding, is not fixedness. It is not a force of stagnation, but a generator of motion, of what James would see as "the immediate flux of life which furnishes the material to our later reflection with its conceptual categories" (2003: 49). The intellectual operations of abstraction and nominalization are what introduce fixity. This is why both Pentecostalism and radical empiricism share a deep distrust of the rationalist biases of dominant intellectual traditions. These tend to break reality into isolated concepts, fixed and finished, whereas intuition and emotion emphasize the evolving and emergent. For James, "what really *exists* is not things made but things in the making. Once made, they are dead" (1909: 263; emphasis in the original). Similarly, Pentecostal theology instructs against the completeness, the presumed closure, of God's revelation. It opposes the cessationist doctrine that miracles and spiritual gifts came to an end after the apostolic age (Yong 2002: 247–49). The history of Pentecostalism suggests that speaking in tongues, healing, and prophesying transpire no less today than they were recorded to transpire in biblical times.[19]

If the flux of the Holy Spirit, like the flux of preconceptual experience, exceeds any particular point in time, perhaps it exceeds any particular point in space. The force behind Pentecostalism would then be unbound to the institutional structures of any given Pentecostal church. This is the most compelling implication of Pentecostalism's principle of relationality. As van Wyk notes about the UCKG, "the church's membership was not stable . . . most people attended the church for relatively short periods. Those who left the church often joined other local churches, frequently returned to the UCKG, and then left again" (2014: 235). From the perspective of Pentecostal pneumatology, Yong's (2003) view of the Holy Spirit extends even further, not just to other churches but to other religions. He cites as warrant Jesus's own dictum that the Spirit "blows where it chooses" (John 3:8, New Revised Standard Version). This may be yet another point of contact between Makhuwa and Pentecostal worlds, a point where Holy Spirit and ancestral spirits meet. The latter, like the former, are nothing if not mobile, ever migrating between the land of the dead and the land of the living, into and out of people's lives. These movements are also understood to be indeterminate and unpredictable. Though *minepa* can be petitioned, they cannot be pinned down. They, too, blow where they choose.

At the heart of Pentecostal theology is the Holy Spirit. A paradox exists within it, though: its simultaneous promotion of both connection and movement. Against the common understanding that to be with (*okhalano*) something is to be fixed to it, one might argue that to be with Pentecostalism is to be unfixed, that *being with* the Spirit is consistent with *blowing with* the Spirit. Connecting to phenomenological realities peripheral to oneself is the essence of religious conversion, James contends. Given his radically empiricist privileging of movement over stasis, James would be satisfied to know that connection, in Pentecostalism, looks a lot like kinesis.

Pentecostalism Beyond Pentecostalism

The titles of the three preceding sections—"Firmness and Flexibility," "Being and Becoming," and "Connection and Kinesis"—pair together conceptual antinomies. The argument of each section reveals precisely how the words in each pair belong together: the first in every case serves to qualify the second. Thus, to be *firmly* Pentecostal is to be flexible, to *be* Pentecostal is to be ever becoming, and to *connect* to Pentecostalism is to be moved by its kinetic Spirit. Even people, such as Jorge, who align themselves with Pentecostalism's rhetoric of rupture are not static and fixed as a result. Far from refuting the thesis of this book, then, Jorge's anomalous case extends it. Not even he is well captured by the label "Pentecostal"—a term with which I never heard him identify. For him, as for others, "to be Pentecostal" is to be irreducible, even to Pentecostalism. Movement, change, and circularity are internal to, indeed constitutive of, the tradition. Perhaps uniquely within contemporary Christianity, Pentecostalism spurs movement and dynamism from within, promoting a practical experimentalism at odds with its ideological rigidity.

Movement and dynamism are not discouraged by the more ideologically driven leaders of Pentecostal churches. Even with their firm handshakes and upright postures, pastors dance only slightly less ecstatically than their congregants. They speak in tongues and roll on floors, they jump, they cry, and they shout. None of this Dionysian fervor is inappropriate, they would say. If done within the confines of the church, under the auspices of the Spirit, these are the truest signs of grace.

Major studies of these experiential dimensions of Pentecostalism deploy paradigms of embodiment to critique conventional approaches to the study of religion (Csordas 1994; Lindhardt 2011b). Pentecostals, it is commonly agreed, call attention not so much to formalized meanings and systematized beliefs as to the lived body and its affective engagements. In the Pentecostal services I attended, sermons were of course preached and testimonies were offered, but the words uttered seemed intended to *do* things more than to *signify* things.[20] Preachers and worshippers consistently operated at the limits of language. The corporeal outweighed the cognitive, as one would expect for a tradition in which "one does not praise God with the mind (or spirit) alone" (Albrecht 1999: 148).

In his contribution to a somatic turn in Pentecostal studies, Martin Lindhardt makes reference to both phenomenology and Pierre Bourdieu's practice theory. Clearly, however, Lindhardt's analysis aligns more with the latter. Key for Bourdieu is his definition of *habitus* as "systems of durable, transposable dispositions" (1977: 72). "The adjectives 'durable' and 'transposable' are essential here," Lindhardt argues. "People do not 'take off' the ritually cultivated embodied and linguistic dispositions for experiencing the sacred and reordering the behavioral environment, as one might take off a particular ritual garment at the end of a service" (2011a: 19). Thus emphasizing the pervasive and enduring nature of specifically Pentecostal dispositions, Lindhardt highlights the entrenchment of ritual effects, their penetration into all aspects of the individual Pentecostal's life.[21]

It is important to note that while both phenomenology and practice theory bring the lived body into anthropology, they do so quite differently. The former highlights the indeterminacies of lived experience (Merleau-Ponty 1962; Csordas 1993), while the latter highlights the durability of dispositions derived from preexisting social structures. In his suspicions about what he sees as the autonomous subject presumed by phenomenology, Bourdieu transfers the greater store of agency to objective, external forces. This overcorrection (see Throop and Murphy 2002) is arguably what makes him so relevant to paradigms of cultural anthropology that similarly bestow upon cultural traditions and social structures the very capacities they deny to individuals themselves. As anthropologist Saba Mahmood has argued in her critique of Bourdieu, dispositions come to be naturalized and inscribed not through unconscious imbibing alone (2005: 136–39). Often, they require and result from deliberate and industrious practice, from training and discipline. Seen this way, it is not that traditions are ineffectual for those shaped by them, but that people have at least a degree of control over what traditions ever come around to shaping them.[22]

Phenomenologists would have no problem recognizing the interplay of prediscursive experience with "the multiplicity of cultural meaning in which we are always and inevitably immersed," as Thomas Csordas does in his elaboration of a *cultural* phenomenology (1994: vii). But they would recognize that multiplicity pertains not just to a single culture but to the "multiple realities" (Schutz 1945) or the multiple idioms, cultural and religious, that an individual inhabits and has some say in negotiating. Phenomenology's concept of the lifeworld, whose key feature is its irreducibility to any fixed or singular worldview, points to the repertoire of resources upon which people eclectically draw in their practical, everyday engagements—engagements that compel regular alterations and oscillations not unlike how (to use Lindhart's image) one might switch between ritual garments.

From this perspective, it is ironic that the boundaries Pentecostals are known for blurring—between inside and outside, between the ritual and the everyday (Lindhardt 2011a: 19–21)—tend to be quite pronounced by those who study them. A truly phenomenological approach to the study of Pentecostalism could not confine itself to the study of Pentecostalism. Whereas cultural anthropologists in general, and anthropologists of Christianity in particular, stress cultural particulars predicated on discursive discontinuities, phenomenological anthropologists call attention to human universals predicated on bodily continuities: "While words and concepts distinguish and divide, bodiliness unites" (Jackson 1989: 135). Thus, phenomenology contributes to Pentecostal studies by rendering Pentecostalism less autonomous, distinctive, and determinative than it tends to appear in studies predefined as studies of Pentecostalism.

Throughout this book I have argued that Pentecostal and indigenous traditions are corporeally continuous in ways that defy Pentecostalism's rhetoric of rupture. The Makhuwa are disposed toward transformative, mobile practices prior to encountering Pentecostalism, and thus converting to Pentecostalism is consistent with staying Makhuwa. The most striking implication, however, has to do not with what precedes Pentecostal conversion but with what succeeds it—a continuation of this mobile manner of being such that seamless transitions into the tradition give way to seamless transitions out of it. This observation runs counter to the major thrust of scholarship in the anthropology of Pentecostalism, which emphasizes how and with what effect Pentecostalism both demands and receives singular allegiance. Every preceding chapter of this book has attempted to show how the lifeworld of those I worked with, characterized as it is by mobility and mutability, is crucial for understanding their counterintuitive patterns of Pentecostal conversion. The pluralistic way of being that continues to characterize Makhuwa converts' post-Pentecostal selves, though, manifests not *despite* the particularities of Pentecostalism. It is a Pentecostal feature as well. Thus, the qualities of transience that bring people to Pentecostal churches get reinforced in Pentecostal churches. In turn, these same qualities may lead them beyond Pentecostal churches.

Unbinding the Bound

The Pentecostal propensity for fluidity—the tradition's portable practices and transposable messages—has been cited as key to Pentecostalism's global success (Csordas 2009; Meyer 2010). However, in northern Mozambique, where Pentecostalism has not met with success, the very same factors nevertheless pertain. As anthropologist Robert Hefner put it in his brief consideration of Pentecostal decline: "Pentecostalism has the distinction of being both enormously successful but also, sociologically speaking, protean and unstable" (2013a: 27). Being protean and unstable is what allows Pentecostalism to meet the Makhuwa where they are—not at the level of ideology, identity, and a philosophy of being, but at the level of practice, existence, and a philosophy of becoming. But the fact that experimentalism and pragmatism are affirmed in so much of Pentecostalism makes of it a "revolving door" (Hefner 2013a: 28). By promoting mobility and dispersal from within, Pentecostalism sows the seeds of its own dissolution. What enables the churches to rise today may be just what leads them to fall tomorrow.

This paradox presents researchers with an important lesson, one increasingly needed in an academic culture where subfields proliferate within subfields, where the expectation to specialize requires training in, or "conversion" to, one area of research and rupture from others. Just as identifying oneself as a scholar of Pentecostalism would make one less likely to go where the tradition does not thrive, so too identifying oneself as an anthropologist of Christianity would make one less likely to note the totality of people's lives. William James, one of the few truly eclectic scholars in modern Western intellectual history, would call attention here to the wider fields of being to which subfields necessarily remain closed.[23] With hopes of remaining open to those wider fields, I choose to identify less as an anthropologist of Christianity, a narrow specialization, than as a friend of Abílio, a man on the move. I close this chapter by catching up with him.

In the final weeks of my fieldwork year, with the sugar-apple trees just coming into bloom, the time came for Abílio's reprimand to be lifted. For the previous four months I saw him every week at church, but always seated silently in the back. This, again, was his punishment for propitiating the ancestors: no singing, no clapping, no preaching. In the ADA church, the lifting of the reprimand is easily the most celebratory of occasions. It is called the ritual of liberation. That Sunday, for the first time since he came out to issue the reprimand, Pastor Simões, the district pastor, returned to Kaveya village. After his sermon, he called Abílio to the front, placed his hand atop Abílio's head, prayed his typically thunderous prayer, and declared the period of punishment complete.

"You are liberated!" he yelled, and I joined the congregation in applause and ululations. Abílio smiled his broad smile and, as the voices of all turned from cacophonic yells to euphoric songs, he grabbed the nearest *nlapa* drum. He pounded away for several minutes, then set the drum aside and ran forward to join the dancers. The intensity and integrity of Abílio's devotion were beyond dispute. Anyone there that day, hearing him praise God at full volume, watching him worship with all his body, would be hard pressed to say there is anything superficial about his faith.

Afterward, I approached Nório, the church deacon, to learn his thoughts on what had just transpired. We clasped hands and laughed heartily, still uplifted by the mood.

"It looked like our brother was dead, and now he's come back to life!" I said.

"Yeah, yeah, yeah," Deacon Nório replied, too animated to bother dissenting. Then, with the subtlest rephrasing, he corrected me: "He was bound, and now he's free!"

It was an important clarification. Undesired though death is, it is not resisted in northern Mozambique as intensely as it is in Western societies. Death, a passage rather than a cessation, actually preserves mobility, the fundamental property of the Makhuwa self. "From Namuli we come, to Namuli we return." It is therefore not so much that Abílio was dead and now "born again" as he was bound and now free, seated and now dancing, immobile and now mobile. Not just passage unto death, then, but passage unto Pentecostalism preserves Makhuwa mobility.

There is a certain irony to the district pastor having come all the way from town to officiate at this event. For we can know one thing for sure: Abílio, now back on his feet, will move again (or, by the Spirit, *be* moved again). What threatens to leave pastors, and scholars, as confounded as ever is that there is no telling where that next move will be.

Conclusion

"Africa is on the move, a new Africa is emerging." So said former United States president Barack Obama in 2015 on his final presidential visit to the continent.[1] He was commenting on Africa's widespread economic gains, gains that promised to eradicate poverty, curtail endemic diseases, and overcome legacies of misrule. The *Economist* and *Time* magazines have also conveyed this optimism in recent years, both under the headline "Africa Rising."[2] Skeptics point out that Africa's new wealth is far from fairly distributed; but operative for the narrative's proponents and critics alike is the old Hegelian picture of sub-Saharan Africa—of a "traditional" past, marked by stability and continuity, catalyzed by a "modern" present introducing movement and change.

In this book, I have sought to trouble the dubious yet enduring distinctions encoded in such a picture, distinctions that in Africa and elsewhere have served to underwrite colonial and neocolonial rule. I have done so by critically exploring one of the most heralded harbingers of the new in Africa today: Pentecostal Christianity. With respect to the Makhuwa of Mozambique, my argument has been twofold. First, people's scarce involvements with Pentecostalism demand that triumphalist accounts of its "explosion" be tempered. Second, converts' fluid involvements with Pentecostalism demand that commonplace understandings of "tradition" be abandoned. Among the Makhuwa, fluidity and flexibility stem primarily from rituals, metaphors, and histories often labeled traditional and considered primitive or premodern. These, however, shape the people I worked with by inculcating not conservative dispositions but dispositions toward change.[3]

If it is true, then, that Africa is now on the move, now rising, now emerging, this may well be because it has never been—nor is it likely ever to be—otherwise. Moreover, if the analytical paradox holds for the Makhuwa world, it does so no less for the Pentecostal. The prospects for Pentecostalism among the Makhuwa will, it seems, depend largely on whether it adapts to Makhuwa traditions of change or, just as helpfully, reclaims its own.

Natality Reborn

In the scholarship on Pentecostalism—as well as that on globalization, modernization, and (increasingly) Africa as a whole—it is by now well established that the contemporary world is not well captured by once-dominant models of hybridization. Anthropologist Charles Piot accounts best for the current condition: "Today, a diffuse and fragmented sovereignty is replacing authoritarian political culture; tradition is set aside and cultural mixing looked down upon; Africanity is rejected and Euro-modernity embraced; futures are replacing the past as cultural reservoir. Postcolonial theory's focus on hybrid culture, on the ways in which pasts haunt the present, on the cultural impulse to appropriate and indigenize that which is outside, stops short in analyzing this new—post-postcolonial—terrain" (2010: 16). Among the Makhuwa, however, not much in this is new. For them, breaking with the past has long been as sure a way as any of preserving the past. That is because the "past" is itself diffuse and fragmented.

Numerous spheres of Makhuwa "traditional" life presume disparate domains and clear borders between them. A great deal of ritual effort is expended on establishing distinctions—between men and women, the uninitiated and the initiated, the living and the dead, the village and the bush. Of course, such distinctions are regularly flaunted. At initiation rituals, women mimic men and men act like boys; at *makeya* ceremonies, the dead join the living and the living the dead; and in daily affairs, men hunt for meat and women gather wood, doing so by venturing to and from the bush. The frequency of such crossings—of traversals and reversals—demonstrates not the absence of borders but their permeability, indeed the way in which well-being is predicated on a continual negotiation between closure and openness, containment and the refusal to be contained.

Pentecostalism plays on this double sense of borders. Preachers warn adherents to stay within the lines, not to "backslide" into heathenism. Yet the ritual practices contradict the rhetoric. For while there is a discursive divide between Pentecostalism and everything outside of it, the tradition's experiential and embodied dynamics reinforce more than they contravene the fundamental Makhuwa experience of the fluctuating self. Thus, what is notable about the Makhuwa context is not so much the epistemic divide between Pentecostalism, on the one hand, and indigenous practices and beliefs, on the other. What matters is that, despite the distinct domains, people move bidirectionally between them, oscillating as they always have with alacrity and ease.

"Why do people convert?" This, the most common of analytical concerns, may not be the best question we could be asking. For it assumes that conversion is an anomaly. We generally conceive of religious conversion as the outcome of some crisis or calamity. But what appear to outsiders as momentous shifts may be experienced by insiders as unexceptional. Writing about the effects of merging polities on Kachin self-perception, anthropologist Edmund Leach states: "It is only the external observer who tends to suppose that [such] shifts . . . must be of shattering significance" (1954: 287). Ascribing shattering significance to religious change reveals at least as much about us as it does about those we work with. It bespeaks a bourgeois tendency to locate well-being in secure and stable identities, in tethering ourselves to something firm: brick homes, political structures, religious cultures.

Yet might there be other ways to see things? Is it possible that there are people for whom movement across borders, engagement with alterity, and exposure to the new are, despite their dangers, preconditions for well-being?

The normalizing of stasis over flux fits the substantive view of reality we inherit, ultimately, from Plato's directive to fix our gaze on the eternal and the immutable. Since then, the Western intellectual tradition has had a hard time dealing with change. One of its better-known attempts, from the philosophy of science, posits the existence of two durable paradigms within each of which "normal science" occurs; the shift from one to another is occasioned by "revolutionary science" (Kuhn 1962). Presumed in this model is an absolute distinction between ordinary change and revolutionary change. What the Makhuwa case offers is the possibility of frameworks that collapse that distinction, where movements within paradigms are continuous with movements between them. These would be frameworks that facilitate their own piecemeal and experimental revision, that render radical transformation a banal extension of everyday life.[4]

In anthropological terms, the cultivated dispositions Pierre Bourdieu calls the *habitus* may not merely reproduce the social order. Bourdieu at times gives this impression. Yet even if bodily dispositions faithfully replicate objective structures, might certain structures have pliability and transformability built into them? Such structures would inculcate not dispositions *in spite of which* a degree of agency remains, but dispositions toward agency, toward mobility, toward discontinuity. In this case, people would embrace an experimental stance toward the world not against their conditioning but because of it.

It is to underscore this possibility that I invoke the idea of "existential mobility." As discussed in the Introduction, the significance of the term lies not only in the second word, which suggests the self's irreducibility to one or another framework, but also in the first, which suggests passion for that which one engages. As Christian existentialist Gabriel Marcel (1964) argues, creativity is entirely compatible with fidelity. In everyday dealings with the world, each of the cultural or religious formations constituting one's repertoire may be foregrounded at one time and backgrounded at another. Engagement with a tradition does not preclude disengagement, especially insofar as the tradition in question promotes mobility from within. Such is the case with the Makhuwa tradition, notable for its "capacity for simultaneous transformation and permanence" (Obarrio 2014: 230). The more grounded one is in Makhuwa ways, the more likely one is to transcend them.

Thus some of the most widely assumed antinomies dissolve and fall away—roots versus routes, structure versus agency, continuity versus discontinuity. In an essay on conversion, philosopher Pierre Hadot (1968) points to an internal opposition stemming from the two Greek terms, *epistrophe* and *metanoia*, corresponding to the Latin *conversio*. Suggested by the Makhuwa case is a reconciliation even of that opposition, the possibility that a return to one's origin (*epistrophe*) might in fact be a return to a state of rebirth (*metanoia*), that to convert to one's true self is to convert to convertibility.

Founding anthropologist of Christianity Joel Robbins argues that anthropology's long-standing continuity bias excludes a "theory of truly radical cultural change" and therefore perpetuates the ethnocentric view of non-Western societies as stagnant. As a corrective, Robbins writes that "people really do learn new things and cultures really do change" (2003: 231). This concern with novelty is commendable, existential even. But does the capacity to learn new things require the presence of Pentecostalism or other forms of "modernity"? The notion that radical change springs from globalizing forces that originate in the Western world may in fact be the ethnocentric position, as specious as politicians' and journalists' celebrations of Africa *now* being on the rise, *now* being on the move.

This book contests not the foregrounding of radical renewal in and through Pentecostalism but the implication that there is something radically new about radical renewal. Perhaps surprisingly, it is Pentecostal theologians who give the lie to Pentecostal exceptionalism. Wolfgang Vondey (2010) and Nimi Wariboko (2012) write of their tradition as but one expression of such human universals as creativity, freedom, and play. Like Ruth Marshall (2009), a leading proponent of the rupture paradigm, Wariboko also draws extensively on Hannah Arendt's notion of natality—the capacity to begin things anew (Arendt 1971: 247). Unlike most social scientists of Pentecostalism, however, Wariboko refuses to restrict natality to any single culture or religion. This is in keeping with Arendt's use of the term; she presents it, after all, in a book titled *The Human Condition*. Thus, although social scientists (including anthropologists) studying Pentecostalism have valuably challenged anthropology's continuity bias, their association of "born again" experiences exclusively with "born again" Christians only recapitulates the problem. Despite recasting natality as "the pentecostal principle" (deliberately with a lowercase *p* to uncouple the idea from the institution), Wariboko much better captures the existential point when he writes, "The pentecostal principle predates pentecostalism and is likely to outlive it" (2012: 4).

I present my research as empirical evidence for this critical insight. In northern Mozambique, Pentecostalism does less to introduce natality than to reinforce a preexistent capacity for it. With its dances and trances, exorcisms and ecstasies, Pentecostalism restages without displacing the fundamental Makhuwa experience of the mobile and mutable self. This conclusion is not a simplistic return to discredited models of hybridization and continuity. For what gets continued in this case is precisely the disposition toward *dis*continuity. And what gets conveyed by this case are crucial insights about what it is to be human: about changing as a means of enduring, becoming as a mode of being, and converting as a way of life.

Pentecostal Intransigence

Makhuwa men and women manifest this disposition in different ways corresponding with three broad relations I observed them to maintain with the newly arrived Pentecostal churches. First, among the few who appear to commit exclusively and exhaustively, rebirth continues within the faith. Though possibly abiding by the tenet of permanent and irreversible rupture, these people do not become immobile as a result. This is because the religion to which they convert is, at least experientially, a religion of renewal. In all the ways discussed in Chapter 6, Pentecostalism allows people who commit themselves singularly to it to remake themselves continually through it.

Second, a good number of people deploy their disposition toward mobility by oscillating between Pentecostal churches and proscribed ancestral spaces. They convert, revert, and convert again. They return to the ancestral spirits as readily as they turn to the Holy Spirit; as new imperatives arise, they turn yet again. These patterns of circularity are cultivated through the Makhuwa lifeworlds and worldviews, myths and rites, histories and habitations discussed in the first five chapters of this book. Those who relate to Pentecostalism in this passing and partial (yet nonetheless fervent) manner do so, therefore, as an expression of their Makhuwa selfhood. Yet it may just as well be that they do so as an expression of their Pentecostal selfhood. Again, as Chapter 6 argues, Pentecostalism's own particularities cultivate patterns of circularity. The kinesthetic experiences it promotes may easily exceed the bounds of its own rigid discourse. Whatever the source—Makhuwa or Pentecostal (or both)—this mobile manner of relating to Pentecostalism is key to understanding its underwhelming presence in northern Mozambique.

The relationship with Pentecostalism I have least explored is that of simple avoidance. Many people, not just those who already live at a distance from the new churches, opt to stay away from them. This reluctance to engage may seem to refute my contention that the Makhuwa experiment eagerly with any and all options before them. They are not, however, eager to experiment with those things known to tamp their experimentalism. Analogously, as seen in Chapter 2, even the most well-intentioned development projects are warily received insofar as moving to the roadsides is seen—as it is promoted—as a way of becoming stabilized and sedentarized.

In the short time Maúa's Pentecostal churches have been trying to resettle people religiously, the churches too have garnered a suspect reputation. They are increasingly known not so much for demanding discontinuity as for demanding the discontinuity of a discontinuous way of being. People unfamiliar with the discourse of Pentecostal churches are willing to give them a chance. These are the men and women at the heart of this book, those who move in, but also move out. There are many, however, familiar with the discourse of Pentecostal churches. These are the ones who simply avoid them altogether. They prefer to stay put, which is to say they prefer to stay mobile.

They prefer to stay mobile by staying put in one of the two religions that have met with success in the region: Islam and Catholicism. As discussed in Chapter 4, neither of these is opposed to the kinds of multiplicity with which the Makhuwa customarily carry out their lives. Of course, this was not always the case. Both religions arrived in the region, not unlike Pentecostalism, with ideological rigidity and impermeable borders. However, both learned (Islam soon upon its arrival, Catholicism after many decades) to abandon their opposition to ancestral practices and embrace a logic more akin to that of the Makhuwa. Regarding similar developments elsewhere in Mozambique, Harry West writes with felicitous phrasing that the Makonde "did not merely 'convert to Catholicism'; they also 'converted Catholicism to themselves'" (2005: 126).

Catholicism and Islam are nowadays spoken of not just as *ittini* but as *ittini sa amaye* (mother religions), yet another variation on the theme of centripetal motherhood traced throughout this book. Release from mother is always followed by return to mother. One may leave Catholicism or Islam and expect to be welcomed back.

"Mother" religions are so designated because they have come to be seen as Makhuwa religions. Pentecostalism, by contrast, has not. I often heard it described as the church of the whites/foreigners (*ekereja y'akunya*). This is ironic in that all of the Pentecostal pastors and members I encountered were African. Even more ironic is that the designation of *ekereja y'akunya* is not given to the Catholic Church, despite its propagation through European missionaries up to and including its current leader in Maúa. But that man, Padre Giuseppe Frizzi, is embraced as Makhuwa. He has learned the language (speaking it "better than we do," many say), participated in healing rituals, shown honor to the ancestors, and even revived initiation rites that once were nearly stamped out. Affection for him was widespread during my fieldwork year; even self-identifying Pentecostals referred to him as *bambo ahu* (our priest). What Padre Frizzi did, and what he helped do for Catholicism, was undergo a Makhuwa rebirth.

A parallel point could be made about the party-state run by the Mozambican Liberation Front (Frelimo), which survived Mozambique's transition to liberal democracy in the early 1990s while similar socialist regimes of Eastern Europe did not. There are many reasons for it to have survived (see Pitcher 2002), but one of them may well be its willingness to undergo its own rebirth—to come around to recognizing and respecting what it previously labored to confiscate: healing traditions, sorcery practices, chieftaincies, and the like. The Frelimo state "converted," one might say, not only by allowing customary practices but also by adopting customary logics—most pertinently, the logic of convertibility itself.[5]

In a context where local traditions have long fostered inclusion and mobility, and where nonlocal regimes (religious and political) survived insofar as they assumed the same for themselves, the biggest obstacle to Pentecostal success may be its reluctance to follow suit. Pentecostal intransigence is why the majority of people in Maúa do not even bother with the few Pentecostal churches in their midst. Why would they when they can affiliate with that which affirms, rather than denies, their mobile manner of being?

Seen in this light, the future of Pentecostalism among the Makhuwa looks bleak. It appears likely to remain a marginal presence—attractive to a few members from the local population, who bring to it their polyontological mobility, and to *vientes* (newcomers) who were already evangelized elsewhere. Of course, my speculations may be wildly off. As communication technologies and road networks continue advancing, and as Maúa continues integrating with wider political economies, the traffic of new people and new ideas will likely only increase. As a result, more of the local population may venture beyond the district, there encountering ways of being to bring back with them. *Vientes* may also increasingly appear—as teachers, government workers, merchants, and, of course, evangelists. If and when they reach the critical mass they lack today, these *vientes* may end up transmitting not only new ideas and new institutions but also new priorities such as fixity, stability, and the principle of "having" over that of "being with." At that point, the ruptured mode of Pentecostal participation could very well become more locally attractive, and the Pentecostal churches more successful as a result.[6] One should note, however, that for over a century various outside influences—Muslim clerics and Catholic missionaries, Portuguese colonizers and Frelimo modernizers, regional traders and multinational corporations—have been descending upon the local population without drastically altering the Makhuwa predilection for pluralism. A tipping point may one day be reached, but for the time being, this seems unlikely.

Alternatively, Pentecostalism may follow the path of Islam, Catholicism, and Frelimo and assume for itself something of the Makhuwa propensity for mobility and mutability. This would require the kind of ideological reversal that the worldwide Catholic Church underwent at its Second

Vatican Council in the 1960s and that the national Frelimo state underwent at its Sixth Party Congress in 1991. Bellicose though Pentecostal "spiritual warfare" is, such a reversal may not be farfetched when one considers that early Catholic evangelists and early Frelimo modernists similarly demanded discontinuity of those they sought to reform—that is, until the reformers became the reformed. Furthermore, Pentecostalism has the virtue of carrying within its origins and at the margins of its discourse a spirit of renewal, a resistance to reification, and an aversion to centralization. By softening its animosity toward Makhuwa "tradition," Pentecostalism would follow the path of Catholicism and Frelimo but would also tap into its own congenital charisma, its originating dynamic of renewal and rebirth.

Most signs, however, point to it taking the opposite tack, becoming even more hard-line than it already is. Historians of Pentecostalism have noted a shift that Max Weber first spoke of as the routinization of charisma: the rise of institutional bureaucracies at the cost of visionary energies ([1922] 1978: 246–54). One of the original members of Kaveya's African Assembly of God (Assembléia de Deus Africana, or ADA) church told me he has become disillusioned for just this reason, seeing its priorities change drastically in the course of his lifetime. Before, he explained, pastors, healers, and prophets (all collaborating more or less equally) used their spiritual gifts to bring healing and security to the community. Today, the younger, more male, and more credentialed leaders are primarily concerned with enriching themselves and consolidating their authority.[7]

What began as a loosely structured movement with antinomian tendencies, appealing especially to women and outcasts, has over time become increasingly exclusive and exclusionary. Anthropologist Robert Hefner sees this as a present and possibly persisting trend: "what was at first a non- or interdenominational movement with multiple authority figures . . . may give way to a clear denominational pattern of exclusive affiliation and strict or even authoritarian pastoral control" (2013a: 8–9). The suggestion that there is something new to this reveals that Pentecostalism originally made more room for the kind of experimental flexibility with which Makhuwa men and women conduct their lives. Early American Pentecostal leaders were remarkably inclusive, open even to what they took to be the Spirit working in non-Christian religions (Richie 2013: 58–66). Against this history Pentecostal churches are, institutionally at least, becoming more rigid, more insistent on singular allegiance, and, in the process, more alien to Makhuwa ways.

Converting Pentecostalism?

In Maúa, evidence for Pentecostalism's routinization can be found in the churches' integration with the local branch of the Christian Council of Mozambique (Conselho Cristão de Moçambique, or CCM), an ecumenical Protestant organization.[8] The local coordinator was Costa, an elder in Maúa's only mainline Protestant denomination (the Evangelical Church of Christ in Mozambique). Along with ten or so lay leaders and pastors, I had the chance to attend what was only the second meeting since Costa revitalized the Maúa CCM branch following years of dormancy. Clarity on the group's mission was still needed. Costa called the meeting largely with that purpose in mind.

It took place one Saturday morning, beginning at nine o'clock sharp, in an elegant, white-walled building formerly home to a foreign NGO. The pastors of the district's two Pentecostal churches were both wearing the same spotless finery they used to command respect at their Sunday services. As much as at those services, I was struck at this meeting by the force of the words they shared. "We are militants for Christ," Pastor Simões of the ADA said, "and our task is to battle against the devil and the people enslaved by the devil, the people who do not know Christ." Pastor Manuel of the Evangelical Assembly of God (Evangélica Assembléia de Deus) church peppered similarly bellicose comments with such biblical readings as: "Outside are the dogs, those who practice magic arts, the sexually immoral, the murderers, the idolaters and everyone who loves and practices falsehood" (Rev. 22:15, New Revised Standard Version).

The meeting had the feel of a call to arms. The outsider enemies were identified as Maúa's Catholics, those who claimed to follow Christ but who continued to consume alcohol, commit sexual improprieties, and worship "idols." The archenemies were identified as Padre Frizzi and his catechists for permitting such sinfulness, for making the religious path as easy as possible so as to make their churches as full as possible. Assessments of Maúa's enslavement to the devil gave way to debates over how best to go about saving it, how to convert its inhabitants not just to a particular religion but to a particular way of being religious—one that is unambiguously singular, exhaustive, and absolute. For three hours the meeting carried on like this, the heat of the rhetoric diminishing little as the heat of the day spiked.

It was the starkest example of the combined bureaucratic and exclusionary trends that have, in recent decades, conspired against Pentecostalism's founding impulse—the impulse toward creativity, freedom, and renewal. As a result of these trends, theologian Harvey Cox argues, Pentecostals today "are facing a dilemma they may not survive. At least they may not be able to survive it and still remain true to their origins" (1995: 17). In Maúa district, there are many reasons to wonder whether Pentecostalism will survive, but there is no doubting that what Wariboko calls the "pentecostal principle" has always been alive and well. If the Pentecostal churches reclaim it, they may yet come into their own among the Makhuwa. They may yet survive; they may even thrive. But it will take a massive conversion—not of the Makhuwa to Pentecostalism but of Pentecostalism to the Makhuwa.

This may be under way.

Energy levels were fading at that Saturday's CCM meeting as noon sluggishly approached. I expected Costa to adjourn the meeting, to send everyone off to rest and relax with what remained of the day. Instead he told a riddle. It took the form of a story: "Let's say my mother has become sick. And at the same time she is sick, my wife is also. I'm not around because I had to be away for a few days. On my way home, I meet someone who tells me, 'Hey, your mother has died and your wife has died.' I'm still on my way home. To which site will I go, the compound of my wife or the compound of my mother?" It seemed a bizarre story to tell, having nothing to do with Costa's soul-saving zeal during the previous three hours. I asked afterward why he chose to tell this story when he did. He said he had been concerned that not everyone spoke up during the meeting. He wanted to end on a high note so that next time everyone would feel comfortable contributing. Indeed, the discussion that followed—about striking the right balance between obligations to the natal household and obligations to the marital household—reenergized the gathering. Everyone spoke with gusto and even joy, despite the story's somber theme. Provocation of such palaver is a primary purpose of African dilemma tales. Another is that, by encouraging multiple points of view, discussions around such tales provide a means of coming to terms with the irresolvable predicaments of human existence (Bascom 1975).

I was struck that everyone in attendance—mostly Pentecostals—debated the conundrum intensely, yet without foreclosing perspectives different from their own. One person's immediate response—"I will first go to my wife, out of respect"—prompted an immediate counter—"No, you have to go to your mother"—and a set of passionate justifications. There was widespread approval for that answer until someone else laid out an equally compelling claim: "Most important is to go to your wife because there you have children. You have to be there to console your children." This and other reasons for going to the wife's burial were taken as seriously as those for going to the mother's. The tide of the debate shifted, though with neither answer displacing the other. Whatever the consensus provisionally reached, it was always inevitably undone.

The line of responses that generated the most enthusiasm attempted a reconciliation. "Now, between your mother's home and your wife's home, what's the distance?" one person asked. "Yes," another voiced his support, "ask about the distance." The discussion turned to ascertaining this and other details, to fine-tuning the initially vague scenario so as to devise a strategy for attending both funerals, for solving the dilemma by dissolving it. Depending on the distance between compounds, and on other such contingencies, you could go to one set of kin first, just to assure them you will return to make the expected contributions after having done so for the other set of kin. It was a solution that drew on what I have been calling the skill of polyontological mobility, the capacity to be in two places and be in them fully—not simultaneously (which is impossible), but serially. In the end, however, even this line of responses was beset by too many uncertainties for a consensus to emerge.

Costa allowed the debate to go on like this for quite some time, well into the lunch hour. He eventually brought it to a close with a smile on his face. "The thing is," he said, "this story has no solution." Everyone laughed, as if relieved to be reminded of the insolubility of life's deepest quandaries, of the limits to what one can be expected to know and do in any given situation. As impassioned as the debate over this dilemma tale was, when it was over, everyone seemed content for having participated in it, even without having resolved it.

It was a striking conclusion to a meeting whose tone up to then had been diametrically different. The dilemma tale diverged from what preceded it by being hypothetical, of course, but also in its urgency and immediacy. How to fulfill conflicting responsibilities arising from critical situations seemed a qualitatively different question than that of which religion is true. The latter led to absolute certainties, while the former called forth indeterminacy. The latter demonized deviations, while the former accommodated all.

Embracing and, indeed, reveling in the dilemma tale's ambiguities, the Pentecostal evangelists proved themselves capable of seeing things as I knew their congregants and hoped-for converts do. They were tapping into the distinctly, but not uniquely, Makhuwa tradition of natality. They were making what struck me as the very conversion required of Pentecostalism—required if it is ever to put down roots among a people on the move.

NOTES

Introduction

1. Citing a variety of anthropological theorists, Piot notes the following counterarguments: globalization is not new, nation-states remain strong, continuities may outweigh discontinuities, and scholars should be wary of the ideology of the moment (2010: 13).

2. The related term, charismatic Christianity, designates movements within Catholic and Protestant churches that have adopted Pentecostal practices and beliefs relating to spiritual gifts. In the scholarly literature, Pentecostalism and charismatic Christianity are often grouped and discussed together, for good analytical reasons. But because my research site was home to Pentecostal but not charismatic movements, I use in this book the shorthand term Pentecostalism (and variants thereof). For the sake of clarity and brevity, I do so even when discussing phenomena equally applicable to charismatic movements. For more on these and other taxonomic niceties, see Anderson 2010.

3. For an overview, see Robbins 2010: 158–63.

4. See, e.g., van Dijk 1998; Meyer 1998, 1999; Robbins 2003, 2007; Engelke 2004, 2010; Daswani 2013, 2015.

5. The most sophisticated ethnographic studies of Christian rupture, however, demonstrate that it is not so simple (see, e.g., Meyer 1999; Robbins 2004). Breaks with the past play out paradoxically: the very process of demonizing and expelling ancestral deities also affirms their reality, presence, and power. Robbins frames his ethnographic illustration of this point in terms of Marshall Sahlins's (1985) insight that, while radical cultural change certainly occurs, even it relies on extant cultural frameworks to gain traction (Robbins 2004: 6–11). Perhaps significantly, Sahlins—and the nuance he brings—appears to drop from Robbins's analysis in his more programmatic calls for an anthropology of Christianity based on discontinuous change (e.g., Robbins 2003, 2007, 2010).

6. Highlighting indigenous models of change need not be seen as a return to the hybridity model or to anthropology's continuity bias. It may, instead, be seen as a recognition that change (conversion, migration, transformation) has particular and often pregnant meanings in "traditional" societies. It is an approach that asks not only what Christianity does to local cultures, but also what local ways of knowing and being do to Christianity. Examples of how indigenous models of change inform Christian conversion can be found in Horton 1971; Cucchiari 1988; Rutherford 2006; Vilaça and Wright 2009.

7. See especially the consistency with which edited volumes on Pentecostalism are framed in these terms (e.g., Hefner 2013b; Miller, Sargeant, and Flory 2013; Lindhardt 2015). The violence of the "explosion" metaphor, perhaps not coincidentally, correlates with the equally

destructive connotations of "break" and "rupture" often used to describe Pentecostal conversion. Linda van de Kamp (2016) takes violence as a central theme in her ethnographic study of Mozambican Pentecostalism.

8. For studies of Pentecostalism in the north of Mozambique, see Morier-Genoud 2000; Kantel 2007; Brown 2011. For studies of Pentecostalism in Mozambique's southern and central regions, see Pfeiffer 2005; Gaspar 2006; Cruz e Silva 2008; Schuetze 2010; van de Kamp 2016.

9. This information was freely given to me by IURD pastors themselves, people who would be more prone to overstating than understating the success of their evangelistic efforts.

10. Among the rare exceptions, see Oro 2004; Freston 2013; Morier-Genoud 2014.

11. Others, likewise, have written of "Pentecostal disaffiliation" (Gooren 2010: 124–25), "post-Pentecostal/Charismatic Christians" (Jacobsen 2011: 56), and a possible "Pentecostal 'walk-out'" (Maxwell 2006b: 390).

12. Numerous reasons for this neglect have been suggested. They include Christians' simultaneously insufficient and excessive alterity from the cultural contexts of Western anthropologists (Robbins 2003), the political quietism if not conservatism of many of its most successful branches (Harding 1991), and anthropologists' theoretical inability to handle projects of radical change such as that of Christian conversion (Robbins 2007).

13. In a thoughtful essay on the maturation of the subfield he founded, Robbins, to his great credit, acknowledges this lacuna. Moreover, and like those I earlier cited, he gestures toward the need to fill it: "now that the anthropological impulse to analyze away the Christianity of the people anthropologists study has been largely stilled, there is room to ask what the anthropology of Christianity might learn from research on ambivalent or only tenuously committed Christians" (2014: S166).

14. In his sympathetic critique of Ferguson, anthropologist Francis B. Nyamnjoh (2001) argues for such seamlessness in migrants' movements between rural and urban settings. He finds that, for a variety of reasons, even successful and cosmopolitan city dwellers retain ties to their rural villages. Thus, few urban workers would experience the need to return home as Ferguson's informants appear to: as a demoralizing defeat.

15. Anthropologist Mario Aguilar writes that conversion in Africa "cannot be limited to changes in religious affiliation from a local religious tradition to a world religion. African processes of conversion are fluid, and they also include processes of reconversion to religious practices socially present in the eras preceding the world religions" (1995: 526). The point here is not that cultural continuities obtain despite such rupturing events as Pentecostal conversion, valuable though this point is (see Cole 2010; Chua 2012). Rather, it is that breaks with the past do not preclude breaks back to the past. Thus, indeed, conversions can be circular.

16. Michael Herzfeld has written compellingly about the distinctive value of ethnographic biography: "The tactic of ethnographic biography allows us to move along the trajectory of a life that has bisected many histories and of a person who has dwelt in many communities rather than staying (as most conventional ethnography does) within a single place" (1997: 1).

17. They have also driven much of religious studies, at least historically, until its recent and influential turn toward materiality, practice, embodiment, and emplacement (see Vasquez 2011; Meyer 2014).

18. For concise overviews, see Jackson 1996; Desjarlais and Throop 2011.

19. Ethnographies that bring existential or phenomenological perspectives to bear on the study of Christianity include Csordas 1994, 1997; Lester 2005; Seeman 2009, 2014, forthcoming; Bielo 2011; Werbner 2011; Luhrmann 2012; Premawardhana 2012, 2015, forthcoming.

20. These are what most get left out in studies of African Christianity, privileging as they do churches and movements over ordinary adherents (Engelke 2004).

21. On this dimension of Négritude thought, see Outlaw 1996: 65–69.

22. See, for starters, Stoller 1989, 1997, 2009; Jackson 1989, 2005, 2013. See also the work of a younger generation of phenomenologically inclined anthropologists of Africa and its diaspora (e.g., Silva 2011; van de Port 2011; Lucht 2012), among whom I count myself.

23. For similar critiques of the anthropology of Christianity, see Englund 2007: 482; Hann 2007; Peel 2016: 107–9.

24. For articulations of this critique, see Englund and Leach 2000: 227–30; van Wyk 2014: 27.

25. See van der Veer 1996: 9; Cannell 2006: 14–22; Keane 2007; Bialecki, Haynes, and Robbins 2008: 1146–47; Robbins 2010: 168–69.

26. For novel forms of sociality, see Coleman 2006; Engelke 2010; Haynes 2017; Ikeuchi 2017. For renewed forms of sociality, see Lindhardt 2010; Mosko 2010; Daswani 2011.

27. This approach resonates also with the method of situational analysis developed by the Manchester School (see Evens and Handelman 2006). For an original application of this method to the anthropological study of Pentecostalism, see Daswani 2015.

28. See, e.g., Schielke 2010; Das 2013; Meyer and Janson 2016.

29. For a promising parallel effort, described as an anthropology of religious *butinage* (a French word drawn from the image of bees buzzing about in pursuit of nectar), see Gez et al. 2017.

30. See Maxwell 2006b: 390; Englund 2007: 480–81; Drønen 2013.

31. These include Hage 2005, 2009; Lucht 2012; Jackson 2013; Silva 2015.

32. Michael Lambek (2015), in his sympathetic critique of existential anthropology, offers ethnographic and theoretical support for this kind of "both/and" methodological pluralism.

33. The history of this church, including of its transnational expansions, is the subject of Maxwell 2006a.

34. The 2007 national census indicates the Muslim population in Maúa district to be 49.6 percent and the Catholic population to be 48.9 percent. The (distant) third most represented religion (at 0.5 percent) is given as *Evangélica* (Instituto Nacional de Estatística 2012: 18). This category includes Pentecostals and members of the one non-Pentecostal, non-Catholic church present in the district: the Evangelical Church of Christ in Mozambique (Igreja Evangélica de Cristo em Moçambique). This older Protestant denomination shares in common with the Pentecostal tradition a degree of opposition to ancestral traditions—although with considerably less hostility and vitriol. It also shares in common with the Pentecostal churches of Maúa a relatively minuscule presence. There is only one congregation in the entire district and it attracts only slightly more worshippers than do the Pentecostal churches. Given the important differences between Pentecostal and Protestant denominations and the need for analytic focus, I did not make the Evangelical Church of Christ in Mozambique a site of investigation. It appears only once more in this study, indirectly, when I discuss one of its lay leaders (see the Conclusion).

35. See, e.g., Green 2003; West 2005: 109–32; López 2016.

36. This accords with one ancient Greek word for conversion, *epistrophe*, which connotes turning or returning, in contrast with another, *metanoia*, which suggests something more like rebirth and the transformation of interior attitudes (Hadot 1968; Foucault 2005: 205–27).

Chapter 1

1. A different version of this narrative went to press before I had a chance to learn the naming preference of Luisinha's parents. In that version (Premawardhana, forthcoming), I followed ethnographic writing conventions by giving Luisinha a pseudonym. When I next met her parents, in August 2016, they asked me to use Luisinha's real name, as a way of honoring her memory. I am happy to be able to oblige in this text.

2. Claude Lévi-Strauss in particular posed the anthropological project as that of documenting the cultures of non-Western "primitives" prior to their impending extinction. Without the work of anthropologists, "The day will come when the last primitive culture will have disappeared from the earth, compelling us to realize only too late that the fundamentals of mankind are irretrievably lost" (1966: 124). This imagined disappearance was hastened by the homogenizing effects of colonialism, not the least of which were colonial-era motor roads and railroads.

3. See, e.g., Appadurai 1988; Rosaldo 1989; Gupta and Ferguson 1992, 1997. An antecedent for this anthropological shift can be traced to Max Gluckman's (1958) classic account of the opening of a road bridge in Zululand, while nonanthropological parallels can be found among such prominent literary theorists as Edward Said (1994) and Stephen Greenblatt (2010).

4. Africanist anthropologists, beginning especially with Johannes Fabian (1983), have been at the forefront of challenging the Hegelian picture.

5. Noting the pervasiveness of this attitude among historians and geographers, John B. Jackson argues for seeing roads not merely as leading to places but as places themselves—generative sites of leisure, sociality, and excitement (1994: 190).

6. Among those for whom such thinking is scarcely present, I single out Padre Giuseppe Frizzi, an Italian-born Catholic priest who has worked for nearly three decades in Maúa district. His detailed linguistic (Filippi and Frizzi 2005) and ethnological (Frizzi 2008) research among the Makhuwa has been generative for my own work, and I critically but appreciatively engage it at various points in this book.

7. According to Renato Rosaldo, "Most anthropological studies of death eliminate emotions by assuming the position of the most detached observer" (1989: 15). Extrapolating from his profoundly personal experience of loss and grief in the field, Rosaldo argues that scholarly writing aiming at objectivity and neutrality inevitably removes itself from the commonplace idioms of the everyday. Death, for the anthropologist as technician, becomes a matter of ritual rather than bereavement, of formalized routines rather than open-ended practices of empathy, care, and concern.

8. Derived through the Swahili *sadaka* and ultimately the Arabic *sadaqah* (voluntary charity), this word used for the funerary rites of the Makhuwa suggests, according to Edward Alpers, "the partial Islamization of pre-Islamic religious practices" among the Makhuwa (2000: 313).

9. This narrative has been challenged by biblical scholars who argue that Paul was not, as is commonly thought, converted by Christ to a new religion. He was, rather, called by Christ to a prophetic mission; he remained Jewish throughout his life (Stendahl 1976).

10. The formative factor may more generally be Christian ideas of time: the linearity and irreversibility implied in Christianity's central narrative of Jesus Christ's birth, crucifixion, death, and resurrection, each understood as a unique, unrepeatable event. Historian Mircea Eliade, in his study of "archaic" societies' cyclical temporalities, remarks that "Christian thought tended to transcend, once and for all, the old themes of eternal repetition" (1954: 137).

11. To what extent Renamo should be seen as foreign and to what extent internal to Mozambique is a matter of historiographic debate. Against the prevailing nationalist ideology, anthropologist Christian Geffray (1990a) argues that one of the reasons Renamo proved capable of gaining support in the countryside is because of Frelimo's policies that disenfranchised peasant populations. One policy in particular, that of agricultural collectivization (to be discussed in Chapter 2) arose out of Frelimo's project of socialist reform. The appearance of the hoe along with the rifle in Mozambique's 1983 flag could therefore be seen as an expression of this effort to "modernize" and appropriate the output of Mozambique's largely agrarian population.

12. The Makonde African National Union (MANU) was the most significant proto-nationalist force during the late colonial period. Its significance beyond the Makonde people is illustrated by its name change: to the Mozambique African National Union. The 1960 massacre of MANU supporters on the Mueda plateau—heartland of the Makonde—is cited as one of the chief catalysts of the war of independence. MANU later merged with two other proto-nationalist organizations to become Frelimo (West 2005: 134–36).

13. Historian Patrick Chabal distinguishes between "the northern Makonde people (integrated with Frelimo) and their Makua neighbours (who were not)" (2002: 114).

14. Significantly, outside the continent as well, the history of settlement is no less a history of movement, a paradox that philosopher Kwame Anthony Appiah has captured nicely: "In geological terms, it has been a blink of an eye since human beings first left Africa, and there are few spots where we have not found habitation. The urge to migrate is no less 'natural' than the urge to settle" (2006: xviii). Whether within Africa or "out of Africa," migration has long been an utterly unexceptional mode of human being.

15. The Makhuwa subgroups (Makhuwa-Metto and Makhuwa-Xirima) residing in Maúa district, each of which speaks its own dialect, testify through their very names to this migratory past. Metto literally means "legs," the root "et" itself denoting "movement" in many Bantu languages, while Xirima derives from the word *exerema*—slope or embankment, a likely reference to the slopes of Mount Namuli down which the first humans descended and up which spirits (*minepa*) reascend after death.

16. However, this did not prevent people from maintaining the circular pattern of mobility. Stephen Lubkemann notes this at the transnational scale, in his study of wartime migrations among central Mozambicans. Arguing against the view expressed in humanitarian discourse that refugees would—and should—return "home" permanently after the war, Lubkemann notes that, "most Machazian men living in the periurban townships of South Africa at the end of the war did not see the reestablishment of a home in Mozambique as an option that precluded them from also maintaining households in South Africa." Lubkemann refers to these transnational life strategies, involving regular crossings and recrossings between South Africa and Mozambique as a "revolving-door" phenomenon (2008: 266–74).

17. The threat of warfare infuses present experience as well. Troubling signs began to emerge in 2013, immediately following my main fieldwork period, that over twenty years of

relative peace and stability may be unraveling. A sporadic and low-intensity return to political violence—between the Frelimo government and Renamo opposition—has since then played out in Mozambique's central and northern provinces (see Bertelsen 2016). As I send this book to press, in early 2017, tensions appear to be less dire and widespread than they were during the devastating civil war between the same two factions. Nevertheless, the friends I visited in August 2016, on my most recent return to Maúa district, appeared as poised as ever to deploy the time-honored tactics of flight and evasion that I describe in this chapter and the next.

18. On Africa's long history of flexible mobility, see Kopytoff 1987; de Bruijn, van Dijk, and Foeken 2001; Nyamnjoh 2013; Mavhunga 2014; Silva 2015.

19. For an elaboration, see H. West 2004.

20. While every telling of this myth entails a retelling, this one best approximates the renditions I most heard during my fieldwork year. A slight but significant variation has been documented by the Spanish Catholic priest and anthropologist Francisco Lerma Martínez (1989: 40–43). In this version, the first person was a man, not a woman. I presented this discrepancy to my research assistants, who suggested that Lerma Martínez's informants hid from him the version that would have been most familiar to them so as to make the Makhuwa origin myth conform to the biblical account. There, of course, the woman (Eve) derives from man (Adam), not the reverse. Foregrounded in the version told to me is the primacy of the feminine—specifically, as alluded to within the myth itself, the primacy of menstrual blood. The theme of womanhood is central for the matrilineal Makhuwa, as evidenced by its recurrence throughout this book (specifically in Chapters 3 and 5). For still different versions of the Makhuwa origin myth, see de Castro 1941: 9–13; Macaire 1996: 19–24.

21. Luisinha's *munepa* had visited both Fátima and Fátima's mother in dreams, in which she informed them she was hungry. Without hesitation Fátima's family back in Kaveya organized an *esataka* ceremony. Jemusse and Fátima contributed sacks of rice and three chickens, though they themselves did not attend. This was not an uncommon modus vivendi worked out by Pentecostals, a kind of participation in funerary rites that would satisfy both communities of obligation (spiritual kin and biological kin) without making one way of living, and of dying, exclusive of the other.

Chapter 2

1. By comparison, the densest province is Maputo Province at fifty-eight persons per square kilometer, and the national average is thirty persons per square kilometer (Instituto Nacional de Estatística 2013: 20).

2. On this point, see Newitt 1995: 508; Lubkemann 2008: 51–54; Funada-Classen 2012: 115–16.

3. Newitt notes that the peculiarly narrow shape of Mozambique was especially conducive to the latter, as most populations lived in relative proximity to the frontiers of British Africa (1995: 414).

4. For further detail on the communal villages and their dissonance with the priorities and prerogatives of rural populations, see Hall and Young 1997: 73–114; Bowen 2000: 43–44; Pitcher 2002: 85–89; West 2005: 175–76; Lubkemann 2008: 141–45.

5. As political scientist M. Anne Pitcher notes, "For some smallholders, only a change in name differentiated what they did in the colonial period from what they did in the postcolonial period. . . . Otherwise, little changed except for the persons who profited from their production" (2002: 93).

6. See Pitcher 2002: 88. For a diagram of a typical *aldeia comunal*, formerly an *aldeamento*—this one in the district of Maúa—see Lerma Martínez 1989: 30, fig. 9.

7. For a description of these practices in Nampula Province, see Pitcher 2002: 98; and in Manica Province, see Lubkemann 2008: 142, 195.

8. A considerable body of research complicates the common celebration of postwar Mozambique as exemplarily stable, peaceful, and pluralistic, calling attention instead to the ongoing confrontations between state institutions and traditional authorities. See, e.g., Bertelsen 2003, 2016; Kyed 2009; Igreja 2014.

9. Established by the United Nations in 2000 and agreed to by all (at the time) 189 UN member nations, the Millennium Development Goals included as their most prominent objective that of eradicating extreme hunger and poverty by 2015.

10. A clinic once located near Kaveya village could likely have saved Luisinha's life had the district government not shut it down just two years before the fatal snakebite discussed in Chapter 1.

11. A 2005 wildlife management working paper confirms the threat posed in the north of Mozambique generally, and in Maúa district specifically: "The occurrence of human-elephant conflict in the province [of Niassa] is widespread. The intensity of conflict is probably greatest close to Niassa Reserve but there are low densities of elephant and persistent human-elephant conflict around Majune, Maua [*sic*] and Nipepe which are more than 150km from the Niassa Reserve" (Anderson and Pariela 2005: 16).

12. This is the "Lei de Florestas e Fauna Bravia," Law no. 10/99. The criminalization of local hunting is best expressed in the introduction of the term "poaching" in Anglophone countries such as neighboring Zimbabwe. This is the term for the illegitimate killing of animals, even when it involves hunting traditions developed and practiced sustainably by peasant populations for millennia. In other words, it is a term meant to proscribe all hunting except that sanctioned by the state (Mavhunga 2014: 6–7).

13. As a recent report on the economics of lion hunting in Africa suggests, there is nothing uncommon about the lack of financial recompense for those communities most affected by trophy hunting (Economists at Large 2013).

14. Since my primary fieldwork period (2011–12), the politics around this issue have fortunately shifted in villagers' favor. I remember in 2012 sitting with Maúa's agriculture secretary in his district office—two massive elephant tusks emanating from copper bases on either side of his desk—while he explained how villagers could not possibly be trusted to use firearms responsibly. By the time of my first return visit, in 2014, his successor had the gaudy office display removed, a move that bespoke a more substantive shift enacted by the new district administration: it now permitted defensive hunting among appointed community members, and provided them with limited quantities of arms and ammunition. A full analysis of why this policy shift occurred when it did lies beyond the scope of my present argument. The happy bottom line is that by 2016, my last visit to Maúa before sending this book to press, elephant-human conflicts had effectively ceased (whether permanently or not remains to be seen).

15. For a discussion of these structures, see Macaire 1996: 362–65. They are just a bit sturdier than the makeshift lean-to structures built in the bush by those who fled communal villages (Lubkemann 2008: 195).

16. The physical act of moving would not have been the problem. Given the minimal labor that goes into home construction, reconstructing our village base elsewhere could have

been done with ease. The problem would have been disappointing Jemusse and Fátima, and relinquishing a bit of the bond we had been building with them. Thankfully, within a few weeks, the visitor reached the quota of produce he needed and set off back to Nampula.

17. That is partially why anthropologist Elia Ciscato chooses the segmented spiral as his interpretive key for conveying the dynamism of Makhuwa personhood (2012: 35–39).

18. With respect to the anthropological study of time, Alfred Gell similarly argues for the copresence of circularity and linearity. He questions the frequency with which these two conceptions of time are opposed, since circular time—in which moments of time recur—does not logically preclude a linear sequencing of events. The recurrence of an event necessarily transpires at a time that follows its original occurrence. Thus, "it is only with respect to . . . a linear time-axis that any event could ever be said to have 'repeated' itself" (Gell 1992: 35).

19. This copresence of the curvilinear and the rectilinear is pronounced elsewhere among the Makhuwa—in circular winnowing sieves into which are braided concentric jagged edges, or in such cylindrical objects as rolled-up mats, handbags, and baskets that develop from rectangular bases (Gerdes 2000: 101–29; Gerdes 2010: 233).

20. Political scientist Éric Morier-Genoud (1996, 2009) provides the clearest overviews of Mozambique's postcolonial transitions as they relate to state policies toward religion.

21. The sense of roots as anchors is, of course, commonplace. Its invocation by African American intellectuals (e.g., Gates 2009), however, has an ironic ring to it in light of the Makhuwa interpretation of "roots" to be elaborated here. The irony is in the search for genealogical "roots" in the African continent, where "rootedness" may not in all cases matter in quite the same way. Cultural theorist Paul Gilroy makes a persuasive case for attending equally to the significance of roots *and* routes within the regional complex of the black Atlantic, so as to "undermine the purified appeal of either Africentrism or the Eurocentrisms it struggles to answer," and to do so by acknowledging "the flows, exchanges, and in-between elements that call the very desire to be centred into question" (1993: 190).

22. Among the Nyanja, also of Niassa Province, similar conceptions of the vitalizing and mobilizing properties of blood circulation play out in local explanations of the digestive process (Huhn 2013).

23. Mario Aguilar takes a similar approach in his study among the Waso Boorana of Kenya. Aguilar attributes the fluidity of their passages between Islam and traditional practices to aspects of the lifeworld falling outside the domain of religion per se. Particularly important for the Waso Boorana are strategies of diversification pertaining to their subsistence economy. "The reasons for this process of religious diversification throughout their history," Aguilar notes, "are to be found in their own way of diversifying their herds, in order to face drought, famine and political changes" (1995: 526).

24. In Southeast Asia, all-weather roads and modern information technologies have enabled political states and capital markets to extend their sovereignty almost infinitely, to achieve something close to a "final enclosure" (Scott 2009: 10–11).

Chapter 3

1. Both Deleuze (1988) and Braidotti (2011) provide helpful historical overviews of this process-oriented philosophy.

2. As much as anywhere, one sees this in southern Africa, along the borders separating South Africa from its relatively impoverished neighbors, including Mozambique (McDonald 2000).

3. James's concern is to guard against ontologizing change and motion to the point of excluding any possible experience of stability. It is to prevent multiplicity from turning into the very singularity that would be undone (Game 1997).

4. Thomas Tweed (2006) has elaborated a theory of religion that juxtaposes crossing and dwelling, arguing that both movement across space (crossing) and finding a place (dwelling) characterize what religion is and does. In a sympathetic critique, Manuel Vasquez pushes Tweed to temper his reliance on such aquatic metaphors as "flows" and "confluences" with a fuller accounting of the politics of segregation, surveillance, and control (2011: 286–97).

5. This point is a leitmotif in Jackson's work among the Kuranko (see, e.g., 2005: 60–64). Border passages are also crucial for the work of healers who procure their most potent therapeutic substances not only by venturing into the bush but also by circulating across long distances that may even include the crossing of national or other juridical borders (Luedke and West 2006).

6. For other examples of Catholic sponsorship of African initiation rites, see Rasing 1995; Cox 1998; West 2005: 115–16.

7. According to T. O. Beidelman, who observed the wild pig ritual in Ngulu initiation (Tanzania), the hunt at once represents sexual congress and epitomizes male control over both the disorderliness of femininity and the destructiveness of wildlife (1964: 371).

8. That initiatory teachings are accompanied by such ordeals as sleep deprivation is vital, given that an overriding purpose of initiation rites is to learn how to accept and endure adversity (Jackson 2005: 143).

9. Elsewhere Beidelman writes of the Tanzanian rites he studied that "Kaguru ceremonies of initiation resemble Western notions of history and autobiography" (1997: 133), implying with this a teleological and irreversible progression.

10. Nor do mothers cease to be precious for their sons. As with the Akan of Ghana, so too with the Makhuwa, even into adulthood: "a mother is the most cherished person in a man's life" (Oduyoye 1995: 46). It would be hard to overstate the importance of motherhood and the mother-child bond among African peoples generally (Stephens 2013). The Makhuwa compare mothers to *mutholo* trees, the sacred trees beneath which ancestral offerings are made and ancestral blessings are sought. The saying *W'amay'awe mahelé: anvuluweliwa etala* (The maternal home is like pearl millet in times of famine) suggests that the life-giving sustenance provided by mothers is not limited to gestation and birth. As monumental as the moment of birth is, it is not regarded as quite the dramatic rupture it is in societies where prolonged physical separation is immediate and literal. Although the newborn is clearly no longer within the mother's body, he or she rarely loses touch with that body. Whether cooking, hoeing, fetching firewood, or dancing, Makhuwa women carry their infants—even their toddlers—on their backs in tightly wrapped *capulana* slings. The continued contact of skin on skin points to a certain incrementalism even to parturition, the first and arguably most radical transition in every human existence (van Gennep [1909] 1960: 41–64).

11. Among scholars of pilgrimage too (mostly under the influence of van Gennep and Turner), consideration of what happens upon return is uncommon. For critical appraisals of this flaw, and of the Western conception of time it reflects, see Frey 2004; Kaell 2014.

12. Here a note on Makhuwa female initiation is warranted. Because of my gender, I was permitted access only to the male initiation ceremony; the roughly coterminous girls' initiation was off limits. Published accounts of Makhuwa female initiation (Arnfred 1990, 2011;

Medeiros 1997; Sheldon 2002: 134–35) record numerous instructional aspects—on, for example, domestic duties, rules of hygiene, and proper respect for adults. Arguably of greatest importance, however, is instruction on relations, especially sexual relations, with men. While in the patrilineal regions of central and southern Mozambique girls learn to serve men and suppress female expression, in the matrilineal north the rites serve as sites of female camaraderie and enjoyment. Thus, in the north, the fiercest opposition to these rites' bans by the colonial-era Catholic Church and the socialist-era Frelimo state came from women themselves. Furthermore, while genital manipulation has long played a role, this is not the controversial surgical intervention known as genital cutting or, polemically, as genital mutilation. It is, rather, the elongation of the labia, intended to get the girl "acquainted with her own sexual potential at an early age" and to prepare her for what any man with whom she has intercourse knows to do: similarly to stimulate the labia so as to enhance the erotic experience of both partners (Arnfred 2011: 43). Suggested by studies of the Makhuwa (see also those of the Baganda in Tamale 2005) is a significant contrast to those that fixate—at times pornographically (see Nnaemeka 2005)—on the ordeal of genital cutting, portraying it as essential to African female initiation and portraying African female initiation as thus irredeemably barbaric. Of relevance to the argument of this chapter, one sees in Makhuwa female initiation—no less than in the male initiation rites I observed—the elevated standing of the feminine. There is a positive reverence for female sexuality, for that which bears most directly on one of the cardinal values held by the Makhuwa, the value of *oyara* (procreation or regeneration).

13. See, e.g., Meigs 1984; de Heusch 1985; Silverman 2003.

14. In the important volume revising earlier anthropological readings of menstrual blood, from whose introduction I drew the preceding quotation, see especially Alma Gottlieb's (1988) ethnographic chapter on menstrual practices among the Beng of Côte d'Ivoire. For the Beng, menstrual blood symbolizes not female pollution but human fertility.

15. In fact, because *wula* refers specifically to the experience of first menstruation, distinct from *watala* (to menstruate), "Namuli" may refer to the first menstruation—appropriate given that Mount Namuli bore the first humans into the world.

16. For example, Scott's emphasis on "the element of historical and strategic choice" (2009: 179) behind migration patterns leads him to make such statements as this: "The key act of dissimilation is the assertion 'We are a nonstate people. We are in the hills swiddening and foraging because we have placed ourselves at a distance from the valley state'" (2009: 174). That Scott put this declaration of choice and intention in quotation marks yet without attributing it to an actual person underscores his problematic invocation of what Timothy Mitchell calls "the unexpected figure of the rational peasant" (1990: 548). This is likewise what Lila Abu-Lughod refers to as the misattribution to those we study of "forms of consciousness or politics that are not part of their experience" (1990: 47).

17. I borrow the term "proteanism" from psychiatrist Robert Jay Lifton, who argues in *The Protean Self: Human Resilience in an Age of Fragmentation* (1993) for a view of subjectivity as continually subject to reinvention. Michael Brown (1996), in his own critique of the anthropological infatuation with resistance, cites Lifton in support of his argument that human actions easily interpretable as opposition to domination may be experienced by actors themselves as an expansion or transcendence of the self. Brown offers as an example the same kinds of identity play I discuss in this section. I concur with both Brown and Lifton, though

I find problematic Lifton's assumption that proteanism is exceptionally characteristic of contemporary, postmodern America. Counterintuitively, and as evidence from this book suggests, the mutability of the self is perhaps even more readily observable in "traditional" African societies (see, e.g., McGovern 2013: 27–62). That Brown bases his rereading of resistance on ethnographic work done on both American channeling and Asháninka prophecy supports this critique of American exceptionalism.

18. It is important to consider that initiation rites are as much for the already initiated as for the initiates (La Fontaine 1985: 104).

19. Anthropologist Signe Arnfred confirms that this duality also obtains in female initiation rites among the Makhuwa: "The same occasion, which for the initiates is a frightening and harrowing event focused on the serious business of introduction to adulthood, for the older women is an opportunity for unending childishness and types of exalted behaviour, which under normal conditions they would never allow themselves" (2011: 145).

20. Drawing on fieldwork from southern Mozambique, Morten Nielsen (2012) likewise aims to collapse the distance theorists typically presume to exist between "inside" and "outside," preferring instead to stress the fuzziness of the assumed distinction and the capacity of human beings to enfold exteriority, starting from within.

Chapter 4

1. This is true of African languages more generally (Brenner 1989; Shaw 1990).

2. For Africans living along Mozambique's coast, incorporation into this broader world began possibly as far back as the eighth century. However, in the hinterland location where I lived and worked, Swahili acculturation came only in the nineteenth century (Newitt 1995: 437–38; Bonate 2010).

3. As early as the sixteenth century, Jesuits and Dominicans installed a Roman Catholic presence in parts of what is now known as northern Mozambique. There is no evidence of their presence in the region where I worked, however, and their efforts were minimally successful anyway due to their dissolution and expulsion (Newitt 1995: 122–26). Only with the Consolata order's arrival in 1926 did Catholicism spread among the local population.

4. Today, *musikitti* is especially heard in villages where Catholic churches and schools have been most influential; elsewhere, *ejuma* is more commonly used. This difference may not be surprising in light of scholars' insight that it is in apologetic and polemical discourses occasioned by encounters with Western colonialism and Christianity that Islam developed much of its systematic reification (Smith 1963: 115–18). Of course, *musikitti* derives ultimately from the Arabic *masjid*, and mosque architecture is of great significance to Islam. But, differently from Christian churches, the *masjid* is tied more to the act of prayer than to a necessarily enclosed structure (Hillenbrand 1994: 31).

5. This is abundantly evident in their prodigious scholarship on the Makhuwa, much of which I cite throughout this book. See, e.g., Lerma Martínez 1989; Ciscato 1989, 2012; Filippi and Frizzi 2005; Frizzi 2008; Brambilla 2009.

6. Each ethnolinguistic group, or "tribe," was itself reified as such largely due to the epistemological interventions of a host of outsiders, especially missionaries and anthropologists (Vail 1989; Ranger 1989; Amselle 1998; Peel 2000; Harries 2007).

7. It is ironic, therefore, that some theorists of globalization and transnationalism have suggested that modernity is distinguished by incessant mobility unimpaired by borders and boundaries. In fact the greatest impact of colonial modernity was the imposition of a global

system of nation-states that use ports of entry and travel documents to order and discipline otherwise mobile people (Salazar and Smart 2011: iii).

8. Indeed, the postcolonial Frelimo regime was considerably blunter in its opposition to local culture (which it deemed "obscurantist") than was the colonial-era Catholic Church (Lubkemann 2008: 132). Of greatest epistemological consequence, though, was the dualism of such thinking. As M. Anne Pitcher notes, "After 1977 [the year Frelimo declared itself a Marxist-Leninist party and implemented its program of socialist modernization], one was either progressive or reactionary, Mozambican or foreign, modern or traditional" (2002: 57). Despite such dichotomies, institutions deemed obscurantist did not disappear. Rather they operated clandestinely, drawing people to them secretly at night rather than openly in the light of day (Honwana 2002: 169–73).

9. Smith therefore takes his perspicacious genealogy of religion a step too far by moving that the word "religion" be dropped (1963: 50). Missing from his analysis is an account of how phenomenologically consequential the category has become for many people, including many of those previously without it.

10. Indeed, in the context of ethnopolitical struggles that have only intensified in the postcolonial era, an anti-syncretic emphasis on boundaries, purities, and strategic essentialisms has become as prominent a mode of religious being as any (Stewart and Shaw 1994).

11. For examples of hybridity in popular Christianity, see Orsi 1985; Taylor 1996; Tweed 1997.

12. In Kaveya village, for example, no ritual has been organized since the one attended by Florêncio and described in Chapter 3. That was in 2009. Besides the challenge of reviving the ritual after decades of government prohibition, other reasons given to me by village chiefs as to why initiation ceremonies are so uncommon today include their increasing costs (or, more basically, the increasing monetization of goods and services for people still relatively marginal to monetary markets) and the concern that spending weeks in the bush leaves not only ritual participants but also family members, compounds, and farms vulnerable to elephant invasions. For the elevation, in recent years, of this preoccupation with elephants, see Chapter 2.

13. For evidence of the encyclopedic thoroughness of Padre Frizzi's ethnographic work, see Frizzi 2008.

14. This should not be confused with the notion of multiple ontologies advanced in recent anthropological theory. For a critique of how the "ontological turn" has replicated sociocultural anthropology's long-standing fallacy of conflating theories of knowledge with modes of being, see Jackson and Piette 2015: 19–20.

15. For a classic illustration of this type of compartmentalized multiplicity—multiplicity that is premised on bounded zones and thus irreducible to the totalizing structure of syncretism or hybridity—see Spicer 1954.

16. Juan Obarrio furnishes evidence that the resurgence of the customary in neoliberal Mozambique is lived in similar ways. Take, for example, a person Obarrio refers to as "the president-judge," who both presides over one of northern Mozambique's community courts (an entity of the state) and, at a separate time and in a separate space, conducts divination and healing sessions. According to Obarrio, "There were very few continuities between his two fields of activity: divination and justice. Instead of both spaces being interconnected,

channeling conflicts and cases from one to the other, actually a deep fracture existed between the world of invisible justice and the world of legible law" (2014: 146). Obarrio's example suggests a critique, similar to McIntosh's, of hybridity thinking—in the context of his study, the efforts of the neoliberal state to revive the customary and conjoin it to the juridical. The president-judge's ability to inhabit these two worlds across "a deep fracture" owes largely to the postcolonial state's efforts, during its socialist phase, to disqualify such "obscurantist" activities as divination. An epistemology of separation into spheres was introduced, though it was not necessarily received along with the implication that one sphere be renounced. This would have confounded the Frelimo state in its socialist phase. But because the epistemology of separation remains salient into the present (still without the originally intended implication), there is less interest on the part of people like the president-judge to bring "the traditional" and "the modern" into a unitary frame than in letting disparate domains remain disparate. This, Obarrio argues, confounds the Frelimo state in its neoliberal phase.

17. A parallel to such conversion patterns may be found in migration trends following European powers' late nineteenth-century imposition of national borders on Africa. These borders are constructed, yet real; and they are real, yet permeable. They may be traversed, and they may be re-traversed. Indeed, as evidence from the region of my fieldwork shows, they regularly are (Englund 2002).

18. This point finds expression in existentialist Gabriel Marcel's reflections on the necessarily provisional nature of convictions. One cannot possibly anticipate all future scenarios, some of which may cause one's convictions to shake. To decide in advance to remain constant whatever the future holds would require great hubris or an untenable willingness to cease reflection. Thus, Marcel argues, the best one can say regarding one's convictions is that, *at the present moment*, one cannot imagine their being altered (1964: 131–33).

19. On intellectualist, meaning-oriented aspects of conversion, see Horton 1971, 1975a, 1975b; Hefner 1993.

20. The answer, for George Devereux (1967), is clear: anthropological systematizing offers anthropologists a means of coping with the unique anxieties faced in the course of fieldwork—in the move from familiar to foreign circumstances, a move usually accompanied by the loss of any semblance of comprehension and control.

21. Medical anthropologists have long challenged the notion of people, particularly in precarious circumstances, aligning themselves with a single medical system. John Janzen (1978), for example, situates the "quest for therapy" in lower Zaire within a context of "medical pluralism." Likewise, Arthur Kleinman writes of health seekers in China as unbound by the reductionist logic of Western biomedicine. For them, "the use of all available treatment interventions is pragmatic" (1980: 93). Studies of health-seeking strategies amid Mozambique's own medically pluralistic context include Luedke 2006; Granjo 2009; Chapman 2010.

22. On African pragmatism generally, see Jackson 1989; Whyte 1997. On African pragmatism as it relates to the practice of religion, see Kirsch 2004; Englund 2007; van Wyk 2014.

23. James Scott uses the Greek term *mētis* to describe this kind of practical skill, acquired intelligence, and vernacular knowledge (1998: 309–41). By virtue of its essential plasticity, this practical logic—applied situationally by people on the margins of power—contrasts sharply with the totalizing, abstract, and theoretical logic underpinning top-heavy projects of social engineering.

Chapter 5

1. The curvilinear shape of the crucifix is distinctive to Makhuwa art, encouraged by Padre Giuseppe Frizzi as an expression of the non-Cartesian qualities of Makhuwa culture (see Chapter 2).

2. Neuza's retreat into the bush for the purpose of prayer resonates with what Richard Werbner (1985) and Isabel Mukonyora (2006, 2007) both observed in their studies of Zimbabwe's Masowe Apostles. Werbner refers to this African Initiated Church as the Wilderness Church because its members literally wandered to the edges of settlements to conduct worship. Mukonyora calls this a diasporic practice *internal* to the African continent, one that women particularly enacted in response to the patriarchy of Shona ancestral rituals. "Not only were women accustomed to working outdoors," Mukonyora writes, "but they sometimes wandered into the bush because men had excluded them from parts of their ritual activities" (2006: 71).

3. Suggested in this tale is a critique of modern liberalism's view of unfettered autonomy as the only route to human flourishing. Submission and surrender—to God's will, in the case described here—may be a mode of agency, a means of attaining contentment and fulfillment amid the struggles of daily life. The scholarship recasting women's empowerment through—not against—nonliberal regimes of religious power is vast and compelling (see, e.g., Griffith 1997; Mariz and Machado 1997; Mahmood 2005).

4. See Christian Geffray's (1990b) exhaustive study of Makhuwa matrilineality, which has been historically so prominent that the spread of a more patriarchal model of social organization via Islam, in the nineteenth century, did little to alter it (Bonate 2010: 582–83).

5. For more on the *apwiyamwene*, see Lerma Martínez 1989: 74–76; Medeiros 2007: 103–5.

6. The literature on women-centered leadership in "traditional" (supposedly patriarchal) societies and religions is considerable. It includes, for example, Queen Mothers in Akan polities of Ghana (Oduyoye 1995), female authority and agency in African diaspora religious traditions (Stewart 2004; Hucks 2006; Harding 2006), and "gynocracies" among the Pueblo Indians of the American Southwest (Allen 1986).

7. Questionnaire data about the receipt and control of household income, collected in Makhuwa districts in 1994, support these observations. Among the women surveyed, a majority reported seeing the income their husbands made, and 75 percent reported keeping it until it was needed for purchases (Pitcher 1996b: 106).

8. Signe Arnfred, who conducted extensive fieldwork among the Makhuwa of Ribáuè (inland Nampula Province), observed much the same. She writes: "It was evident from living in Ribáuè that women more than men are the ones with a 'direct line' to the spirit world. . . . In an all night spirit-ceremony which I attended in the mountains, both men and women were present, but all those in charge of proceedings were women, as were those who fell into a trance and through whom the spirits spoke" (2011: 237).

9. In such a residence pattern, explains Arnfred, in addition to men relocating to the woman's compound, at which they are first received as strangers, "after divorce it is the man who moves out; the woman stays in the house with the children" (2011: 46).

10. Indeed, as Malyn Newitt contends, Islam in particular proved attractive to Makhuwa men in the nineteenth century for the new forms of authority and control it offered them: "Islam—with its patrilineal and patriarchal institutions—offered unique opportunities to men in matrilineal societies to establish new patterns of social and political relations" (1995: 438).

11. See, e.g., Cucchiari 1990; Brusco 1995; Butler 2007; Casselberry 2017.

12. This gender separation in fact is written into the words that have come to translate spatial directions: the right hand side is spoken of as *mono wolopwana* (literally, arm of man) while the left hand side is spoken of as *mono wothiyana* (literally, arm of woman).

13. Mozambique, particularly its central and southern regions, is the site of extensive research on Pentecostalism's appeal to women and on women's deployment of Pentecostalism in the context of neoliberalism and globalization (Pfeiffer, Gimbel-Sherr, and Augusto 2007; Schuetze 2010; van de Kamp 2016).

14. A similar argument has been made about tribal and ethnic ideologies. These too were colonial constructions in which men, more than women, saw reason to invest. In strikingly similar terms to those at the center of this chapter, Leroy Vail observed among the Tswana of southwestern Africa that "ethnicity's appeal was strongest for men . . . and the Tswana proverb to the effect that 'women have no tribe' had a real—if unintended—element of truth in it" (1989: 15).

15. Moreover, these are generally the forces that manifest at night, as do women healers (a point made earlier in this chapter). Arnfred nicely connects this fact of differing temporalities—diurnal vs. nocturnal—to the contrast between men's and women's spheres of power and influence. "Government programmes of development take place in broad daylight. This is when the men of Frelimo, of the local government—and also of the Catholic/Protestant churches—take over. . . . When night falls and when Europeans go to bed—this is when a different life takes over" (2011: 17–18).

16. The oral and embodied nature of ancestral religiosity has been explored throughout this book. I document parallel features of Pentecostalism in Chapter 6.

17. With respect to girls' educational access, the disparity between northern rural districts such as Maúa and the rest of the country is long-standing. As Kathleen Sheldon has observed about the Portuguese colonial period, "The rate of female education was not the same for the country as a whole. . . Enrollment figures for all of Mozambique demonstrate that in areas more distant from the capital city girls constituted one-third or less of the student population" (2002: 98).

18. This was the case at least for boys, who were taught carpentry and furniture making, iron work, and other crafts that integrated them into the colonial and later postcolonial economy. Girls' education, during the colonial period especially, focused on lessons of domestic economy (Sheldon 2002: 90–91). Thus, of importance is the disparity between boys and girls not only in access to education, but also in the kind of education each had access to.

19. Regional differences in Mozambique's economic development were always immense. Colonial-era Mozambique's period of greatest modernization was largely confined to the cities of Beira and Lourenço Marques (contemporary Maputo). Thus, Newitt notes, "Vast areas of the country saw little or nothing of this modern development. Most of the north had no roads, no railways, no airstrips, no telecommunications and no power supplies. Although forced cotton growing continued throughout the 1940s and the plantation companies continued to recruit large numbers of workers for the sugar plantations, the north of Mozambique remained pre-eminently a land of peasant farmers and peasant communities ruled in traditional fashion by the bizarre coming together of matrilineal Makua homesteads with patriarchal Islamic chieftaincies" (1995: 469–70).

20. This irony has played out in numerous societies around the world. See, e.g., Leacock 1981; Allen 1986; Amadiume 1987; Oduyoye 1995.

21. Although these 1997 census data (available in *Perfil do Distrito de Maúa* 2005: 11) are somewhat outdated, still the vast majority of inhabitants in the district with whom I interacted in 2011 and 2012 were not conversant in Portuguese.

22. See, e.g., Fortes 1987; Jackson and Karp 1990; Piot 1991; Comaroff and Comaroff 2001.

23. These foremothers, Walker argues, did not (could not) expect a room of their own but made space for themselves by creating gardens out of whatever rocky soils they landed on. Without a room of their own, these mothers were consigned to hardship and anonymity, but this was the precondition, the enabling parameter, for their creativity, for their ability to dwell not in possessions but in possibilities.

24. Critical theorists from Hannah Arendt (1944) to Edward Said (1984) have noted the paradoxically privileged status of the outsider, the exile, and the pariah—those who, by virtue of their forced detachment from acceptable sociopolitical orders, achieve the critical distance necessary to contest their orthodoxies.

Chapter 6

1. It was not the only dance; the *eyinlo* repertoire is vast (Frizzi 2008: 1535–675).

2. That this recalling of the ancestor occurred with bare feet dancing upon bare soil confirms the point argued in Chapter 4—that there is a grounded, terrestrial quality even to Makhuwa conceptions of the afterlife.

3. In these churches, one is not allowed "to cry," it was often said. It was an interesting word choice because while there was crying at *esataka* ceremonies, there was little outward display of grief at this *eyinlo*. Yet crying is in fact the etymological root of the word: *eyinlo* derives from the verb *winla*, to cry (Frizzi 2008: 1535). While joy was on the surface, sorrow was, even etymologically, close at hand. This is akin to philosopher Cornel West's description of the blues sensibility born out of African American slavery. Blues music expresses hope in a tragicomic register, seeking transcendence of dehumanizing situations not through repression or willful forgetting but through an honest confrontation of life at its most sorrowful (2004: 19–21).

4. For the original phrasing of the insight that conversion *to* need not entail conversion *from*, here with respect to Islam in Mayotte, see Lambek 2000: 65–68.

5. I make this point in full agreement with Joel Robbins, leading theorist of the anthropology of Christianity, when he writes that, "even taking into account the difficulty of settling on appropriate grounds for deciding whether the anthropology of Christianity is really something new, it remains the case that several interesting and important questions arise if one argues that it is, and perhaps in intellectually pragmatic terms this makes its novelty worth positing" (2014: S159). Thus, while this book is largely a challenge to foundational premises in the anthropology of Christianity—most significantly the notion that it is epistemologically novel in the same way that it presumes Pentecostal rupture to be phenomenologically novel—the current chapter aims to engage and even contribute to the anthropology of Christianity on its own terms.

6. In a similar vein, Jon Bialecki (2012), responding to the critique that Christianity is not a viable object of anthropological inquiry, offers a compelling analysis that employs the Deleuzian notion of the assemblage. Bialecki argues, against contemporary anthropology's tendency to reject abstractions and universals of any sort, that assemblage and the theory of

"virtual realism" within which it is properly embedded offer a means to conceive totalities—such as Christianity—virtually: not as unitary actualities but as heterogeneous potentialities.

7. Body *hexis* is anthropologist Pierre Bourdieu's term for the performative dimension of the *habitus* (1977: 87–95).

8. In a discussion of Pentecostalism's kinesthetic approach to worship, Daniel Albrecht provides a fairly exhaustive compendium of what this includes: swaying, dancing, clapping, applauding, raising hands, joining hands, extending hands, falling "under the power," bowing, kneeling, and spontaneously standing and sitting (1999: 148). See also Csordas 1997.

9. For more on the intensity and vigor of ADA worship, see Maxwell 2006a: 197–200.

10. For explorations of the African roots of global Pentecostalism, see MacRobert 1992; Asamoah-Gyadu 2005; Kalu 2008.

11. I made the case for Makhuwa existentialism in Chapter 4 under the section title "Heaven Below." That choice of title was intended to reflect Makhuwa men's and women's grounded conception of life and afterlife. It also aimed to evoke Grant Wacker's (2001) influential history of Pentecostalism's rise in the United States, *Heaven Below: Early Pentecostals and American Culture*. Wacker's title conveys his central argument about early Pentecostals' realist and this-worldly approach to the heavenly and the holy, realms that conventionally were and still are largely idealized, abstracted, and placed in opposition to the everyday.

12. According to Smith, the Reformation-inspired transformation of belief into a propositional assertion helped usher in a conception of religion as a system—a "belief system"—which came to be "a concept of polemics and apologetics" premised on the essential incompatibility of one "belief system" and another (1963: 42–43). Talal Asad similarly argues that the elevation of belief over practice is what made it possible to conceptualize religion "as a set of propositions to which believers gave assent, and which could therefore be judged and compared as between different religions" (1993: 40–41).

13. See Chapter 4 for a discussion of the philosophy of *wasasa ekumi*. Recent Africanist scholarship urging attention to the pragmatic over the propositional aspects of faith focuses on Pentecostalism (e.g., Englund 2007; van Wyk 2014), though a longer line of scholarship suggests that the downplaying of doctrines and beliefs characterizes African Christianity more generally (e.g., van Binsbergen 1981; Ruel 1997; Kirsch 2004).

14. This is not to understate the bodily training and spiritual preparation that are required of participants in Pentecostal churches. These can be, as Tanya Luhrmann (2012) has argued, quite rigorous and demanding. Nevertheless, they are bestowed more by acts of submission than by drawn-out processes of intellectual formation and therefore make for a more frictionless point of entry.

15. James's work is thus eminently useful for anthropologists, as the radically empiricist ethnographies of Paul Stoller and Michael Jackson abundantly illustrate (see, e.g., Stoller 1989; Jackson 1989, 2009).

16. For references, see where I have discussed this in the section of the Introduction titled "Existential Mobility."

17. The UCKG is the same Brazil-based Pentecostal church discussed in the Introduction, where I identify it by its Portuguese name Igreja Universal do Reino de Deus, or IURD.

18. Pneumatology (from the Greek *pneuma*, meaning "breath") is that branch of Christian theology dealing with the Holy Spirit.

19. For a vivid instantiation of this theology, consider the Friday Masowe Church of Zimbabwe, which shares with other African Initiated Churches "strong family resemblances"

to Pentecostalism (Engelke 2010: 180). As described by Matthew Engelke (2007), members of this church consider the written Bible—insofar as it represents the binding or closing of God's revelation—as inferior to and even an interference with the "live and direct" encounters they seek with the ongoing, dynamic work of the Holy Spirit.

20. Pentecostal language becomes materialized and embodied by, for example, originating from beyond, rather than from within, the self (Bialecki 2011), by being placed into circulation as if a tangible thing (Coleman 2006), and by materially affecting both speakers and hearers (van Wyk 2014: 141–70). From elsewhere in northern Mozambique, anthropologist Harry West (2007) has similarly argued that the Makonde understand their discourse of sorcery not as metaphorical but as bringing into being the reality of which it speaks.

21. For similar applications of Bourdieu to Pentecostal ritual studies, see Csordas 1997; Coleman and Collins 2000.

22. While endorsing Mahmood's critique of Bourdieu's passive conception of subject formation, I differ with Mahmood regarding what keeps her bound to Bourdieu: her expectation of the enduring quality of any given *habitus*, her view that "it becomes a permanent feature of a person's character" (Mahmood 2005: 136). If, as Mahmood argues, one is not simply born into a certain *habitus* but may play a role in learning it, it seems one may conceivably play a role in unlearning it and/or learning another.

23. See James's (1903) memorable—and memorably titled—essay on the perils of academic specialization, "The Ph.D. Octopus."

Conclusion

1. "Remarks by President Obama to the People of Africa," July 28, 2015, https://obamawhitehouse.archives.gov/the-press-office/2015/07/28/remarks-president-obama-people-africa.

2. *Economist*, December 3, 2011; *Time*, December 3, 2012.

3. Whether such dispositions characterize other societies or are unique to the Makhuwa I leave an open question. It is unanswerable within the scope of this book. It does seem, however, from the number of studies of (again, ironically labeled) "traditional" people referenced throughout this book, that there is no reason to consider the Makhuwa exceptional in this regard.

4. For a philosophical framing of this possibility, see Unger 2007.

5. Nevertheless, the Frelimo state's continued antagonism toward the mobile proclivities of the Makhuwa preserves the gulf that has long separated the state and the peasantry (as argued in Chapter 2). This is likely a factor in the recent rise, throughout central and northern Mozambique, of a new political party: the Democratic Movement of Mozambique (Movimento Democrático de Moçambique).

6. A parallel story may play out with respect to Islam, with merchants from coastal regions and even one I met from Somalia bringing to Maúa a more rigid, reformist version of Islam that, like Pentecostalism, opposes ancestral practices but also, like Pentecostalism, has scarcely caught on. Were this to change, were Islamic identity to become more rigid at the same time Christian identity does, the result might be polarization to the point of conflict, as seen elsewhere in sub-Saharan Africa. Matthews Ojo (2007) has documented the deleterious consequences of clashing religious ideologies resulting from Pentecostal attempts to evangelize in the predominantly Muslim regions of Nigeria. For disconcerting hints that such interreligious strife may be under way among the Makhuwa, at least among the Makhuwa of urban and coastal Nampula, see Morier-Genoud 2000.

7. David Maxwell (2006a) has thoroughly documented the shift toward bureaucracy, bourgeois respectability, and the gospel of money in his historical survey of the Zimbabwe Assemblies of God Africa church, from which the ADA emerged.

8. The CCM is the main Protestant ecumenical body of the country and, like the World Council of Churches, of which it is an affiliate, does not include the Catholic Church. Pentecostal churches are also not affiliated, but in Maúa, given the small non-Catholic Christian presence, the local convener has deemed it fit to break with protocol and invite participation by Maúa's two Pentecostal churches.

WORKS CITED

Abu-Lughod, Lila. 1990. The Romance of Resistance: Tracing Transformations of Power through Bedouin Women. *American Ethnologist* 17 (1): 41–55.

———. 1993. *Writing Women's Worlds: Bedouin Stories.* Berkeley: University of California Press.

Aguilar, Mario. 1995. African Conversion from a World Religion: Religious Diversification by the Waso Boorana in Kenya. *Africa* 65 (4): 525–43.

Ahmad, Attiya. 2017. *Everyday Conversions: Islam, Domestic Work, and South Asian Migrant Women in Kuwait.* Durham: Duke University Press.

Albrecht, Daniel E. 1999. *Rites in the Spirit: A Ritual Approach to Pentecostal/Charismatic Spirituality.* Sheffield: Sheffield Academic Press.

Allen, Paula Gunn. 1986. *The Sacred Hoop: Recovering the Feminine in American Indian Traditions.* Boston: Beacon Press.

Allina, Eric. 2012. *Slavery by Any Other Name: African Life under Company Rule in Colonial Mozambique.* Charlottesville: University of Virginia Press.

Alpers, Edward A. 1975. *Ivory and Slaves: Changing Pattern of International Trade in East Central Africa to the Later Nineteenth Century.* Berkeley: University of California Press.

———. 1997. Slave Trade: Eastern Africa. In *The Encyclopedia of Africa South of the Sahara,* edited by John Middleton. Vol. 4. New York: Scribner's.

———. 2000. East Central Africa. In *The History of Islam in Africa,* edited by Nehemia Levtzion and Randall Lee Pouwels. Athens: Ohio University Press.

Amadiume, Ifi. 1987. *Male Daughters, Female Husbands: Gender and Sex in an African Society.* London: Atlantic Highlands.

———. 1997. *Re-inventing Africa: Matriarchy, Religion, and Culture.* London: Zed Books.

Amselle, Jean-Loup. 1998. *Mestizo Logics: Anthropology of Identity in Africa and Elsewhere.* Stanford: Stanford University Press.

Anderson, Allan. 2010. Varieties, Taxonomies, and Definitions. In *Studying Global Pentecostalism: Theories and Methods,* edited by Allan Anderson, Michael Bergunder, André Droogers, and Cornelis van der Laan. Berkeley: University of California Press.

Anderson, J. L., and F. Pariela. 2005. *Strategies to Mitigate Human-Wildlife Conflict, Mozambique.* Rome: Food and Agriculture Organization of the United Nations.

Anzaldúa, Gloria. 1987. *Borderlands/*La Frontera: *The New Mestiza.* San Francisco: Aunt Lute Books.

Appadurai, Arjun. 1988. Putting Hierarchy in Its Place. *Cultural Anthropology* 3 (1): 36–49.

———. 1996. *Modernity at Large: Cultural Dimensions of Globalization.* Minneapolis: University of Minnesota Press.

Appiah, Kwame Anthony. 2006. *Cosmopolitanism: Ethics in a World of Strangers*. New York: W. W. Norton.

Arendt, Hannah. 1944. The Jew as Pariah: A Hidden Tradition. *Jewish Social Studies* 6 (2): 99–122.

———. 1971. *The Human Condition*. Chicago: University of Chicago Press.

Arnfred, Signe. 1990. Notes on Gender and Modernization: Examples from Mozambique. In *The Language of Development Studies*, edited by Agnete Weis Bentzon. Copenhagen: New Social Science Monographs.

———. 2011. *Sexuality and Gender Politics in Mozambique: Rethinking Gender in Africa*. Oxford: James Currey.

Asad, Talal. 1993. *Genealogies of Religion: Discipline and Reasons of Power in Christianity and Islam*. Baltimore: Johns Hopkins University Press.

Asamoah-Gyadu, J. Kwabena. 2005. *African Charismatics: Current Developments within Independent Indigenous Pentecostalism in Ghana*. Leiden: Brill.

Austin, Diane J. 1981. Born Again . . . and Again and Again: Communitas and Social Change among Jamaican Pentecostalists. *Journal of Anthropological Research* 37 (3): 226–46.

Bascom, William Russell. 1975. *African Dilemma Tales*. The Hague: Mouton.

Beidelman, T. O. 1964. Pig (Guluwe): An Essay on Ngulu Sexual Symbolism and Ceremony. *Southwestern Journal of Anthropology* 20 (4): 359–92.

———. 1965. Notes on Boys' Initiation among the Ngulu of East Africa. *Man* 65: 143–47.

———. 1997. *The Cool Knife: Imagery of Gender, Sexuality, and Moral Education in Kaguru Initiation Ritual*. Washington, D.C.: Smithsonian Institution Press.

———. 2005. Circumcision. In *Encyclopedia of Religion*, edited by Lindsay Jones. 2nd ed. Detroit: Macmillan Reference.

Berger, Peter L. 2012. A Friendly Dissent from Pentecostalism. *First Things* 227: 45–50.

———. 2013. Afterword. In *Global Pentecostalism in the 21st Century*, edited by Robert W. Hefner. Bloomington: Indiana University Press.

Bergson, Henri. 1998. *Creative Evolution*, translated by Arthur Mitchell. Mineola, N.Y.: Dover.

Bertelsen, Bjørn Enge. 2003. "The Traditional Lion Is Dead": The Ambivalent Presence of Tradition and the Relation between Politics and Violence in Mozambique. *Lusotopie* 2003: 263–81.

———. 2016. *Violent Becomings: State Formation, Sociality, and Power in Mozambique*. New York: Berghahn.

Bettelheim, Bruno. 1954. *Symbolic Wounds: Puberty Rites and the Envious Male*. Glencoe, Ill.: Free Press.

Bhabha, Homi. 1994. *The Location of Culture*. London: Routledge.

Bialecki, Jon. 2011. No Caller I.D. for the Soul: Demonization, Charisms, and the Unstable Subject of Protestant Language Ideology. *Anthropological Quarterly* 84 (3): 679–703.

———. 2012. Virtual Christianity in an Age of Nominalist Anthropology. *Anthropological Theory* 12 (3): 295–319.

Bialecki, Jon, and Girish Daswani. 2015. What Is an Individual? The View from Christianity. *Hau: Journal of Ethnographic Theory* 5 (1): 271–94.

Bialecki, Jon, Naomi Haynes, and Joel Robbins. 2008. The Anthropology of Christianity. *Religion Compass* 2 (6): 1139–58.

Bielo, James S. 2011. *Emerging Evangelicals: Faith, Modernity, and the Desire for Authenticity*. New York: New York University Press.

Bonate, Liazzat. 2010. Islam in Northern Mozambique: A Historical Overview. *History Compass* 8 (7): 573–93.

Bourdieu, Pierre. 1977. *Outline of a Theory of Practice.* Translated by Richard Nice. Cambridge: Cambridge University Press.

———. 1990. *The Logic of Practice.* Translated by Richard Nice. Stanford: Stanford University Press.

———. 1991. Rites of Institution. In *Language and Symbolic Power*, edited by John B. Thompson and translated by Gino Raymond and Matthew Adamson. Cambridge: Harvard University Press.

———. 2000. *Pascalian Meditations.* Translated by Richard Nice. Stanford: Stanford University Press.

Bourne, Joel K. 2014. The Next Breadbasket. *National Geographic* 226 (1): 47–73.

Bowen, Merle L. 2000. *The State against the Peasantry: Rural Struggles in Colonial and Postcolonial Mozambique.* Charlottesville: University Press of Virginia.

Braidotti, Rosi. 2011. *Nomadic Theory: The Portable Rosi Braidotti.* New York: Columbia University Press.

Brambilla, Simona. 2009. Evangelizzare il Cuore: L'Evangelizzazione Inculturata tra i Macua Scirima del Mozambico: Uno Studio Antropologico e Psicologico. Ph.D. diss., Pontifical Gregorian University.

Brenner, Louis. 1989. "Religious" Discourses in and about Africa. In *Discourse and Its Disguises: The Interpretation of African Oral Texts*, edited by Karin Barber and P. F. Farias. Birmingham: Centre of West African Studies, University of Birmingham.

Brown, Candy Gunther. 2011. Global Awakenings: Divine Healing Networks and Global Community in North America, Brazil, Mozambique, and Beyond. In *Global Pentecostal and Charismatic Healing*, edited by Candy Gunther Brown. New York: Oxford University Press.

Brown, Michael F. 1996. On Resisting Resistance. *American Anthropologist* 98 (4): 729–35.

Brusco, Elizabeth E. 1995. *The Reformation of Machismo: Evangelical Conversion and Gender in Colombia.* Austin: University of Texas Press.

———. 2010. Gender and Power. In *Studying Global Pentecostalism: Theories and Methods*, edited by Allan Anderson, Michael Bergunder, André Droogers, and Cornelis van der Laan. Berkeley: University of California Press.

Buckley, Thomas, and Alma Gottlieb. 1988. A Critical Appraisal of Theories of Menstrual Symbolism. In *Blood Magic: The Anthropology of Menstruation*, edited by Thomas Buckley and Alma Gottlieb. Berkeley: University of California Press.

Butler, Anthea. 2007. *Women in the Church of God in Christ: Making a Sanctified World.* Chapel Hill: University of North Carolina Press.

Cairns, Malcolm, ed. 2007. *Voices from the Forest: Integrating Indigenous Knowledge into Sustainable Upland Farming.* Washington, D.C.: Resources for the Future.

Cannell, Fenella. 2006. The Anthropology of Christianity. In *The Anthropology of Christianity*, edited by Fenella Cannell. Durham: Duke University Press.

Casey, Ruairi. 2015. Niassa Is Finding Its Feet: The Fight against Poverty in Mozambique's Most Remote Province. Viewed December 10, 2015. Available from http://www.newstalk.com/niassa-mozambique.

Casselberry, Judith. 2017. *The Labor of Faith: Gender and Power in Black Apostolic Pentecostalism.* Durham: Duke University Press.

Castles, Stephen, and Mark J. Miller. 1998. *The Age of Migration: International Population Movements in the Modern World*. 2nd ed. Basingstoke: Macmillan.

Chabal, Patrick. 2002. *A History of Postcolonial Lusophone Africa*. Bloomington: Indiana University Press.

Chapman, Rachel Rebekah. 2010. *Family Secrets: Risking Reproduction in Central Mozambique*. Nashville: Vanderbilt University Press.

Chidester, David. 1996. *Savage Systems: Colonialism and Comparative Religion in Southern Africa*. Charlottesville: University Press of Virginia.

Chua, Liana. 2012. *The Christianity of Culture: Conversion, Ethnic Citizenship, and the Matter of Religion in Malaysian Borneo*. New York: Palgrave Macmillan.

Ciscato, Elia. 1989. *Ao Serviço deste Homem: Apontamentos de Iniciação Cultural*. Kampala: St. Paul Book Center.

———. 2012. *Introdução à Cultura da Área Makhuwa Lomwe*. Lisbon: Fundação AIS.

Clifford, James. 1997. *Routes: Travel and Translation in the Late Twentieth Century*. Cambridge: Harvard University Press.

Cole, Jennifer. 2010. *Sex and Salvation: Imagining the Future in Madagascar*. Chicago: University of Chicago Press.

Coleman, Simon. 2003. Continuous Conversion? The Rhetoric, Practice, and Rhetorical Practice of Charismatic Protestant Conversion. In *The Anthropology of Religious Conversion*, edited by Andrew Buckser and Stephen D. Glazier. Lanham, Md.: Rowman and Littlefield.

———. 2006. Materializing the Self: Words and Gifts in the Construction of Charismatic Protestant Identity. In *The Anthropology of Christianity*, edited by Fenella Cannell. Durham: Duke University Press.

———. 2011. Introduction: Negotiating Personhood in African Christianities. *Journal of Religion in Africa* 41 (3): 243–55.

Coleman, Simon, and Peter Collins. 2000. The "Plain" and the "Positive": Ritual, Experience and Aesthetics in Quakerism and Charismatic Christianity. *Journal of Contemporary Religion* 15 (3): 317–29.

Coleman, Simon, and Rosalind I. J. Hackett. 2015. Introduction: A New Field? In *The Anthropology of Global Pentecostalism and Evangelicalism*, edited by Simon Coleman and Rosalind I. J. Hackett. New York: New York University Press.

Collins, Patricia Hill. 1990. *Black Feminist Thought: Knowledge, Consciousness, and the Politics of Empowerment*. Boston: Unwin Hyman.

Comaroff, Jean, and John L. Comaroff. 1991. *Of Revelation and Revolution. Vol.1, Christianity, Colonialism, and Consciousness in South Africa*. Chicago: University of Chicago Press.

———. 1997. *Of Revelation and Revolution. Vol. 2, The Dialectics of Modernity on a South African Frontier*. Chicago: University of Chicago Press.

———. 2001. On Personhood: An Anthropological Perspective from Africa. *Social Identities* 7 (2): 267–83.

Comaroff, John. 2010. The End of Anthropology, Again: On the Future of an In/Discipline. *American Anthropologist* 112 (4): 524–38.

Cox, Harvey. 1995. *Fire from Heaven: The Rise of Pentecostal Spirituality and the Reshaping of Religion in the Twenty-First Century*. Cambridge: Da Capo Press.

———. 2009. *The Future of Faith*. New York: HarperOne.

Cox, James, ed. 1998. *Rites of Passage in Contemporary Africa: Interaction between Christian and African Traditional Religions*. Cardiff: Cardiff Academic Press.

Crapanzano, Vincent. 1981. Rite of Return: Circumcision in Morocco. *Psychoanalytic Study of Society* 9: 15–36.

Cruz e Silva, Teresa. 2001. *Protestant Churches and the Formation of Political Consciousness in Southern Mozambique (1930–1974)*. Basel: Schlettwein.

———. 2008. Evangelicals and Democracy in Mozambique. In *Evangelical Christianity and Democracy in Africa*, edited by Terence Ranger. Oxford: Oxford University Press.

Csordas, Thomas. 1993. Somatic Modes of Attention. *Cultural Anthropology* 8 (2): 135–56.

———. 1994. *The Sacred Self: A Cultural Phenomenology of Charismatic Healing*. Berkeley: University of California Press.

———. 1997. *Language, Charisma, and Creativity: Ritual Life in the Catholic Charismatic Renewal*. Berkeley: University of California Press.

———. 2009. Introduction: Modalities of Transnational Transcendence. In *Transnational Transcendence: Essays on Religion and Globalization*, edited by Thomas J. Csordas. Berkeley: University of California Press.

Cucchiari, Salvatore. 1988. "Adapted for Heaven": Conversion and Culture in Western Sicily. *American Ethnologist* 15 (3): 417–41.

———. 1990. Between Shame and Sanctification: Patriarchy and Its Transformation in Sicilian Pentecostalism. *American Ethnologist* 17 (4): 687–707.

Cunningham, Hilary. 2004. Nations Rebound? Crossing Borders in a Gated Globe. *Identities: Global Studies in Culture and Power* 11: 329–50.

Dalakoglou, Dimitris. 2010. The Road: An Ethnography of the Albanian-Greek Cross-Border Motorway. *American Ethnologist* 37 (1): 132–49.

Das, Veena. 2013. Cohabiting an Interreligious Milieu: Reflections on Religious Diversity. In *A Companion to the Anthropology of Religion*, edited by Janice Boddy and Michael Lambek. Oxford: John Wiley and Sons.

Daswani, Girish. 2011. (In-)dividual Pentecostals in Ghana. *Journal of Religion in Africa* 41 (3): 256–79.

———. 2013. On Christianity and Ethics: Rupture as Ethical Practice in Ghanaian Pentecostalism. *American Ethnologist* 40 (3): 467–79.

———. 2015. *Looking Back, Moving Forward: Transformation and Ethical Practice in the Ghanaian Church of Pentecost*. Toronto: University of Toronto Press.

de Bruijn, Mirjam, Rijk van Dijk, and Dick Foeken, eds. 2001. *Mobile Africa: Changing Patterns of Movement in Africa and Beyond*. Leiden: Brill.

de Castro, Soares. 1941. *Os Achirimas: Ensaio Etnográfico*. Lourenço Marques: Imprensa Nacional de Moçambique.

de Certeau, Michel. 1984. *The Practice of Everyday Life*. Translated by Steven Rendall. Berkeley: University of California Press.

de Heusch, Luc. 1985. *Sacrifice in Africa: A Structuralist Approach*. Translated by Linda O'Brien and Alice Morton. Bloomington: Indiana University Press.

DeBernardi, Jean. 1999. Spiritual Warfare and Territorial Spirits: The Globalization and Localisation of a "Practical Theology." *Religious Studies and Theology* 18 (2): 66–96.

Deleuze, Gilles. 1988. *Bergsonism*. Translated by Hugh Tomlinson and Barbara Hammerjam. New York: Zone Books.

Deleuze, Gilles, and Félix Guattari. 1987. *A Thousand Plateaus: Capitalism and Schizophrenia.* Translated by Brian Massumi. Minneapolis: University of Minnesota Press.

Desjarlais, Robert, and C. Jason Throop. 2011. Phenomenological Approaches in Anthropology. *Annual Review of Anthropology* 40: 87–102.

Devereux, George. 1967. *From Anxiety to Method in the Behavioral Sciences.* The Hague: Mouton.

Dewey, John. 1929. *The Quest for Certainty: A Study of the Relation of Knowledge and Action.* New York: Putnam.

DNFFB (Direcção Nacional de Florestas e Fauna Bravia). 1999. *Política e Estratégia de Desenvolvimento de Florestas e Fauna Bravia.* Maputo: Ministério de Agricultura.

do Rosário, Lourenço, ed. 2004. *II Congresso sobre a Luta de Libertação Nacional-Guerra Colonial, 27 Anos Depois, A Reflexão Possível.* Maputo: Edições ISPU.

Dreyfus, Hubert L. 2009. The Roots of Existentialism. In *A Companion to Phenomenology and Existentialism*, edited by Hubert L. Dreyfus and Mark A. Wrathall. Oxford: Wiley-Blackwell.

Drønen, Tomas Sundnes. 2013. *Pentecostalism, Globalisation, and Islam in Northern Cameroon: Megachurches in the Making?* Leiden: Brill.

Economists at Large. 2013. *The $200 Million Question: How Much Does Trophy Hunting Really Contribute to African Communities?* Melbourne: Economists at Large.

Ehret, Christopher. 2001. Bantu Expansions: Re-envisioning a Central Problem of Early African History. *International Journal of African Historical Studies* 34 (1): 5–41.

Eliade, Mircea. 1954. *The Myth of the Eternal Return: Or, Cosmos and History.* Princeton, N.J.: Princeton University Press.

Engelke, Matthew. 2004. Discontinuity and the Discourse of Conversion. *Journal of Religion in Africa* 34 (1/2): 82–109.

———. 2007. *A Problem of Presence: Beyond Scripture in an African Church.* Berkeley: University of California Press.

———. 2010. Past Pentecostalism: Notes on Rupture, Realignment, and Everyday Life in Pentecostal and African Independent Churches. *Africa* 80 (2): 177–99.

Englund, Harri. 2002. *From War to Peace on the Mozambique-Malawi Borderland.* Edinburgh: Edinburgh University Press.

———. 2007. Pentecostalism Beyond Belief: Trust and Democracy in a Malawian Township. *Africa* 77 (4): 477–99.

Englund, Harri, and James Leach. 2000. Ethnography and the Meta-narratives of Modernity. *Current Anthropology* 41 (2): 225–48.

Evens, T. M. S., and Don Handelman, eds. 2006. *The Manchester School: Practice and Ethnographic Praxis in Anthropology.* New York: Berghahn.

Fabian, Johannes. 1983. *Time and the Other: How Anthropology Makes Its Object.* New York: Columbia University Press.

Ferguson, James. 1999. *Expectations of Modernity: Myths and Meanings of Urban Life on the Zambian Copperbelt.* Berkeley: University of California Press.

———. 2013. Declarations of Dependence: Labour, Personhood, and Welfare in Southern Africa. *Journal of the Royal Anthropological Institute* 19 (2): 223–42.

Filippi, M. F., and G. Frizzi. 2005. *Dicionário Xirima-Português e Português-Xirima.* Maúa, Mozambique: Centro de Investigação Xirima.

Firmino, Gregório Domingos. 2001. *Situação Linguística de Moçambique: Dados do II Recenseamento Geral da População e Habitação de 1997.* Maputo: Instituto Nacional de Estatística.

Fortes, Meyer. 1987. *Religion, Morality and the Person.* Cambridge: Cambridge University Press.

Foucault, Michel. 1972. *The Archaeology of Knowledge: And the Discourse on Language*, translated by A. M. Sheridan Smith. New York: Pantheon Books.

———. 2005. *The Hermeneutics of the Subject*, translated by Graham Burchell. New York: Palgrave Macmillan.

Freston, Paul. 2005. The Universal Church of the Kingdom of God: A Brazilian Church Finds Success in Southern Africa. *Journal of Religion in Africa* 35 (1): 33–65.

———. 2013. The Future of Pentecostalism in Brazil: The Limits to Growth. In *Global Pentecostalism in the 21st Century*, edited by Robert W. Hefner. Bloomington: Indiana University Press.

Frey, Nancy. 2004. Stories of Return: Pilgrimage and Its Aftermaths. In *Intersecting Journeys: The Anthropology of Pilgrimage and Tourism*, edited by Ellen Badone and Sharon R. Roseman. Urbana: University of Illinois Press.

Frizzi, Giuseppe. 2008. *Murima ni Ewani Exirima: Biosofia e Biosfera Xirima.* Maúa, Mozambique: Centro de Investigação Xirima.

———. 2009. Biosofia e Biosfera Xirima: Localidade e Alteridade Cultural em Diálogo Propositivo com a Globalidade. Unpublished manuscript.

———. 2014. Ettini. Unpublished Manuscript.

Funada-Classen, Sayaka. 2012. *Origins of War in Mozambique: A History of Unity and Division.* Translated by Masako Osada. Somerset West, South Africa: African Minds.

Game, Ann. 1997. Time Unhinged. *Time and Society* 6 (2/3): 115–29.

Gaspar, Dowyvan Gabriel. 2006. "É Dando que se Recebe": A Igreja Universal do Reino de Deus e o Negócio da Fé em Moçambique. Master's thesis, Universidade Federal da Bahia.

Gates, Henry Louis. 2009. *In Search of Our Roots: How Nineteen Extraordinary African Americans Reclaimed Their Past.* New York: Crown.

Geffray, Christian. 1990a. *La Cause des Armes au Mozambique: Anthropologie d'une Guerre Civile.* Paris: Karthala.

———. 1990b. *Ni Père ni Mère: Critique de la Parenté, le Cas Makhuwa.* Paris: Seuil.

Gell, Alfred. 1992. *The Anthropology of Time: Cultural Constructions of Temporal Maps and Images.* Oxford: Berg.

Gerdes, Paulus. 2000. *Le Cercle et le Carré: Créativité Géométrique, Artistique et Symbolique de Vannières et Vanniers d'Afrique, d'Amérique, d'Asie et d'Océanie.* Paris: L'Harmattan.

———. 2010. *Otthava: Making Baskets and Doing Geometry in the Makhuwa Culture in the Northeast of Mozambique.* Maputo: Centre for Mozambican Studies and Ethnoscience, Universidade Pedagógica.

Gez, Yonatan N., Yvan Droz, Edio Soares, and Jeanne Rey. 2017. From Converts to Itinerants: Religious *Butinage* as Dynamic Identity. *Current Anthropology* 58 (2): 141–59.

Gilroy, Paul. 1993. *The Black Atlantic: Modernity and Double Consciousness.* Cambridge: Harvard University Press.

Gluckman, Max. 1958. *Analysis of a Social Situation in Modern Zululand.* Manchester: Manchester University Press.

Gonçalves, Euclides. 2013. Orientações Superiores: Time and Bureaucratic Authority in Mozambique. *African Affairs* 112 (449): 602–22.

Gooren, Henri Paul Pierre. 2010. *Religious Conversion and Disaffiliation: Tracing Patterns of Change in Faith Practices*. New York: Palgrave Macmillan.

Gordon, Lewis. 2000. *Existentia Africana: Understanding Africana Existentialist Thought*. New York: Routledge.

Gottlieb, Alma. 1988. Menstrual Cosmology among the Beng of Ivory Coast. In *Blood Magic: The Anthropology of Menstruation*, edited by Thomas Buckley and Alma Gottlieb. Berkeley: University of California Press.

Granjo, Paulo. 2009. Saúde, Doença e Cura em Moçambique. In *Migração, Saúde e Diversidade Cultural*, edited by Elsa Lechner. Lisbon: Imprensa de Ciências Sociais.

Green, Maia. 2003. *Priests, Witches and Power: Popular Christianity after Mission in Southern Tanzania*. Cambridge: Cambridge University Press.

Greenblatt, Stephen. 2010. *Cultural Mobility: A Manifesto*. New York: Cambridge University Press.

Griffith, R. Marie. 1997. *God's Daughters: Evangelical Women and the Power of Submission*. Berkeley: University of California Press.

Gruber, Jacob W. 1970. Ethnographic Salvage and the Shaping of Anthropology. *American Anthropologist* 72 (6): 1289–99.

Gupta, Akhil, and James Ferguson. 1992. Beyond "Culture": Space, Identity, and the Politics of Difference. *Cultural Anthropology* 7 (1): 6–23.

———. 1997. Discipline and Practice: "The Field" as Site, Method and Location in Anthropology. In *Anthropological Locations: Boundaries and Grounds of a Field Science*, edited by Akhil Gupta and James Ferguson. Berkeley: University of California Press.

Hackett, Rosalind. 2003. Discourses of Demonization in Africa and Beyond. *Diogenes* 50 (3): 61–75.

Hadot, Pierre. 1968. Conversion. In *Encyclopaedia Universalis*. Paris: Encyclopaedia Universalis France.

Hage, Ghassan. 2005. A Not So Multi-sited Ethnography of a Not So Imagined Community. *Anthropological Theory* 5 (4): 463–75.

———. 2009. Waiting Out the Crisis: On Stuckedness and Governmentality. In *Waiting*, edited by Ghassan Hage. Carlton: Melbourne University Publishing.

Hall, Margaret, and Tom Young. 1997. *Confronting Leviathan: Mozambique since Independence*. Athens: Ohio University Press.

Hanlon, Joseph. 1996. *Peace without Profit: How the IMF Blocks Rebuilding in Mozambique*. Oxford: Irish Mozambique Solidarity and the International African Institute.

Hann, Chris. 2007. The Anthropology of Christianity Per Se. *European Journal of Sociology* 48 (3): 383–410.

Harding, Rachel E. 2006. É a Senzala: Slavery, Women, and Embodied Knowledge in Afro-Brazilian Candomblé. In *Women and Religion in the African Diaspora*, edited by R. Marie Griffith and Barbara Dianne Savage. Baltimore: Johns Hopkins University Press.

Harding, Susan. 1991. Representing Fundamentalism: The Problem of the Repugnant Cultural Other. *Social Research* 58: 373–93.

Harries, Patrick. 2007. *Butterflies and Barbarians: Swiss Missionaries and Systems of Knowledge in South-East Africa*. Oxford: James Currey.

Harris, Olivia. 2006. The Eternal Return of Conversion: Christianity as Contested Domain in Highland Bolivia. In *The Anthropology of Christianity*, edited by Fenella Cannell. Durham: Duke University Press.

Harrison, Gualtiero, and Matilde Callari Galli. 1971. *Né Leggere Né Scrivere: La Cultura Analfabeta: Quando l'Istruzione Diventa Violenza e Sopraffazione.* Milan: Feltrinelli.

Haynes, Naomi. 2017. *Moving by the Spirit: Pentecostal Social Life on the Zambian Copperbelt.* Oakland: University of California Press.

Hefner, Robert W. 1993. World Building and the Rationality of Conversion. *Conversion to Christianity: Historical and Anthropological Perspectives on a Great Transformation*, edited by Robert W. Hefner. Berkeley: University of California Press.

———. 2013a. The Unexpected Modern: Gender, Piety, and Politics in the Global Pentecostal Surge. In *Global Pentecostalism in the 21st Century*, edited by Robert W. Hefner. Bloomington: Indiana University Press.

Hefner, Robert W., ed. 2013b. *Global Pentecostalism in the Twenty-first Century.* Bloomington: Indiana University Press.

Hegel, Georg Wilhelm Friedrich. [1837] 1956. *The Philosophy of History.* Translated by J. Sibree. New York: Dover.

Heidegger, Martin. 1962. *Being and Time*, translated by John Macquarrie and Edward Robinson. New York: Harper.

Herzfeld, Michael. 1997. *Portrait of a Greek Imagination: An Ethnographic Biography of Andreas Nenedakis.* Chicago: University of Chicago Press.

Hillenbrand, Robert. 1994. *Islamic Architecture: Form, Function, and Meaning.* New York: Columbia University Press.

Hobsbawm, Eric, and Terence Ranger, eds. 1992. *The Invention of Tradition.* New York: Cambridge University Press.

Honwana, Alcinda. 2002. *Espíritos Vivos, Tradições Modernas: Possessão de Espíritos e Reintegração Social Pós-Guerra no Sul de Moçambique.* Maputo: Promédia.

Hood, Robert E. 1990. *Must God Remain Greek? Afro Cultures and God-Talk.* Minneapolis: Fortress Press.

Horton, Robin. 1971. African Conversion. *Africa* 41 (2): 85–108.

———. 1975a. On the Rationality of Conversion, Part I. *Africa* 45 (3): 219–35.

———. 1975b. On the Rationality of Conversion, Part II. *Africa* 45 (4): 373–99.

Hovland, Ingie. 2013. *Mission Station Christianity: Norwegian Missionaries in Colonial Natal and Zululand, Southern Africa, 1850–1890.* Leiden: Brill.

Hucks, Tracey E. 2006. "I Smoothed the Way, I Opened Doors": Women in the Yoruba-Orisha Tradition of Trinidad. In *Women and Religion in the African Diaspora: Knowledge, Power, and Performance*, edited by R. Marie Griffith and Barbara Dianne Savage. Baltimore: Johns Hopkins University Press.

Huhn, Arianna. 2013. The Tongue Only Works without Worries: Sentiment and Sustenance in a Mozambican Town. *Food and Foodways* 21 (3): 186–210.

Igreja, Victor. 2014. Memories of Violence, Cultural Transformations of Cannibals, and Indigenous State-Building in Post-conflict Mozambique. *Comparative Studies in Society and History* 56 (3): 774–802.

Ikeuchi, Suma. 2017. Accompanied Self: Debating Pentecostal Individual and Japanese Relational Selves in Transnational Japan. *Ethos* 45 (1): 3–23.

Instituto Nacional de Estatística. 2012. *Estatísticas do Distrito de Maúa*. Maputo: Instituto Nacional de Estatística.

———. 2013. *Anuário Estatístico 2012—Moçambique*. Maputo: Instituto Nacional de Estatística.

Isaacman, Allen F. 1996. *Cotton Is the Mother of Poverty: Peasants, Work, and Rural Struggle in Colonial Mozambique, 1938–1961*. Portsmouth, N.H.: Heinemann.

Isaacman, Allen F., and Barbara Isaacman. 2013. *Dams, Displacement, and the Delusion of Development: Cahora Bassa and Its Legacies in Mozambique, 1965–2007*. Athens: Ohio University Press.

Jackson, John B. 1994. *A Sense of Place, a Sense of Time*. New Haven: Yale University Press.

Jackson, Michael. 1989. *Paths toward a Clearing: Radical Empiricism and Ethnographic Inquiry*. Bloomington: Indiana University Press.

———. 1996. Introduction: Phenomenology, Radical Empiricism, and Anthropological Critique. In *Things as They Are: New Directions in Phenomenological Anthropology*, edited by Michael Jackson. Bloomington: Indiana University Press.

———. 2005. *Existential Anthropology: Events, Exigencies and Effects*. New York: Berghahn.

———. 2009. *The Palm at the End of the Mind: Relatedness, Religiosity, and the Real*. Durham: Duke University Press.

———. 2012. *Between One and One Another*. Berkeley: University of California Press.

———. 2013. *The Wherewithal of Life: Ethics, Migration, and the Question of Well-Being*. Berkeley: University of California Press.

Jackson, Michael, and Ivan Karp, eds. 1990. *Personhood and Agency: The Experience of Self and Other in African Cultures*. Washington, D.C.: Smithsonian Institution Press.

Jackson, Michael, and Albert Piette. 2015. Anthropology and the Existential Turn. In *What Is Existential Anthropology?* edited by Michael Jackson and Albert Piette. New York: Berghahn.

Jacobsen, Douglas G. 2011. *The World's Christians: Who They Are, Where They Are, and How They Got There*. Chichester: Wiley-Blackwell.

James, William. 1903. The Ph.D. Octopus. *Harvard Monthly* 36: 1–9.

———. 1909. *A Pluralistic Universe*. New York: Longmans, Green.

———. 1950. *The Principles of Psychology. Vol. 1*. New York: Dover.

———. 1985. *The Varieties of Religious Experience: A Study in Human Nature*. New York: Penguin.

———. 2003. *Essays in Radical Empiricism*. Mineola, N.Y.: Dover.

Janzen, John M. 1978. *The Quest for Therapy in Lower Zaire*. Berkeley: University of California Press.

Jones, Ben. 2011. *Beyond the State in Rural Uganda*. Edinburgh: Edinburgh University Press.

Kaell, Hillary. 2014. *Walking Where Jesus Walked: American Christians and Holy Land Pilgrimage*. New York: New York University Press.

Kalu, Ogbu. 2008. *African Pentecostalism: An Introduction*. Oxford: Oxford University Press.

Kantel, Donald R. 2007. The "Toronto Blessing" Revival and Its Continuing Impact on Mission in Mozambique. D.Min. diss., Regent University.

Keane, Webb. 2007. *Christian Moderns: Freedom and Fetish in the Mission Encounter*. Berkeley: University of California Press.

Kierkegaard, Søren. 1985. *Fear and Trembling*, translated by A. Hannay. London: Penguin.

———. [1849] 1989. *The Sickness unto Death*, translated by A. Hannay. London: Penguin.

Kirsch, Thomas G. 2004. Restaging the Will to Believe: Religious Pluralism, Anti-syncretism, and the Problem of Belief. *American Anthropologist* 106 (4): 699–709.

Kleinman, Arthur. 1980. *Patients and Healers in the Context of Culture: An Exploration of the Borderland between Anthropology, Medicine, and Psychiatry*. Berkeley: University of California Press.

Kollman, Paul. 2005. *The Evangelization of Slaves and Catholic Origins in Eastern Africa*. Maryknoll, N.Y.: Orbis Books.

Kopytoff, Igor. 1987. The Internal African Frontier: The Making of African Political Culture. In *The African Frontier: The Reproduction of Traditional African Societies*, edited by Igor Kopytoff. Bloomington: Indiana University Press.

Kottak, Nicholas Charles. 2002. Stealing the Neighbor's Chicken: Social Control in Northern Mozambique. Ph.D. diss., Emory University.

Kuhn, Thomas S. 1962. *The Structure of Scientific Revolutions*. Chicago: University of Chicago Press.

Kyed, Helene Maria. 2009. Traditional Authority and Localization of State Law: The Intricacies of Boundary Making in Policing Rural Mozambique. In *State Violence and Human Rights: State Officials in the South*, edited by Andrew M. Jefferson and Steffen Jensen. New York: Routledge-Cavendish.

La Fontaine, Jean Sybil. 1985. *Initiation*. Middlesex, England: Penguin.

Lambek, Michael. 1993. *Knowledge and Practice in Mayotte*. Toronto: University of Toronto Press.

———. 2000. Localising Islamic Performances in Mayotte. In *Islamic Prayer across the Indian Ocean: Inside and Outside the Mosque*, edited by David Parkin and Stephen C. Headley. Richmond: Curzon Press.

———. 2015. Both/And. In *What Is Existential Anthropology?* edited by Michael Jackson and Albert Piette. New York: Berghahn.

Leach, Edmund. 1954. *Political Systems of Highland Burma: A Study of Kachin Social Structure*. Cambridge: Harvard University Press.

Leacock, Eleanor. 1981. *Myths of Male Dominance: Collected Articles on Women Cross-Culturally*. New York: Monthly Review Press.

Lerma Martínez, Francisco. 1989. *O Povo Macua e a Sua Cultura*. Lisbon: Ministério da Educação, Instituto de Investigação Científica Tropical.

———. 2009. *Religiões Africanas Hoje: Introdução ao Estudo das Religiões Tradicionais em Moçambique*, 3rd ed. Maputo: Paulinas.

Lester, Rebecca J. 2005. *Jesus in Our Wombs: Embodying Modernity in a Mexican Convent*. Berkeley: University of California Press.

Lévi-Strauss, Claude. 1966. Anthropology: Its Achievements and Future. *Current Anthropology* 7 (2): 124–27.

———. 1992. *Tristes Tropiques*, translated by John and Doreen Weightman. New York: Penguin.

Lienhardt, Godfrey. 1961. *Divinity and Experience: The Religion of the Dinka*. Oxford: Oxford University Press.

———. 1985. Self: Public, Private, Some African Representations. In *The Category of the Person: Anthropology, Philosophy, History*, edited by Michael Carrithers, Steven Collins, and Steven Lukes. Cambridge: Cambridge University Press.

Lifton, Robert Jay. 1993. *The Protean Self: Human Resilience in an Age of Fragmentation*. New York: Basic Books.

Lindhardt, Martin. 2010. "If You Are Saved You Cannot Forget Your Parents": Agency, Power, and Social Repositioning in Tanzanian Born-Again Christianity. *Journal of Religion in Africa* 40 (3): 240–72.

———. 2011a. Introduction. In *Practicing the Faith: The Ritual Life of Pentecostal-Charismatic Christians*, edited by Martin Lindhardt. New York: Berghahn.

Lindhardt, Martin, ed. 2011b. *Practicing the Faith: The Ritual Life of Pentecostal-Charismatic Christians*. New York: Berghahn.

———. 2015. *Pentecostalism in Africa: Presence and Impact of Pneumatic Christianity in Postcolonial Societies*. Leiden: Brill.

López V., Álvaro. 2016. *A Política Religioso-Missionária do Estado Novo em Portugal e a Evangelização do Niassa: 1926–1962*. Prior Velho: Paulinas.

Lubkemann, Stephen C. 2008. *Culture in Chaos: An Anthropology of the Social Condition in War*. Chicago: University of Chicago Press.

Lucht, Hans. 2012. *Darkness before Daybreak: African Migrants Living on the Margins in Southern Italy Today*. Berkeley: University of California Press.

Luedke, Tracy J. 2006. Presidents, Bishops, and Mothers: The Construction of Authority in Mozambican Healing. In *Borders and Healers: Brokering Therapeutic Resources in Southeast Africa*, edited by Tracy J. Luedke and Harry G. West. Bloomington: Indiana University Press.

Luedke, Tracy J., and Harry G. West, eds. 2006. *Borders and Healers: Brokering Therapeutic Resources in Southeast Africa*. Bloomington: Indiana University Press.

Luhrmann, Tanya M. 2012. *When God Talks Back: Understanding the American Evangelical Relationship with God*. New York: Alfred A. Knopf.

Macaire, Pierre. 1996. *L'Héritage Makhuwa au Mozambique*. Paris: Harmattan.

MacRobert, Iain. 1992. The Black Roots of Pentecostalism. In *Pentecost, Mission, and Ecumenism: Essays on Intercultural Theology: Festschrift in Honour of Professor Walter J. Hollenweger*, edited by Jan A. B. Jongeneel. Frankfurt am Main: Peter Lang.

Mahmood, Saba. 2005. *Politics of Piety: The Islamic Revival and the Feminist Subject*. Princeton, N.J.: Princeton University Press.

Malkki, Liisa H. 1995. *Purity and Exile: Violence, Memory, and National Cosmology among Hutu Refugees in Tanzania*. Chicago: University of Chicago Press.

Maples, Chauncy. 1882. Makua Land, Between the Rivers Rovuma and Luli. *Proceedings of the Royal Geographical Society* 4 (2): 79–90.

Marcel, Gabriel. 1951. *Being and Having*, translated by Katharine Farrer. Boston: Beacon Press.

———. 1962. *Homo Viator: Introduction to a Metaphysic of Hope*, translated by Emma Crauford. New York: Harper.

———. 1964. *Creative Fidelity*, translated by Robert Rosthal. New York: Farrar, Straus.

Mariz, Cecília Loreto, and María das Dores Campos Machado. 1997. Pentecostalism and Women in Brazil. In *Power, Politics and Pentecostals in Latin America*, edited by Edward L. Cleary and Hannah W. Stewart-Gambino. Boulder: Westview Press.

Marshall, Ruth. 2009. *Political Spiritualities: The Pentecostal Revolution in Nigeria*. Chicago: University of Chicago Press.

Mavhunga, Clapperton C. 2013. Cidades Esfumaçadas: Energy and the Rural-Urban Connection in Mozambique. *Public Culture* 25 (2): 261–71.

———. 2014. *Transient Workspaces: Technologies of Everyday Innovation in Zimbabwe*. Cambridge: MIT Press.

Maxwell, David. 2006a. *African Gifts of the Spirit: Pentecostalism and the Rise of a Zimbabwean Transnational Religious Movement*. Athens: Ohio University Press.

———. 2006b. Writing the History of African Christianity. *Journal of Religion in Africa* 36 (3/4): 379–99.

McBride, Jennifer M. 2012. *The Church for the World: A Theology of Public Witness*. Oxford: Oxford University Press.

McDonald, David A., ed. 2000. *On Borders: Perspectives on International Migration in Southern Africa*. New York: St. Martin's Press.

McGovern, Mike. 2013. *Unmasking the State: Making Guinea Modern*. Chicago: University of Chicago Press.

McGuire, Meredith B. 2008. *Lived Religion: Faith and Practice in Everyday Life*. Oxford: Oxford University Press.

McIntosh, Janet. 2009. *The Edge of Islam: Power, Personhood, and Ethnoreligious Boundaries on the Kenya Coast*. Durham: Duke University Press.

Medeiros, Eduardo. 1997. Notas para o Estudo dos Ritos de Iniciação da Puberdade em Moçambique. In *Educação, Empresas e Desenvolvimento em Moçambique*, edited by Feliciano de Mira. Evora: Pendor.

———. 2000. Reestruturação do Poder Político Makhuwa-Mmetthu sob o Domínio da Companhia do Nyassa, 1894–1929. In *A África e a Instalação do Sistema Colonial (c. 1885–c.1930)*, edited by M. E. Santos. Lisbon: Centro de Estudos de História e Cartografia Antiga.

———. 2007. *Os Senhores da Floresta: Ritos de Iniciação dos Rapazes Macuas e Lómuès*. Porto: Campo das Letras.

Meigs, Anna S. 1984. *Food, Sex, and Pollution: A New Guinea Religion*. New Brunswick: Rutgers University Press.

Merleau-Ponty, Maurice. 1962. *Phenomenology of Perception*. Translated by Colin Smith. New York: Humanities Press.

Meyer, Birgit. 1998. "Make a Complete Break with the Past": Memory and Post-colonial Modernity in Ghanaian Pentecostalist Discourse. *Journal of Religion in Africa* 28 (3): 316–49.

———. 1999. *Translating the Devil: Religion and Modernity among the Ewe in Ghana*. Edinburgh: Edinburgh University Press.

———. 2004. Christianity in Africa: From African Independent to Pentecostal-Charismatic Churches. *Annual Review of Anthropology* 33 (1): 447–74.

———. 2010. Pentecostalism and Globalization. In *Studying Global Pentecostalism: Theories and Methods*, edited by Allan Anderson, Michael Bergunder, André Droogers, and Cornelis van der Laan. Berkeley: University of California Press.

———. 2014. An Author Meets Her Critics: Around Birgit Meyer's "Mediation and the Genesis of Presence: Toward a Material Approach to Religion." In *Religion and Society* 5: 205–30.

Meyer, Birgit, and Marloes Janson, eds. 2016. Studying Islam and Christianity in Africa: Moving Beyond a Bifurcated Field. Special issue, *Africa* 86 (4).

Miller, Donald E., Kimon H. Sargeant, and Richard Flory, eds. 2013. *Spirit and Power: The Growth and Global Impact of Pentecostalism.* Oxford: Oxford University Press.

Mitchell, Timothy. 1990. Everyday Metaphors of Power. *Theory and Society* 19 (5): 545–77.

Morier-Genoud, Éric. 1996. Of God and Caesar: The Relation between Christian Churches and the State in Post-colonial Mozambique, 1974–1981. *Le Fait Missionnaire* 3: 1–79.

———. 2000. The 1996 "Muslim Holidays" Affair: Religious Competition and State Mediation in Contemporary Mozambique. *Journal of Southern African Studies* 26 (3): 409–27.

———. 2009. Mozambique since 1989: Shaping Democracy after Socialism. In *Turning Points in African Democracy,* edited by Abdul Raufu Mustapha and Lindsay Whitfield. Oxford: James Currey.

———. 2014. Renouveau Religieux et Politique au Mozambique: Entre Permanence, Rupture et Historicité. *Politique Africaine* 134: 155–77.

Mosko, Mark. 2010. Partible Penitents: Dividual Personhood and Christian Practice in Melanesia and the West. *Journal of the Royal Anthropological Institute* 16: 215–40.

———. 2015. Unbecoming Individuals: The Partible Character of the Christian Person. *Hau: Journal of Ethnographic Theory* 5 (1): 361–93.

Mukonyora, Isabel. 2006. Women of the Diaspora Within: The Masowe Apostles. In *Women and Religion in the African Diaspora: Knowledge, Power, and Performance,* edited by R. Marie Griffith and Barbara Dianne Savage. Baltimore: Johns Hopkins University Press.

———. 2007. *Wandering a Gendered Wilderness: Suffering and Healing in an African Initiated Church.* New York: Peter Lang.

Natanson, Maurice. 1970. *The Journeying Self: A Study in Philosophy and Social Role.* Reading: Addison-Wesley.

Neumann, Roderick P. 1998. *Imposing Wilderness: Struggles over Livelihood and Nature Preservation in Africa.* Berkeley: University of California Press.

Newitt, Malyn. 1995. *A History of Mozambique.* Bloomington: Indiana University Press.

Nielsen, Morten. 2012. Interior Swelling: On the Expansive Effects of Ancestral Interventions in Maputo, Mozambique. *Common Knowledge* 18 (3): 433–50.

Nietzsche, Friedrich. 1954. Twilight of the Idols. In *The Portable Nietzsche,* edited and translated by Walter Kaufmann. New York: Penguin.

———. 2005. *Thus Spoke Zarathustra: A Book for Everyone and Nobody,* translated by Graham Parkes. Oxford: Oxford University Press.

Nnaemeka, Obioma. 2005. African Women, Colonialist Discourses, and Imperialist Interventions. In *Female Circumcision and the Politics of Knowledge: African Women in Imperialist Discourses,* edited by Obioma Nnaemeka. Westport: Praeger.

Nock, Arthur D. 1933. *Conversion: The Old and the New in Religion from Alexander the Great to Augustine of Hippo.* Oxford: Clarendon Press.

Nyamnjoh, Francis B. 2001. Expectations of Modernity or a Future in the Rear-view Mirror? *Journal of Southern African Studies* 27 (2): 363–69.

———. 2013. Fiction and Reality of Mobility in Africa. *Citizenship Studies* 17 (6–7): 653–80.

Obarrio, Juan. 2014. *The Spirit of the Laws in Mozambique.* Chicago: University of Chicago Press.

Oduyoye, Mercy Amba. 1995. *Daughers of Anowa: African Women and Patriarchy.* Maryknoll, N.Y.: Orbis Books.

Ojo, Matthews A. 2007. Pentecostal Movements, Islam and the Contest for Public Space in Northern Nigeria. *Islam and Christian–Muslim Relations* 18 (2): 175–88.

Oro, Ari Pedro. 2004. A Presença Religiosa Brasileira no Exterior: O Caso da Igreja Universal do Reino de Deus. *Estudos Avançados* 18 (52): 139–55.

Orsi, Robert. 1985. *The Madonna of 115th Street: Faith and Community in Italian Harlem, 1880–1950*. New Haven: Yale University Press.

Outlaw, Lucius. 1996. *On Race and Philosophy*. New York: Routledge.

p'Bitek, Okot. 2011. *Decolonizing African Religion: A Short History of African Religions in Western Scholarship*. New York: Diasporic Africa Press.

Peel, J. D. Y. 2000. *Religious Encounter and the Making of the Yoruba*. Bloomington: Indiana University Press.

———. 2016. *Christianity, Islam, and Orișa Religion: Three Traditions in Comparison and Interaction*. Oakland: University of California Press.

Perfil do Distrito de Maúa, Província de Niassa. 2005. Mozambique: Ministério da Administração Estatal.

Pfeiffer, James. 2005. Commodity Fetichismo, the Holy Spirit, and the Turn to Pentecostal and African Independent Churches in Central Mozambique. *Culture, Medicine, and Psychiatry* 29 (3): 255–83.

Pfeiffer, James, Kenneth Gimbel-Sherr, and Orvalho Joaquim Augusto. 2007. The Holy Spirit in the Household: Pentecostalism, Gender, and Neoliberalism in Mozambique. *American Anthropologist* 109 (4): 688–700.

Piot, Charles. 1991. Of Persons and Things: Some Reflections on African Spheres of Exchange. *Man* 26: 405–24.

———. 1999. *Remotely Global: Village Modernity in West Africa*. Chicago: University of Chicago Press.

———. 2010. *Nostalgia for the Future: West Africa after the Cold War*. Chicago: University of Chicago Press.

Pitcher, M. Anne. 1996a. Chiefs, Companies and Cotton: Observations from Rural Nampula. *Southern Africa Report* 12 (1): 26–30.

———. 1996b. Conflict and Cooperation: Gendered Roles and Responsibilities within Cotton Households in Northern Mozambique. *African Studies Review* 39 (3): 81–112.

———. 2002. *Transforming Mozambique: The Politics of Privatization, 1975–2000*. New York: Cambridge University Press.

Poewe, Karla O. 1981. *Matrilineal Ideology: Male-Female Dynamics in Luapula, Zambia*. London: Academic Press.

Potts, Deborah. 2010. *Circular Migration in Zimbabwe and Contemporary Sub-Saharan Africa*. Oxford: James Currey.

———. 2012. *Whatever Happened to Africa's Rapid Urbanisation?* London: Africa Research Institute.

Premawardhana, Devaka. 2012. Transformational Tithing: Sacrifice and Reciprocity in a Neo-Pentecostal Church. *Nova Religio* 15 (4): 85–109.

———. 2015. Conversion and Convertibility in Northern Mozambique. In *What Is Existential Anthropology?* edited by Michael Jackson and Albert Piette. New York: Berghahn.

———. Forthcoming. Egress and Regress: Pentecostal Precursors and Parallels in Northern Mozambique. *Ethnos: Journal of Anthropology*.

Ranger, Terence. 1989. Missionaries, Migrants, and the Manyika: The Invention of Ethnicity in Zimbabwe. In *The Creation of Tribalism in Southern Africa*, edited by Leroy Vail. London: Currey.

———. 1993. The Local and the Global in Southern African Religious History. In *Conversion to Christianity: Historical and Anthropological Perspectives on a Great Transformation*, edited by Robert W. Hefner. Berkeley: University of California Press.

Rasing, Thera. 1995. *Passing on the Rites of Passage: Girls' Initiation Rites in the Context of an Urban Roman Catholic Community on the Zambian Copperbelt.* Aldershot: Avebury.

Richie, Tony. 2013. *Toward a Pentecostal Theology of Religions: Encountering Cornelius Today.* Cleveland, Tenn.: CPT Press.

Robbins, Joel. 2003. On the Paradoxes of Global Pentecostalism and the Perils of Continuity Thinking. *Religion* 33 (3): 221–31.

———. 2004. *Becoming Sinners: Christianity and Moral Torment in a Papua New Guinea Society.* Berkeley: University of California Press.

———. 2007. Continuity Thinking and the Problem of Christian Culture: Belief, Time, and the Anthropology of Christianity. *Current Anthropology* 48 (1): 5–38.

———. 2010. Anthropology of Religion. In *Studying Global Pentecostalism: Theories and Methods*, edited by Allan Anderson, Michael Bergunder, André Droogers, and Cornelis van der Laan. Berkeley: University of California Press.

———. 2011. Crypto-Religion and the Study of Cultural Mixtures: Anthropology, Value, and the Nature of Syncretism. *Journal of the American Academy of Religion* 79 (2): 408–24.

———. 2014. The Anthropology of Christianity: Unity, Diversity, New Directions: An Introduction to Supplement 10. *Current Anthropology* 55 (S10): S157–71.

Rosaldo, Renato. 1989. *Culture and Truth: The Remaking of Social Analysis.* Boston: Beacon Press.

Ruel, Malcolm. 1997. *Belief, Ritual and the Securing of Life: Reflexive Essays on a Bantu Religion.* Leiden: Brill.

Rutherford, Danilyn. 2006. The Bible Meets the Idol: Writing and Conversion in Biak, Irian Jaya, Indonesia. In *The Anthropology of Christianity*, edited by Fenella Cannell. Durham: Duke University Press.

Sahlins, Marshall. 1985. *Islands of History.* Chicago: University of Chicago Press.

Said, Edward. 1984. Reflections on Exile. *Granta* 13: 159–72.

———. 1994. *Representations of the Intellectual.* New York: Pantheon Books.

Salazar, Noel B., and Alan Smart. 2011. Anthropological Takes on (Im)Mobility. *Identities: Global Studies in Culture and Power* 18 (6): i–ix.

Sartre, Jean-Paul. 1968. *Search for a Method*, translated by Hazel Barnes. New York: Vintage.

Saunders, George. 2010. *Il Linguaggio dello Spirito: Il Cuore e la Mente nel Protestantesimo Evangelico.* Pisa: Pacini Editore.

Schielke, Samuli. 2010. Second Thoughts about the Anthropology of Islam, Or How to Make Sense of Grand Schemes in Everyday Life. *ZMO Working Papers* 2: 1–16.

Schielke, Samuli, and Liza Debevec, eds. 2012. *Ordinary Lives and Grand Schemes: An Anthropology of Everyday Religion.* New York: Berghahn.

Schuetze, Christy. 2010. "The World Is Upside Down": Women's Participation in Religious Movements in Mozambique. Ph.D. diss., University of Pennsylvania.

Schutz, Alfred. 1945. On Multiple Realities. *Philosophy and Phenomenological Research* 5 (4): 533–76.

Scott, James C. 1985. *Weapons of the Weak: Everyday Forms of Peasant Resistance.* New Haven: Yale University Press.

———. 1998. *Seeing Like a State: How Certain Schemes to Improve the Human Condition Have Failed.* New Haven: Yale University Press.

———. 2009. *The Art of Not Being Governed: An Anarchist History of Upland Southeast Asia.* New Haven: Yale University Press.

Seeman, Don. 2009. *One People, One Blood: Ethiopian-Israelis and the Return to Judaism.* New Brunswick, N.J.: Rutgers University Press.

———. 2014. Coffee and the Moral Order: Ethiopian Jews and Pentecostals against Culture. *American Ethnologist* 42 (4): 734–48.

———. Forthcoming. Divinity Inhabits the Social: Ethnography in a Phenomenological Key. In *Theologically Engaged Anthropology*, edited by J. Derrick Lemons. Oxford: Oxford University Press.

Seibert, Gerhard. 2005. "But the Manifestation of the Spirit Is Given to Every Man to Profit Withal": Zion Churches in Mozambique since the Early 20th Century. *Le Fait Missionnaire* 17: 125–50.

Shaw, Rosalind. 1990. The Invention of "African Traditional Religion." *Religion* 20 (4): 339–53.

Sheldon, Kathleen E. 2002. *Pounders of Grain: A History of Women, Work, and Politics in Mozambique.* Portsmouth: Heinemann.

Silva, Sónia. 2011. *Along an African Border: Angolan Refugees and Their Divination Baskets.* Philadelphia: University of Pennsylvania Press.

———. 2015. Mobility and Immobility in the Life of an Amputee. In *What Is Existential Anthropology?* edited by Michael Jackson and Albert Piette. New York: Berghahn.

Silverman, Eric. 2003. The Cut of Wholeness: Psychoanalytic Interpretations of Biblical Circumcision. In *The Covenant of Circumcision: New Perspectives on an Ancient Jewish Rite*, edited by Elizabeth Wyner Mark. Hanover, N.H.: Brandeis University Press.

Smith, Wilfred Cantwell. 1963. *The Meaning and End of Religion: A New Approach to the Religious Traditions of Mankind.* New York: Macmillan.

———. 1977. *Belief and History.* Charlottesville: University Press of Virginia.

Soares, Daniel B. 2009. The Incorporation of Geometry Involved in the Traditional House Building in Mathematics Education in Mozambique: The Case of Zambezia and Sofala Provinces. Ph.D. diss., University of the Western Cape.

Spicer, Edward H. 1954. Spanish-Indian Acculturation in the Southwest. *American Anthropologist* 56: 663–78.

Stendahl, Krister. 1976. *Paul among Jews and Gentiles, and Other Essays.* Philadelphia: Fortress Press.

Stephens, Rhiannon. 2013. *A History of African Motherhood: The Case of Uganda, 700–1900.* New York: Cambridge University Press.

Stewart, Charles, and Rosalind Shaw, eds. 1994. *Syncretism/Anti-syncretism: The Politics of Religious Synthesis.* London: Routledge.

Stewart, Dianne M. 2004. Womanist Theology in the Caribbean Context: Critiquing Culture, Rethinking Doctrine, and Expanding Boundaries. *Journal of Feminist Studies in Religion* 20 (1): 61–82.

Stoller, Paul. 1989. *The Taste of Ethnographic Things: The Senses in Anthropology.* Philadelphia: University of Pennsylvania Press.

———. 1997. *Sensuous Scholarship.* Philadelphia: University of Pennsylvania Press.

———. 2009. *The Power of the Between: An Anthropological Odyssey.* Chicago: University of Chicago Press.

Swift, Philip. 2012. Touching Conversion: Tangible Transformations in a Japanese New Religion. *Hau: Journal of Ethnographic Theory* 2 (1): 269–88.

Tamale, Sylvia. 2005. Eroticism, Sensuality and "Women's Secrets" among the Baganda: A Critical Analysis. *Feminist Africa* 5: 9–36.

Taylor, Charles. 2004. *Modern Social Imaginaries.* Durham: Duke University Press.

Taylor, William B. 1996. *Magistrates of the Sacred: Priests and Parishioners in Eighteenth-Century Mexico.* Stanford: Stanford University Press.

Throop, C. Jason, and Keith M. Murphy. 2002. Bourdieu and Phenomenology: A Critical Assessment. *Anthropological Theory* 2 (2): 185–207.

Tsing, Anna L. 1993. *In the Realm of the Diamond Queen: Marginality in an Out-of-the-Way Place.* Princeton, N.J.: Princeton University Press.

Turner, Victor. 1957. *Schism and Continuity in an African Society: A Study of Ndembu Village Life.* Manchester: Manchester University Press.

———. 1962. Three Symbols of Passage in Ndembu Circumcision Ritual: An Interpretation. In *Essays on the Ritual of Social Relations*, edited by Max Gluckman. Manchester: Manchester University Press.

———. 1967. *The Forest of Symbols: Aspects of Ndembu Ritual.* Ithaca: Cornell University Press.

———. 1969. *The Ritual Process: Structure and Anti-structure.* Chicago: Aldine.

Tweed, Thomas A. 1997. *Our Lady of the Exile: Diasporic Religion at a Cuban Catholic Shrine in Miami.* Oxford: Oxford University Press.

———. 2006. *Crossing and Dwelling: A Theory of Religion.* Cambridge: Harvard University Press.

Unger, Roberto Mangabeira. 2007. *The Self Awakened: Pragmatism Unbound.* Cambridge: Harvard University Press.

Urry, John. 2007. Mobilizing Social Life. In *Mobilities*, 3–16. Cambridge: Polity Press.

Vail, Leroy. 1989. Introduction: Ethnicity in Southern African History. In *The Creation of Tribalism in Southern Africa*, edited by Leroy Vail. London: Currey.

van Binsbergen, Wim M. J. 1981. *Religious Change in Zambia: Exploratory Essays.* London: Kegan Paul.

van de Kamp, Linda. 2013. South-South Transnational Spaces of Conquest: Afro-Brazilian Pentecostalism, and the Reproductive Domain in Urban Mozambique. *Exchange* 42 (4): 343–65.

———. 2016. *Violent Conversion: Brazilian Pentecostalism and Urban Women in Mozambique.* Woodbridge: James Currey.

van de Port, Mattijs. 2011. *Ecstatic Encounters: Bahian Candomblé and the Quest for the Really Real.* Amsterdam: Amsterdam University Press.

———. 2015. Reading Bruno Latour in Bahia: Or, How to Approach the "Great, Blooming, Buzzing Confusion" of Life and Being without Going Mad. In *What Is Existential Anthropology?* edited by Michael Jackson and Albert Piette. New York: Berghahn.

van der Veer, Peter. 1996. Introduction. In *Conversion to Modernities: The Globalization of Christianity*, edited by Peter van der Veer. New York: Routledge.

van Dijk, Rijk. 1998. Pentecostalism, Cultural Memory and the State: Contested Representations of Time in Postcolonial Malawi. In *Memory and the Postcolony: African Anthropology and the Critique of Power*, edited by Richard Werbner. London: Zed Books.

———. 2009. Social Catapulting and the Spirit of Entrepreneurialism: Migrants, Private Initiative and the Pentecostal Ethic in Botswana. In *Traveling Spirits: Migrants, Markets and Mobilities*, edited by Gertrud Hüwelmeier and Kristine Krause. New York: Routledge.

van Gennep, Arnold. [1909] 1960. *The Rites of Passage*. Translated by Monika B. Vizedom and Gabrielle L. Caffee. Chicago: University of Chicago Press.

van Wyk, Ilana. 2014. *The Universal Church of the Kingdom of God in South Africa: A Church of Strangers*. New York: Cambridge University Press.

Vasquez, Manuel. 2011. *More Than Belief: A Materialist Theory of Religion*. New York: Oxford University Press.

Vilaça, Aparecida, and Robin M. Wright, eds. 2009. *Native Christians: Modes and Effects of Christianity among Indigenous Peoples of the Americas*. Burlington: Ashgate.

Vondey, Wolfgang. 2010. *Beyond Pentecostalism: The Crisis of Global Christianity and the Renewal of the Theological Agenda*. Grand Rapids: William B. Eerdmans.

Voss Roberts, Michelle. 2010. Religious Belonging and the Multiple. *Journal of Feminist Studies in Religion* 26 (1): 43–62.

Wacker, Grant. 2001. *Heaven Below: Early Pentecostals and American Culture*. Cambridge: Harvard University Press.

Walker, Alice. 1983. In Search of Our Mothers' Gardens. In *In Search of Our Mothers' Gardens: Womanist Prose*, 231–43. San Diego: Harcourt Brace Jovanovich.

Wariboko, Nimi. 2012. *The Pentecostal Principle: Ethical Methodology in New Spirit*. Grand Rapids: William B. Eerdmans.

Weber, Max. [1922] 1978. *Economy and Society: An Outline of Interpretative Sociology*. Translated by Ephraim Fischoff et al. Berkeley: University of California Press.

Werbner, Richard. 1985. The Argument of Images: From Zion to the Wilderness in African Churches. In *Theoretical Explorations in African Religion*, edited by Wim van Binsbergen and Matthew Schoffeleers. London: Routledge and Kegan Paul.

———. 2011. *Holy Hustlers, Schism, and Prophecy: Apostolic Reformation in Botswana*. Berkeley: University of California Press.

West, Cornel. 2004. *Democracy Matters: Winning the Fight against Imperialism*. New York: Penguin.

West, Harry G. 2004. Villains, Victims, or Makonde in the Making? *Ethnohistory* 51 (1): 1–43.

———. 2005. *Kupilikula: Governance and the Invisible Realm in Mozambique*. Chicago: University of Chicago Press.

———. 2007. *Ethnographic Sorcery*. Chicago: University of Chicago Press.

Whyte, Susan Reynolds. 1997. *Questioning Misfortune: The Pragmatics of Uncertainty in Eastern Uganda*. Cambridge: Cambridge University Press.

Woolf, Virginia. 1998. *The Waves*. Oxford: Oxford University Press.

Yong, Amos. 2002. *Spirit-Word-Community: Theological Hermeneutics in Trinitarian Perspective*. Burlington: Ashgate.

———. 2003. *Beyond the Impasse: Toward a Pneumatological Theology of Religions*. Grand Rapids: Baker Academic.

Zaslavsky, Claudia. 1973. *Africa Counts: Number and Pattern in African Cultures*. Boston: Prindle, Weber, and Schmidt.

Zigon, Jarrett. 2009. Phenomenological Anthropology and Morality: A Response to Joel Robbins. *Ethnos* 74 (2): 286–88.

INDEX

Abílio, 74; afterlife and, 101, 104; *makeya* and, 143–45, 147, 157–58
Abu-Lughod, Lila, 182n16
ADA (African Assembly of God, Assembléia de Deus Africana), 21–22, 167–68, 191n7; afterlife and, 33–36; ancestral practices and, 74–75, 118–22, 139–41, 143–44; mobility and, 64–66, 144–46; ritualism and, 107, 109–10, 157–58, 189n9
African Initiated Churches, 13, 186n2, 189n19
agriculture, 53, 56, 113; collectivization and, 55, 65, 177n11; conceptions of land and, 51–52; cotton cultivation and, 54, 132, 187n19; diversification techniques and, 56, 68, 180n23; shifting cultivation and, 53, 56, 113; tobacco cultivation and, 74, 132
Aguilar, Mario, 174n15, 180n23
Albrecht, Daniel, 145, 189n8
Allina, Eric, 54
Alpers, Edward, 176n8
Amadiume, Ifi, 122
Anderson, Allen, 145
anthropology of Christianity, 6, 188n5; critiques of, 14–17, 175n23, 188n6; relationality and, 151–52; rupture and, 7, 37, 106, 162, 173n5; study population of, 11, 174n13
Anzaldúa, Gloria, 137
Appadurai, Arjun, 5, 32
Appiah, Kwame Anthony, 177n14
architecture, 61–64, 179n15; religion and, 21–22, 65, 94, 183n4
Arendt, Hannah, 42, 163, 188n24
Arnfred, Signe, 183n19, 186n8–186n9, 187n15
Asad, Talal, 189n12
Austin, Diane, 149

Bantu languages, 42–43, 177n15
Beidelman, T. O., 84, 86, 181n7, 181n9
Belinha, 121
Berger, Peter, 8, 151
Bergson, Henri, 76
Bialecki, Jon, 188n6
boundedness, 31–32, 75–79; freedom and, 69; initiation and, 73, 89–90; religion and, 93–94, 184n10; rupture and, 90–91
Bourdieu, Pierre, 88, 90, 143, 147, 154–55, 161, 189n7, 190n21–190n22
Bowen, Merle, 54
Braidotti, Rosi, 76, 180n1
Brambilla, Simona, 95
Brown, Michael, 182n17
bush and village/town dialectic, 76–77, 83, 89, 181n5

Cannell, Fenella, 141
capitalism, 14, 32, 133, 135
Cartesianism, 20, 56, 88, 186n1
categorization, 15, 96–97, 137, 148, 152
Catholicism, 22–23, 41, 149, 175n34, 183n3; Consolata missionaries and, 41, 94–95, 183n2; gender and, 128–30; hybridity and, 13, 97–98, 101; inculturation and, 65–66, 95–101, 165–68, 184n6; initiation and, 78–80, 83, 85–86, 98, 181n6, 182n12; Pentecostalism and, 107–8, 118–21; religion and, 112, 124, 126–28, 147
CCM (Christian Council of Mozambique, Conselho Cristão de Moçambique), 168–69, 191n8
Cewalusa, 12–13
Chabal, Patrick, 177n13
circularity, 67–68, 164; ancestors and, 46, 101; body and, 67, 142, 180n22; conversion and, 13–14; 174n15; material

circularity (*continued*)
culture and, 61–64, 180n19; migration and, 11–14, 18, 57, 177n16; ritual and, 47, 77, 139, 145, 147, 154, 181n5; time and, 177n10, 180n18
Ciscato, Elia, 95, 105, 180n17
civil war, 40–41, 59–60, 177n17, 179n8; migrations and, 43–45, 47, 56–57, 177n16
Coleman, Simon, 10, 16, 149
colonialism, 41, 65, 183n7, 187n14; Christianity and, 14, 36, 65, 95; education and, 130–32, 187n17; gender and, 122–24, 135–37, 187n17–187n18; peasantry and, 54–56, 60
Comaroff, Jean and John, 14
Comaroff, John, 15–16
compartmentalization, 98, 100, 184n15
concessionary companies, 31, 54–55, 123
conservation 58–61
conversion, 159–66, 171; circularity and, 11–14, 147, 174n15; convertibility and, 25, 70, 113; etymology of, 162, 176n36; gender and, 117–18, 126, 136–37; indigenous models and, 91–92, 111, 173n6; modernity and, 16, 20, 36–38; Pauline model of, 36, 176n9; religion and, 93, 97, 169; rupture and, 6–8, 66, 140–41, 168, 174n7, 174n12; theories of, 106–7, 114, 149–53, 185n19, 188n4; translations of, 23–24, 29, 50, 67, 73
Costa, 168–70
Cox, Harvey, 8, 148, 169
Crapanzano, Vincent, 84–85, 87
Csordas, Thomas, 155
Cuamba, 12–13, 21, 49, 69, 74, 108–9, 111–12

da Gama, Vasco, 54
dance: *eyinlo* and, 138–40, 147, 188n1; initiation and, 79–80, 83–85; Pentecostalism and, 74, 144–45, 147, 154, 158, 163, 189n8
de Certeau, Michel, 69, 90
Deleuze, Gilles, 76, 180n1, 188n6
Democratic Movement of Mozambique (Movimento Democrático de Moçambique), 190n5
development projects, 31, 54, 61, 134–35, 164, 187n15
Devereux, George, 185n20
Dewey, John, 113
dilemma tales, 169–71
Diniz, 68–69, 76
Dreyfus, Herbert, 104

EAD (Evangelical Assembly of God, Evangélica Assembléia de Deus), 21–22, 33, 128, 142, 168; ancestral practices and, 107–12
economics, 31, 159, 187n19; gender and, 136–37, 186n7, 187n18; modernity and, 37, 56, 132–33; tradition and, 52, 133–35
education, 12–13, 130–33, 135; gender and, 122, 137, 187nn17, 18
elephants, 58–61, 68–70, 77, 179n11, 179n14, 184n12
Eliade, Mircea, 177n10
embodiment, 15, 130, 161, 174n17; initiation and, 73–92; Pentecostalism and, 142–47, 153–56, 190n20
Engelke, Matthew, 190n19
epistemology: embodiment and, 15; pluralism and, 105; politics and, 183n6, 184n8, 185n16; religion and, 95–96, 100, 112
erima (patience and courage), 69, 75
erimu (heaven), 102, 105
esataka (funerary rite), 35–36, 49, 140, 178n21, 188n3
ethnography, 14–15, 18–21, 32, 174n16
ettini (religion), 93–95, 99, 124, 127–30, 136, 165
ettini ya makholo (ancestral religion), 73, 94, 112
Evangelical Church of Christ in Mozambique, 168, 175n34
existential anthropology, 7, 15, 17, 20, 175n32
existential mobility, 10, 16–20, 42, 105, 162
existentialism, 15–20, 102–5, 175n19; Pentecostalism and, 147–50, 163, 189n11. *See also* existential anthropology; existential mobility
eyinlo (ancestral ceremony), 138–40, 143–44, 147, 188n1, 188n3

Fabian, Johannes, 176n4
Fátima, 141; Luisinha and, 30, 34, 178n21; mobility and, 38–39, 41, 44, 48–51, 75; residential compound and, 59, 62, 180n16
Fausto, 101

Ferguson, James, 12, 108–9, 174n14
fertility, 85, 87, 125, 182n14
firearms, 60–61, 68, 179n14; Mozambican flag and, 40, 42, 177n11
Florêncio, 141; initiation and, 73–75, 87, 91–92, 184n12
Foucault, Michel, 4
Frelimo (Frente de Libertação de Moçambique, Mozambican Liberation Front), 37, 165–67; democratic transition of, 165–67; ethnic politics and, 41–42, 177n13; gender and, 182n12, 187n15; modernization and, 41, 65; obscurantism and, 73, 78–79, 96–97, 184n8, 185n16; peasantry and, 37, 51, 55–56, 59, 177n11, 190n5; religion and, 64–66; Renamo and, 40, 43, 178n17; war of independence and, 40, 43, 177n12
Freudianism, 85
Frizzi, Padre Giuseppe, 105, 176n6; gender and, 124, 126; inculturation and, 95, 100, 165, 186n1; initiation and, 79, 98–99; scholarship and, 102, 105, 184n13
fundamentalism, 145

Geffray, Christian, 55, 177n11, 186n4
Gell, Alfred, 180n18
gender, 122–24; economics and, 132–33, 186n7; education and, 130–32, 187n17–187n18; identity and, 187n14; initiation and, 84–90, 124–25, 181n7, 181n12, 182n12, 183n19; mobility and, 25, 136; Mount Namuli and, 125, 178n20; Pentecostalism and, 118–22, 187n13; religion and, 117–18, 126–30, 186n3, 186n8; rematriation and, 124–26
Gerdes, Paulus, 63
Gildon, 12–13
Gilroy, Paul, 180n21
globalization, 5, 15–16, 160, 162; mobility and, 32, 48, 183n7; Pentecostalism and, 6–8, 10, 141, 156, 187n13
Gluckman, Max, 176n3
Gordon, Lewis, 17
Gottlieb, Alma, 182n14
Greek philosophy, 15, 104–5
Greenblatt, Stephen, 176n3

habitus, 88–90, 154, 161, 189n7, 190n22
Hackett, Rosalind, 10
Hadot, Pierre, 162
Hage, Ghassan, 17
Hariwa, 102–3
Harris, Olivia, 150
healing, 2–4, 109–12, 185n21; gender and, 124, 129, 187n15; hybridity and, 99–100; Pentecostalism and, 6, 120–21, 148–50; traditional ceremonies and, 36, 46, 119–20, 124–25, 143, 181n5
Hefner, Robert, 8, 10, 157, 167
Hegel, G. W. F., 32–33, 37, 90, 159, 176n4
Heidegger, Martin, 16, 20, 134
Heraclitus, 76
Herzfeld, Michael, 174n16
Holy Spirit, 23, 129, 164; body and, 144, 147; empowerment and, 149; healing and, 3, 110, 120; mobility and, vi, 152–54; spiritual warfare and, 39–41; theology and, 152–53, 189n18, 190n19
Honwana, Alcinda, 101
hunting, 52–53, 179n12–179n13, 181n7; elephants and, 60–61, 179n14
hybridity, 36, 163, 173n6, 184n11; architecture and, 63–64; Pentecostalism and, 5–7, 13, 160; polyontological mobility and, 97–101, 184n15, 185n16

initiation, 25, 73–75, 79–84, 184n12; adults and, 79–80, 183n18; Catholicism and, 22, 78–79, 98–99, 165, 181n6; circumcision and, 75, 80–82, 84, 86–87; conversion and, 91–92; education and, 130, 132; Frelimo and, 73, 78–79, 96–97; gender and, 88, 123–25, 181n7, 181n12, 183n19; rite of return and, 84–87; role-playing and, 88–90, 160; studies of, 77–79, 84, 86, 181n9; stoicism and, 34, 80, 89, 181n8
intersubjectivity, 105, 134, 151. *See also* subjectivity
Isaacman, Allen, 54–55
Islam, 8, 22; ancestral practices and, 95, 165, 176n8; architecture and, 63, 65, 94, 183n4; conversion and, 180n23, 188n4; gender and, 121, 124, 128–29, 186n4, 186n10, 187n19; initiation and, 86; polyontology and, 100–101, 112; reformist versions of, 190n6; religion and, 94–95, 124, 126–30, 147, 149, 183n4
IURD (Igreja Universal do Reino de Deus, Universal Church of the Kingdom of God), 8–9, 152–53, 174n9, 189n17

Jackson, John B., 176n5
Jackson, Michael, 15, 17–18, 88, 151, 181n5, 189n15
James, William, 76, 101, 114, 150–53, 157, 181n3, 189n5, 190n23
Jemusse, 1, 141; Luisinha and, 30, 33–34, 38, 178n21; mobility and, 38–39, 41, 44, 48–51, 75, 135; residential compound and, 59, 62–64, 180n16
Jorge, 140–41, 147, 149, 154

Kalinka, 62, 118
Kalu, Ogbu, 40
Kaveya, Chief, 58–59, 70, 74
Kayaya, 80, 89
Kierkegaard, Søren, 20
Kirsch, Thomas, 100
Kleinman, Arthur, 185n21

labor: mobility and, 12, 45, 55; monetization and, 132–33, 136
Lambek, Michael, 101, 175n32
Leach, Edmund, 161
Leacock, Eleanor, 122
Leonardo, 1–2, 4, 124
Lerma Martínez, Francisco, 46, 95–96, 178n20
Lévi-Strauss, Claude, 131, 176n2
liberalism, 11, 109, 186n3
Lichinga, 8–10, 12, 18, 21, 23, 108–9, 143, 150
Lienhardt, Godfrey, 16, 104, 111
Lifton, Robert Jay, 182n17
liminality, 78, 83–86
Lindhardt, Martin, 154–55
Lioma village, 59–60, 77
literacy, 50, 130–31, 135
logocentrism, 14, 148
Lubkemann, Stephen, 45, 177n16
Luhrmann, Tanya, 189n14
Luisinha, 29–31, 33–34, 179n10; afterlife of, 35, 38–39, 178n21; choice of pseudonym for, 176n1

Mahmood, Saba, 155, 190n22
makeya (ancestral offering), 47, 63, 144, 160; gender and, 123, 128–29; initiation and, 79; polyontological mobility and, 98, 100, 120; religion and, 95
Makonde people, 41, 44, 165, 177n12, 177n13, 190n20
Manuel, Pastor, 33, 108, 111–12, 142, 148; spiritual warfare and, 22, 168
Marcel, Gabriel, 134, 162, 185n18
marriage, 117–18, 126, 150, 152, 169; polygamy and, 18, 97
Marshall, Ruth, 6, 163
Marx, Karl, 37
Marxism. *See* socialism
matricentrism, 25, 89, 122–24, 181n10, 188n23
Maxwell, David, 191n7
McIntosh, Janet, 100, 185n16
Medeiros, Eduardo, 79, 83, 85
media, 1–5, 7, 11
menstruation, 85–87, 124–25, 182n14–182n15
mētis (practical logic), 185n23
Meyer, Birgit, 6, 14, 65
migration, 7; afterlife and, 48, 153; circularity and, 11–14, 18, 174n14; colonialism and, 96, 182n16, 185n17; conversion and, 24; gender and, 131; history and, 41–45, 177n16; mobility and, 17–18, 177n14; modernity and, 20, 31–32
Mitchell, Timothy, 182n16
modernity, 4; anthropology and, 5–7, 12–13, 15, 31–32, 45; architecture and, 61–65, 134; Frelimo and, 41, 56–57, 66, 78–79, 96–97, 166–67, 177n11, 184n8, 184n16; gender and, 130–33; mobility and, 24, 31, 36–38, 159, 162, 183n7; religion and, 97, 100; subjectivity and, 16, 20, 117, 151–52, 186n3
Morier-Genoud, Éric, 11, 180n20
Mosko, Mark, 152
Mukonyora, Isabel, 186n2
Mukwetxhe, Atata, 38, 49
Muluku (Supreme Being), 102, 104, 111, 124
munepa (ancestral spirit), 104, 129; afterlife and, 46–48, 126; Luisinha and, 35, 39, 178n21; mobility and, 36, 153, 177n15
murette (traditional medicine), 30–31, 111, 119–20. *See also* healing
mutability, 91, 138, 156, 163, 166, 183n17; immutability and, 38, 161
mutholo shrines, 47, 79–80, 88, 128, 181n10
Mutúali, 1–3, 7

Nampula, 22, 62, 110, 190n6
namuku (healer), 47, 77; Catholicism and, 100; gender and, 124, 127

Namuli, Mount, 46–48, 51, 177n15; afterlife and, 101–2, 104–5, 139, 158; circularity and, 63, 79, 145; gender and, 87, 125–26, 178n20, 182n15
natality, 42, 50, 160–63, 171
nation-state formation, 40–42, 96, 180n24
Négritude philosophy, 15, 175n21
neoliberalism, 15, 37, 41, 134, 184n16, 187n13
Neuza, 118–22, 137, 141, 186n2
Newitt, Malyn, 53, 65, 178n3, 186n10, 187n19
Nicodemus, 130, 132–35
Nielsen, Morten, 183n20
Nietzsche, Friedrich, vi, 102
Nock, A. D., 36
nomadism, 13, 24, 29, 54, 66, 93
Nório, Deacon, 1–2, 33, 158
Nyamnjoh, Francis B., 174n14
Nyanja people, 9, 180n22

Obama, Barack, 159
Obarrio, Juan, 184n16
obscurantism, 56, 65, 73, 79, 96–97, 184n8, 185n16
ohiya ni ovolawa (to leave and to enter), 24, 73, 107, 113, 136–37, 149
Ojo, Matthews, 190n6
okhalano (to be with / to have), 25, 105, 117, 133–38, 153
oral tradition, 130–31, 145, 187n16
othama (to move), 24, 29, 50, 53, 67, 70, 73, 136–37, 147
otxentxa ittini (to change religions), 136
oveya metto (to be light-footed), 52, 62, 134
oyara (to procreate), 42, 85, 87, 125, 182n12

pastoralism, 44, 56
patriarchy, 118, 137; mobility and, 186n2; religion and, 127, 129–30, 186n4, 186n10, 187n19; traditional societies and, 122, 186n6
Paul (the apostle), 36–37, 176n9
Paulino, 67, 118–19, 123
pentecostal principle, 163, 169
phenomenology, 13–16, 147, 153; critiques of, 15–16, 19–20; embodiment and, 154–56; ethnography and, 175n19, 175n22
Piot, Charles, 5–6, 12–14, 160, 173n1
Pitcher, M. Anne, 178n5, 184n8
Plato, 104, 161
pluralism, 17, 156, 166; agriculture and, 56; existential-phenomenology and, 15, 104–5, 175n32; medicine and, 185n21; mobility and, 25, 98; religion and, 17, 156, 166
pneumatology, 152–53, 189n18
polyontological mobility, 97–101, 105, 166, 170; gender and, 126; Pentecostalism and, 106, 112–14, 140, 149. *See also* hybridity
Portugal, 54–56, 97, 166, 187n17; concessionary companies and, 31, 123; Frelimo and, 40–41, 43, 51
postcolonial theory, 4–6, 97, 160
poverty, 31, 57, 59–60, 132, 159, 179n9
pragmatism, 113–14, 185n21–185n22, 189n13; Pentecostalism and, 147–50, 157
proteanism, 88, 182n17
Protestantism, 168, 173n2, 175n34, 187n15, 191n8; belief and, 148, 189n12; fundamentalism and, 145; individualism and, 16; Pentecostalism and, 6, 173n2

radical empiricism, 151–53, 189n15
Raimundo, 107–13, 141
rationalism, 15, 105, 113, 182n16; religion and, 104, 148, 152
refugees, 44–45, 64, 177n16
relationality, 105, 133–35, 150–53; religion and, 127, 148; subjectivity and, 16–17, 20, 108–9, 178n21
religion, 93–97, 112, 126–30, 147–48, 184n9; conversion and, 69, 106–7, 135–37, 174n15, 176n9; gender and, 117–118, 122–26, 165, 186n6; reification and, 25, 100–101, 189n12; state and, 64–65, 180n20; theories of, 150–51, 181n4; study of, 8, 14–15, 17, 154, 174n17
Renamo (Resistência Nacional Moçambicana, Mozambican National Resistance), 40, 43, 56, 177n11, 178n17
revolution, 37, 63, 91, 161
Robbins, Joel, 6–7, 14–15, 106–7, 162, 173n5, 174n13, 188n5
roots, 24, 171; African American intellectuals and, 180n21; land and, 42, 44, 62; medicine and, 47, 102, 110; mobility and, 20–21, 45, 64–67, 162; routes and, 31, 162
Rosaldo, Renato, 32, 176n7

rupture, 36, 138, 150, 166, 173n5; anthropology of Christianity and, 14, 36–37, 90, 93, 106, 188n5; childbirth and, 125–26, 181n10; Christianity (beyond Pentecostalism) and, 36, 69; embodiment and, 143, 154, 156; natality and, 163; reversal and, 38, 91; routine and, 50, 91; theories of, 4–8, 13, 157, 174n7

Sahlins, Marshall, 173n5
Said, Edward, 176n3, 188n24
Sartre, Jean-Paul, 17
Saunders, George, 148
Scott, James, 56, 66–67, 88, 107, 131, 182n16, 185n23
sedentarization, 51, 54–58, 65–66, 68, 164
Sheldon, Kathleen, 187n17
Simões, Pastor, 21, 49–50, 144, 149, 157, 168; afterlife and, 39–40, 101, 104, 140; fixity and, 66–67; funerary rites and, 33–36
slavery, 43–45, 53–54, 145, 188n3
Smith, Wilfred Cantwell, 148, 184n9, 189n12
socialism, 37, 184n8; collectivization and, 56–57, 177n11; cultural politics and, 56, 96–97, 182n12, 184n8, 185n16; Pentecostalism and, 11; postsocialism and, 65, 123, 132, 135, 165–66
sorcery, 38–39, 111, 165–66, 190n20; countersorcery and, 41, 49–50
South Africa, 33, 40, 61, 135, 152, 177n16, 180n2
Southern Rhodesia. *See* Zimbabwe
speaking in tongues, 6, 127, 144, 153–54
spiritual warfare, 40–41, 150, 167
Stoller, Paul, 15, 189n15
subjectivity, 160–64; individualism and, 16, 117, 151–52; mobility and, 7, 16–18, 24, 91, 158, 180n17, 182n17; relationality and, 20, 105, 134, 151–53, 190n20; subject formation and, 190n22. *See also* intersubjectivity
Swahili, 22, 183n2
syncretism, 5, 36, 100, 184n10, 184n15. *See also* hybridity

Tanzania, 55–56
Taylor, Charles, 20
traditional societies: Catholicism and, 22, 65, 95–96, 98–101, 126–27; change and, 7, 32, 159, 162, 173n6, 183n17, 190n3; gender and, 122–23, 133, 186n6; Islam and, 22, 95, 126–27; mobility and, 24, 29, 44–45, 48, 90; modernity and, 37, 185n16; Pentecostal views of, 6, 40, 66–67, 93, 97–98
Turner, Victor, 45, 47, 77–78, 84–86, 181n11
Tweed, Thomas, 181n4

Unger, Roberto Mangabeira, 91
United Nations, 57, 60, 179n9
United States, 61, 159, 167, 189n11
Universal Church of the Kingdom of God. *See* IURD

Vail, Leroy, 187n14
van de Kamp, Linda, 174n7
van Gennep, Arnold, 77, 84, 86, 91, 181n11
van Wyk, Ilana, 152–53
Vasquez, Manuel, 181n4
Vondey, Wolfgang, 163

Wacker, Grant, 189n11
Walker, Alice, 136, 188n23
war for Mozambican independence, 40–41, 43, 177n12
Wariboko, Nimi, 163, 169
wasasa ekumi (search for life), 111–13, 149, 189n13
Weber, Max, 167
Werbner, Richard, 186n2
West, Cornel, 188n3
West, Harry, 41, 44–45, 165, 190n20
Woolf, Virginia, 20–21, 136

Yao people, 9
Yong, Amos, 152–53

Zaslavsky, Claudia, 63
Zimbabwe, 21, 40, 179n12; Assemblies of God Africa and, 141, 191n7; Masowe Apostles and, 186n2, 189n19

ACKNOWLEDGMENTS

Heartfelt thanks go first and foremost to the people of Maúa district. I am honored to count many of them not as informants, but as friends. To preserve their anonymity, I have changed most of their names. I do, however, wish to recognize and specially thank my primary collaborators: Paulino Amala, Fausto Mwiraseke, and Leonardo Quido Uisque. I also thank Padre Giuseppe Frizzi of Maúa's Centro de Estudos Xirima for extending his hospitality and expertise and for modeling what a sustained, immersive commitment to the people of Africa looks like. Researchers at the Centro who helped me interpret fieldwork findings include Nicodemus Agostinho Amido, Adriano Saide, Maria Estela Vahiwa, and Marquês Victor. Elsewhere in Mozambique, Padre Elia Ciscato and Bishop Francisco Lerma Martínez shared valuable insights from their decades of work among the Makhuwa, and faculty members affiliated with the Centro de Estudos Africanos of the Eduardo Mondlane University, in Maputo, offered indispensable logistical and intellectual support. Particularly valuable interlocutors there include Carlos Arnaldo, Teresa Cruz e Silva, Teresa Manjate, Miguel Moto, and Armindo Ngunga.

Funding for field research came from multiple sources, namely: the Wenner-Gren Foundation for Anthropological Research; Harvard University's John L. Loeb Fellowship program, Weatherhead Center for International Affairs, and Committee on African Studies; and Colorado College's Humanities Executive Division. Most of this book was written against a Rocky Mountain backdrop in the captivating climes of Colorado. I am extraordinarily grateful to my religion department colleagues and to the dean's office of Colorado College for inviting me to join the college first with a Riley predoctoral fellowship, which resulted in the first draft of this book, and for continuing generously to support my research since. A summer fellowship at the School for Advanced Research, in yet another stunning setting of the American Southwest, also provided welcome stimulation at a critical stage.

Whatever the merits of this book, they owe largely to the influence of numerous fellow scholars. The members of my dissertation committee—Davíd Carrasco, Harvey Cox, Michael Jackson, and Jacob Olupona—deserve deepest thanks for their years of guidance, direction, and inspiration. It is hard to imagine myself on a more satisfying intellectual path than the one on which they set me. My indebtedness to Michael in particular is immeasurable. This project also benefited from the critical and/or encouraging feedback of Afe Adogame, Asad Ahmed, Ronaldo Almeida, David Amponsah, Raimundo Barreto, Robert Baum, Jon Bialecki, James Bielo, Elias Bongmba, Jason Bruner, Annalisa Butticci, Judith Casselberry, Francis X. Clooney, Simon Coleman, Vagner Gonçalves da Silva, Kyrah Malika Daniels, Kate DeConinck, Iracema Dulley, Matthew Engelke, Marla Frederick, Sayaka Funada-Classen, Yonatan Gez, Kathy Giuffre, George González, Santiago Guerra, Nadia Guessous, William Harcombe, Naomi Haynes, Joseph Hellweg, Michael Herzfeld, Andreas Heuser, Arianna Huhn, Suma Ikeuchi, Ben Jones, Anusha Kedhar, Irfan Khan, Frederick Klaits, Smita Lahiri, Michael Lambek, Victoria Levine, Christina Leza, Marc Loustau, Hans Lucht, Adeline Masquelier, Clapperton Chakanetsa Mavhunga, Michael McClymond, Purvi Mehta, Birgit Meyer, Anne Monius, Mario Montaño, Éric Morier-Genoud, Kristy Nabhan-Warren, Dylan Nelson, Jonathan Nkhoma, Ebenezer Obadare, Oludamini Ogunnaike, Kevin O'Neill, Adedamola Osinulu, Chan Sok Park, Kimberley Patton, Lars Pharo, Michael Puett, Katrien Pype, Joel Robbins, Ramon Sarró, Jonathan Schofer, Don Seeman, Stephen Selka, Sónia Silva, Josef Sorett, Abdoulaye Sounaye, Dianne Stewart, Paul Stoller, Jason Throop, Linda van de Kamp, Ilana van Wyk, Ibrahima Wade, David Weddle, Harry West, Sarah Willen, John Williams, Richard Fox Young, and Tyler Zoanni. Also belonging to this list are Maria Cecilia Aguilar Holt and Sarah Hautzinger, brilliant friends who accompanied me through various stages, but deserve special mention for offering detailed feedback on a late draft of the entire book. I also express my appreciation for the generous enthusiasm shown by Penn Press from our moment of first contact, particularly by my editor Peter Agree and two anonymous reviewers.

Portions of this book first appeared in two separate essays and I acknowledge the publishers' permissions to reprint them: "Conversion and Convertibility in Northern Mozambique," in the volume *What Is Existential Anthropology?* (Berghahn Books, 2015); and "Egress and Regress: Pentecostal Precursors and Parallels in Northern Mozambique," in the journal *Ethnos* (Taylor and Francis, 2018). For the photographs appearing in this book, credit and thanks go to Kalinka Caldas Premawardhana. The map was created by Alice Thiede.

What remains is the privilege of thanking my family: Amma and Apuchi for their love and their example, for teaching us the way of care and compassion; and Ayya and Amali, and Now and Albert, for always being there. It is impossible to convey how grateful to Kalinka I am and forever will be. Without her companionship, enthusiasm, and insight no phase of this project would have been possible, and not much in this life would be worthwhile. In the years it took to research and write this book, another collaboration of ours entered the world. His name, Baraka, keeps us connected to Maúa, and reminds us every day just how blessed we are.

CPSIA information can be obtained
at www.ICGtesting.com
Printed in the USA
BVOW09*0226150318
510234BV00002B/2/P